Integrating
Human
Resources
and
Strategic
Business
Planning

Integrating Human Resources *and* Strategic Business Planning

Andrew O. Manzini and John D. Gridley

American Management Association

This book is available at a special
discount when ordered in bulk quantities.
For information, contact Special Sales Department,
AMACOM, a division of American Management Association,
135 West 50th Street, New York, NY 10020.

Library of Congress Cataloging-in-Publication Data

Manzini, Andrew O.
  Integrating human resources and strategic
business planning.

    Bibliography: p.
    Includes index.
    1. Manpower planning.   2. Strategic planning.
I. Gridley, John D.   II. Title.
HF5549.5.M3M356   1987   658.4'012   86-47585
ISBN 0-8144-5882-3

Printing number

10 9 8 7 6 5 4 3 2 1

ACKNOWLEDGMENTS

For a work of this scope we must acknowledge the contribution of many people who, directly or indirectly, influenced either the central concept, which is the cornerstone of the book, or the content of the work itself, in which we describe the practical application of the idea. We are indebted to Professor Elmer H. Burack, who was literally responsible for initiating this work, and whose pioneering efforts to study and write about human resources planning made it possible to single this area out as a discipline in its own right; to Richard Frantzreb, whose "HRP Newsletter" and symposia encouraged the development of the technology, and whose lucid and insightful articles removed much of the mystique associated with the subject and made it practical to apply in many organizations; to Dr. Harry Levinson, who inspired the lead author to use diagnostic methods to identify organizational problems and to seek ways to overcome them; to Peter Barth, President of the Intercultural Group, whose enthusiasm during the early stages of conceptual development and whose efforts to provide us with significant exposure to hundreds of managers in Brazil and the United States greatly encouraged the completion of our work; to Professor Timm Kainen, who gave us the opportunity to present and test the material to many graduate students at three universities, and whose support for the concept provided great encouragement when it was most needed. We are also grateful to the many participants of our public workshops who provided a living laboratory that helped refine the process and to the colleagues and friends who gave so generously of their time and efforts to help us make this happen. In addition, we express our gratitude to John Monaghan, whose research and masterly editorship made possible the production of the manuscript. Finally, we thank Adrienne Hickey, acquisitions and planning editor at AMACOM Books, and Barbara Horowitz, managing editor at AMACOM, for their guidance and support throughout the publishing process.

INTRODUCTION

The human resources planning and development process explained in this book is based on practical business experience. It is the product of a fully supported ten-year effort in one company, Ebasco Services Incorporated, and consultation over an even longer period with dozens of public and private organizations in other industries, including financial institutions, health-care organizations, high-tech companies, and labor-intensive firms, encompassing both large, established concerns and growing entrepreneurial firms. While no two of these organizations are exactly alike, we have found that the salient realities of business-based human resources planning apply across the board, and that is what this book is all about, plus some new ideas for making the process even more effective.

Because this book is a synthesis of practical applications in the real world and is intended to apply to a broad range of differently situated organizations, the "model" for integrated planning should be recognized for what it is: a vehicle to help explain how the integration of major organizational planning systems takes place. The model is essentially didactic, a teaching tool rather than an inflexible blueprint. Its execution, however, is eminently practical and based on reality.

The first thing to strike a casual reviewer of this book, especially one who has picked it up because it has "human resources" in its title, may be the extensive early material on strategic business planning and operational planning. We start with these two pillars of organizational planning with a purpose: An early focus on what the organization is trying to do, and what will be needed to make it happen, is essential to realizing the full potential of the overall process. Our view, which conditions virtually every recommendation and specific approach discussed in this book, is that the links with strategic and operational plans are precisely what keep human resources planning from being an academic exercise.

Thus, even though a human resources professional could conceivably begin with the more "familiar" material starting in Chapter 7 and backtrack later, our recommendation is that this book be used "from left to right." This approach follows the simple logic of business-based planning: We need to know the organization, what it is and plans to be, before attempting to devise relevant human resources forecasts, planning systems, and development programs. Any other approach is unrealistic.

Finally, we urge readers not to be daunted by what may appear to be an enormous task, the development of three major planning systems and their systematic integration in a business-based planning process. For some organizations, the accomplishment of the comprehensive, "ideal" planning and development system may indeed be years away. As discussed in later chapters, however, there is much to be gained from the analysis and improvement of the "parts" that will make up a whole system in successful organizations of the future. In some of these specific parts—notably career planning and the appraisal process—we have made an effort to move beyond the accepted strictures of human resources management practice. Instead of "playing it safe," we have at times been deliberately speculative, provocative, and perhaps controversial— all in an effort to provoke the kind of fresh thinking about our work that will lead each organization to its own level of effective excellence in the management of human resources.

The organization of this book is designed to explain an optimal process, one that puts first things first and proceeds from the analysis of overall corporate objectives and requirements to the particulars of systematic human resources planning and development. As discussed in the final chapter, however, the actual development of this process in any given company cannot always proceed in logical steps. Authors are able to order things in ways that practicing planners—in firms with ongoing needs, established organizational structures, existing planning systems, and other real-world constraints—are not.

For example, strategic planning in your organization may be in a state of flux, with changing long-range objectives that have not been fully identified or clearly agreed upon by a consensus of top management. Does this mean that your human resources planning and development effort should simply ignore strategic planning or do nothing until it is possible to implement the steps recommended in Chapters 4 and 5? Obviously not. A flexible planning approach such as this is designed to accommodate uncertainty and helps underscore the urgency of developing strategic plans—however general and imperfectly detailed—on which to base today's human resources planning and development activity.

Similarly, human resources professionals in other organizations may be faced with operational planning requirements that are "writ in stone" and that represent indecipherable end products of specialized operations research analysis. "It's not my job," the planner might understandably protest, to explore the reasons for human resources demand with the techniques suggested in Chapter 6. Well and good, we say: If the operational planning data that drive human resources demand requirements are accurate, comprehensive, and as detailed as needed to guide integrated human resources planning and development activities, then there may be no need for planners to understand where this information comes from or how it is affected by change. But how will the planner know this for sure if he or she adopts a "hands-off" approach to understanding operational planning?

Other companies, particularly smaller organizations with less than a few hundred employees, may not have the benefit of mechanized human resource information systems such as those described in Chapter 3. This technology should be recognized for what it is: a tool rather than a business planning system. The concepts and general approach that are the bases of this book do not *require* data systems technology to profit your organization. The advent of such systems, however, which in the age of the microcomputer permit the installation of a complete personnel information system covering thousands of employees for a total cost of under $25,000, have brought the full advantages of mechanized data within reach of planners in companies of all sizes. And as discussed in Chapter 3, the cost-effectiveness of such information systems makes certain kinds of planning economically feasible for the first time.

In short, the book is not a catechism that must be "swallowed whole" or not at all. The overall system works, but most of its parts can be made to work better if designed with the "ideal" integrated system in mind.

Nonetheless, our central purpose is to explain and demonstrate the concepts and methodology of a genuinely integrated strategic, operational, and human resources planning system. This unified system provides a practical, "doable" framework for assuring that all human resources programs and policies are designed to operate synergistically with business goals in a cohesive whole. This business-based approach to "the people side" of the organization is the wave of the future, we are convinced, and this book describes how to utilize it.

Following Chapter 1's introductory overview of the integrated planning system proposed by this book, the concepts and origins of this system are explored in Chapter 2, and the technology that makes such an integrated system economically feasible today—for any organization with more than a few hundred employees—is the subject of Chapter 3. Readers who wish to get directly into the "how-to" material, which begins with a discussion of demand factors that emerge from strategic and operational planning, may wish to skip this background material and move directly to Part II (Chapters 4–6). Part III (Chapters 7–9) explores the availability side, the results of human resources planning and development, and the methods of making availability forecasts. Part IV (Chapters 10–11) "closes the gap" and describes systematic techniques for identifying and managing variances between supply and demand. The final chapter offers recommendations to human resources planners faced with the very difficult job of gaining initial support for an integrated system such as this and suggests methods that have proved to be effective in our experience.

Appendix I presents an organizational assessment questionnaire to help the human resources planner determine the extent to which his or her organization needs to upgrade its capabilities in the HR forecasting, planning, and development areas; this is followed by a series of sample planning schedules (Appendixes II–VI) illustrating how the various steps of the human resources planning process would be implemented in practice.

Appendix VII is a case study, complete with graphs and spreadsheet supporting data. It concretely demonstrates how the principles of the integrated human resources planning system herein proposed would be applied in a hypothetical but realistic corporate situation.

CONTENTS

xi

FIGURES

TABLES

PART I
Overview, Historical Perspective, and Today's Technology

The first three chapters of this book, Part I, provide an introductory overview of the integrated planning system, background material on the evolution of human resources planning concepts in this country, and a chapter on the technology that makes integrated HR planning and development economically feasible in complex organizations—the human resource information system (HRIS). Readers seeking only information about how to design and develop their own planning system—and who feel sufficiently knowledgeable about the capabilities of today's HRIS technology—can safely move from the end of Chapter 1 to Chapter 4.

For most of us who have labored long in the field of human resources planning, however, and for others who may be faced with a major change effort requiring a fully developed "rationale" that includes the changing role of human resources management, Chapter 2 provides a valuable historical perspective on "how we got here" and the logical next steps. The long and somewhat checkered history of the planning concepts integrated in this book, and especially the evolution of human resources management as a discrete function in modern organizations, is more than just "interesting reading," we feel. For one thing, this review will provide planners with the background needed to answer the question often asked by top management: If this is such a good idea, why hasn't it been done before?

One reason the kind of integrated planning proposed here has not been successfully achieved in the past is that the personnel information systems that make it possible—at low costs and covering all relevant factors—have not previously been available. Human resource information system technology, the subject of Chapter 3, remains a relatively new phenomenon in organizational

1

life, although most U.S. companies today with more than a few hundred employees have some sort of payroll or personnel system in operation.

Chapter 3 presents an overview of the defining characteristics of an effective HRIS, including microcomputer-based systems, and a brief review of the history of computers in personnel; it then proceeds to a discussion of the various functional "modules" that can be separately developed and utilized to plan and manage various human resources functions—from applicant tracking to succession planning. This material is intended to present the "possibilities" available to planners seeking to mechanize various functions and information flows. Not all of these modules are necessary to the implementation of an integrated planning system.

In fact, computerized information itself is not essential to the development of the planning system proposed here. In most organizations, however, the need for detailed, comprehensive, current data about people and their jobs—and the low cost of today's HRIS technology—make computer assistance an inevitable choice.

1

Introduction and Overview of the Planning System

For a growing number of organizations in the postindustrial economy, human resources planning will become *the* planning system for the years ahead. The need for people with increasingly specialized skills, higher managerial competencies, and commitment to new levels of excellence, with professional qualifications in disciplines that did not exist a few decades ago—at costs commensurate with their contribution to organizational objectives—is and will continue to be the overriding "business" concern of the organization.

In some industries and specific organizations, the need will not be for "more" human resources or even significantly greater numbers of different skills and talents. For example, the organization may have fifty young engineers doing work that—according to strategic plans—will require only five similarly qualified engineers five or ten years from now. In this case, the importance of developing the "right" five—or at least assuring that the five who remain are not simply those who were unable to get a better job elsewhere—is magnified rather than diminished.

The growing importance of human resources to the organization has been reflected in many ways over recent decades, as the "Personnel Manager" responsible for hiring and payroll administration has become the "VP–Human Resources" or some other title reflecting increased stature and a role in corporate planning and decision making.

At the same time, the functions of personnel have been rapidly expanding—especially in the United States, partly in response to regulatory requirements affecting employers—to include such responsibilities as equal employment opportunity programs, health and safety efforts, more complex and variable benefits programs, specialized training and development, and a range of career management and planning programs that had not been considered essential in simpler times, when most managers were "generalists" and the word *professional* meant doctors and lawyers and perhaps major-league athletes.

Some organizations attract excellence. By virtue of what they are and how they do things, one or a few companies in every industry have a reputation that attracts the most dedicated professionals, the most innovative and aggressive managers, the brightest graduates, and the most career-minded employees. This book proposes nothing less than a systematic approach to becoming such an organization, through an integrated, human resources–based strategic planning system that focuses first on organizational capabilities and goals.

Specifications of an "Ideal" Planning System

Several prescriptive specifications—things that should be included in any human resources planning system to make it effective—have guided development of the system described in this book. Our view is that whatever the particular characteristics of the planning system, the extent to which the system meets these specifications will ultimately determine its ability to meet organizational and human resources objectives as a comprehensive, credible, effective planning process. These specifications include the need to:

1. Integrate human resources planning with corporate or business planning, avoiding any semblance of a "stand-alone" personnel system with goals or criteria irrelevant to organizational needs
2. Integrate human resources programs and policies with one another—to "get our act together" in the HR department so that all activities operate synergistically in the pursuit of organizational goals
3. Provide a "what-if" planning capacity, be updatable, and retain the flexibility needed to accommodate changing priorities, new environmental conditions, the impacts of technology, and other inevitable changes affecting the organization and its human resources
4. Provide planning data not only for human resources programs but for the business as a whole, enabling comprehensive data collection and analysis relating human resources data to organizational objectives—whatever they may be
5. Include "qualitative" factors as well as numbers and bottom-line results, such as the organization's core mission and the appraisal system's ability to identify and shape the leaders of tomorrow
6. Consider the goals and aspirations of employees—particularly in career planning—as well as organizational objectives, for pragmatic reasons that recognize the vital importance of merging individual commitment with corporate goals

Clearly, many human resources planning systems fail to meet these specifications, in whole or in part. Often, planners speak of the need to "integrate human resources planning with business planning," for example, but few have devised a systematic approach to *developing* business plans, much less integrating them with human resources plans. Many times, it is not the will that is lacking but the means: How do we get top management to take human resources seriously as a critical planning function essential to the future survival and prosperity of the organization?

Overview of the Integrated Strategic Planning System

The strategic planning system that is the subject of this book is depicted in the flowchart in Figure 1-1. (Sections of this flowchart—in effect, "close-ups"—will be presented at appropriate points throughout the book to illustrate the discussion of aspects of the overall system, seen here in its entirety.) The details of this comprehensive chart are not immutable or necessarily applicable to all organizations. For example, methods of determining day-to-day operational demand forecasts may differ among industries, or specific kinds of human resources programs that shape availability may differ among companies.

What is generic to most organizations is the need for a comprehensive strategic planning system based on the elements of the simplified version of the model shown in Figure 1-2. The primary purpose of this book is to present the rationale and specific techniques for developing and implementing a human resources planning system based on a more sophisticated, organization-specific comparison of human resources demand forecasts and availability forecasts—a flexible system that permits least-cost management interventions to assure the availability of the right people, at the right time, in the right places in the organization throughout the planning cycle.

Demand forecasts, as shown in Figure 1-2, grow out of two distinctly different kinds of planning in the organization: strategic planning, which is the long-range view of where the organization is headed, a picture of the prospective organization and its human resources needs five, ten, or more years away on the planning horizon; and operational planning, the actual human resources requirements for the work of the organization, now and in the immediate future. Contained within each of these planning systems, however, are means of changing demand forecasts: Different strategies will require people at different levels and having different skill mixes, and operational analysis can change productivity levels, allocate human resources differently, and lead to other changes affecting operational demand.

Availability forecasts are, first and foremost, derived from existing human resources and the development programs that will shape the quality of people in the organization in the years ahead. Because the organization's most important (and costly) human resources are managers, professionals, and technical people whose capabilities and commitment are fundamentally organization-specific, acquired over time, and shaped by integrated human resources programs and policies that are based on organizational goals (in this system, inevitably), the focus here is on career development, succession planning, and appraisal systems.

Few organizations today can view "availability" of human resources in any other way. As work requirements become increasingly specialized in the Information Age economy, as the commitment of workers to organizational goals becomes the sine qua non of productivity improvement, and as management innovation and leadership increasingly become the keys to distinguishing successful organizations from their competitors, the "positive" results of effective human resources planning become increasingly apparent. On the negative side, the costs of personnel to the organization—especially benefits-laden managers and professionals—are soaring and must be controlled in ways that do the least damage to organizational service or production goals.

The main parts of the system illustrated in Figure 1-1 are shown in Figure 1-3. A brief overview of these parts is useful, to define terms as they will be employed throughout this book and identify the relationships among the main components of the integrated system. The major parts discussed below are the strategic and operational factors that create demand, the human resources programs that shape availability, and the systematic identification of variance between demand and availability forecasts.

Strategic Planning Based on Organizational Analysis

The strategic planning process begins with an assessment of the organization's mission, objectives, financial goals or constraints, and marketing situation and plans. The next step is the development of environmental scenarios, as shown in Figure 1-4, often in a range from "optimistic" to "pessimistic," dealing with the state of the economy, anticipated regulatory or legal impacts, competitive factors, technological change, or social change with effects on organizational goals and objectives.

Strategies for achieving organizational objectives in a different environment can then be developed and their business implications assessed. The predominant business implication for our present purposes is human resources, the quantity and quality of people needed to accomplish strategic objectives, but the comprehensive system also enables the planner to look at financial resources, market data, and technological change, as well as conduct an overall evaluation of organizational strengths and weaknesses.

For organizations embarking on the development of an integrated strategic planning system for the first time, the initial requirement is an often painstaking analysis of the organization itself, its past history, present strengths and weaknesses, current policies and procedures, and prospective plans. One recommended approach to this kind of organizational diagnosis, using organizational development techniques, locates the "critical mass" of influential managers in the organization and enlists their active participation in both the diagnosis itself and the initial development of the integrated planning system.

Whatever methodology is used to accomplish a clear understanding of organizational capabilities, purpose, and goals, this determination is essential to the definition of strategic planning in the organization. Realizable plans cannot exist without realistic strategies—based on actual or obtainable resources—for their implementation.

Figure 1-2. **Simplified conceptual model for human resources planning and development.**

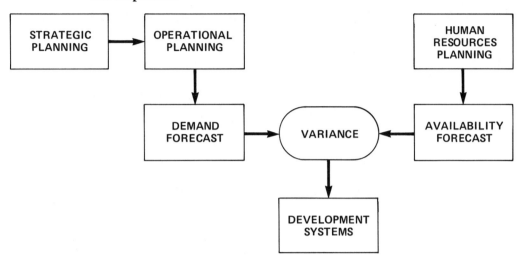

Operational Planning: Baseline of Demand

The integrated planning system that is the basis for this book devotes what may seem an inordinate amount of effort to operations research methods of determining operational human resources variables: the people needed to do the work of the organization, their costs, and the relationships between human resources allocation and output. Many strategic planners with a background in human resources are more than willing to leave these "nuts-and-bolts" issues largely unexamined, to take line managers' word for operational demand requirements and leave the prosaic details of day-to-day operational planning to managers directly involved.

As discussed in Chapter 6, however, strategic planners must have the clearest possible understanding of the concrete realities of operational planning, which is the cornerstone of all human resources planning in the organization. No two organizations are likely to have the same operational requirements or methods of analyzing and forecasting human resources needs, and these organization-specific relationships between work and workers must be clearly understood by planners in a comprehensive, integrated system.

Operational planning is in a sense a short-term microcosm of all human resources planning. Based on production (or service) requirements, utilizing staffing estimates and actual staff requirements, and focusing on human resources as costs that are variable according to output levels and other factors, operational planning often uses sophisticated statistical techniques to determine optimal levels of human resources of various kinds, at different stages of a process or times on a schedule.

This kind of information about immediate and short-term human resources requirements to do the work of the organization is not only the basis for all

Figure 1-3. **Basic structure of the overall human resources planning model.**

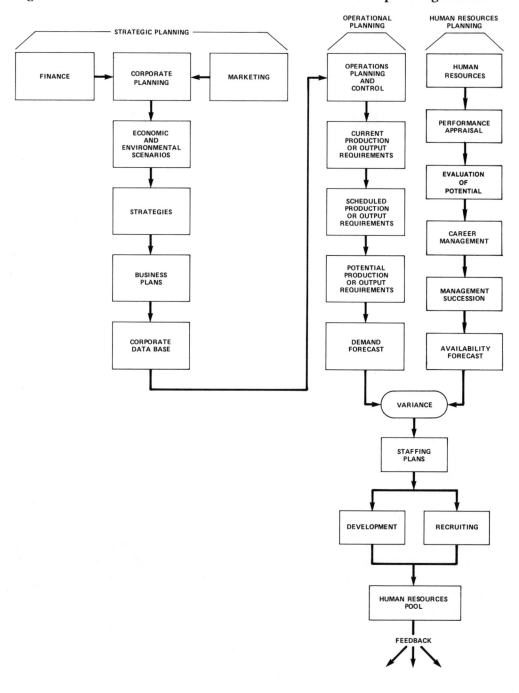

Figure 1-4. Strategic planning elements of the basic model.

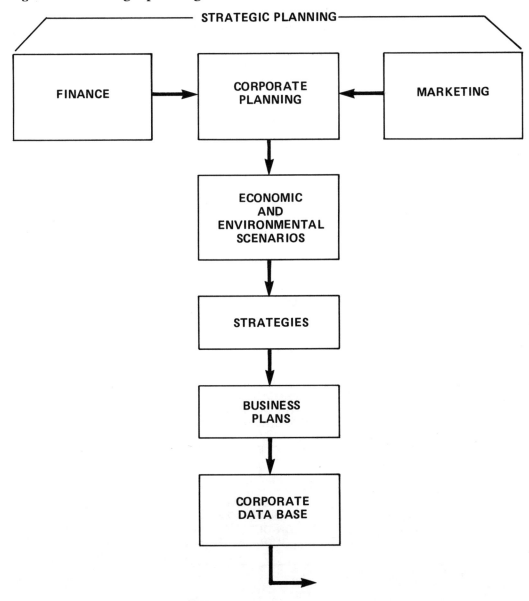
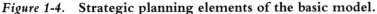

long-range planning. In an integrated system, operational planning also considers the probable human resources demand requirements of strategic plans, the "potential work" of the future, in light of staffing requirements of existing operations. Moreover, the operational planning functions shown in the simplified flowchart in Figure 1-5 permit analysis that may lead to interventions—such as the introduction of a more labor-efficient process—that may be necessary to reach long-range strategic objectives. And changes in the demand requirements of operations, such as a reduced or different workforce resulting from

Figure 1-5.   **Operational planning elements of the basic model.**

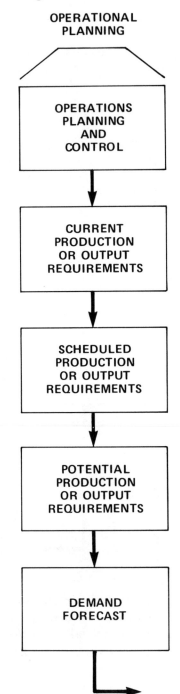

technological advancement, are immediately reflected in the overall planning system.

In many organizations, the task of the strategic planner in determining demand based on operational planning is more than just an information-gathering effort. It may be that the first task of the planner is to "sell" the idea of strategic planning to line managers and others directly involved in operational planning. The way to do this, as discussed in Chapter 11, is to sell "solutions" rather than the system, to point to the operational benefits of an approach that will make the right people available in the right place at the right time—at the least possible cost.

In any case, no strategic planning system can long survive without bottom-up information about the actual human resources demands of real work. Even if the organization is planning to phase out all of its present activities and enter entirely new fields of endeavor, the operational planning demands of those new fields must be examined, understood, and integrated in the overall planning process.

The Availability Side: HR Planning and Development

As shown in the simplified schematic in Figure 1-6, the key personnel elements considered essential to a strategically effective human resources planning system, discussed in Part III of this book, are:

- Performance appraisal systems that are based on organizational objectives, reward contributions to organizational goals, and are systematically designed to be relevant to the work of the organization and to the enhancement of development programs that will make contributions of value to the organization
- A system for evaluating managerial potential that identifies the leadership and professional capabilities needed by the organization of tomorrow, based on strategic plans for a somewhat different organization in a changing environment
- Career management programs that merge the goals of the organization with individual goals and aspirations, in a forthright system that openly communicates the career implications of strategic plans to all employees and systematically directs career plans—as well as developmental experience—along lines dictated by organizational needs
- A succession planning system that addresses management continuity, minimizes disruptive impacts of change, and helps identify managers—in advance—who will accomplish organizational objectives most effectively in the future

Figure 1-6. Human resources planning elements of the basic model.

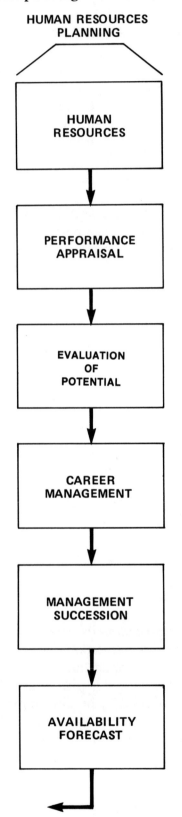

HUMAN RESOURCES
PLANNING

HUMAN
RESOURCES

PERFORMANCE
APPRAISAL

EVALUATION
OF
POTENTIAL

CAREER
MANAGEMENT

MANAGEMENT
SUCCESSION

AVAILABILITY
FORECAST

The emphasis here is on managers and professionals—an increasing share of the workforce generally and always the most critical human resources in the organization. In some organizations, human resources availability will also depend on training programs for hourly workers, skill competencies gained on the job and reflected in seniority ratings, or other kinds of human resources development. The key point is that the idea of human resources "availability" is based on an inward focus: The people who will be needed to meet strategic and operational demands in the future are in the organization or will be fundamentally shaped by organizational human resources programs that can be created today. For most organizations, availability forecasting that looks primarily to external labor markets is likely to be expensive, at best, and possibly disastrous if skills and talents needed to meet strategic goals are not available "at any price." In growing organizations, new people will always be added at entry levels, and the planning system outlined here envisions the judicious hiring of the people who will be needed to replenish an employee population affected by attrition, changing skills requirements, and new corporate directions. The point is not that a system such as this eliminates the need to ever again hire from outside; rather, it is that the most cost-effective, *surest* path to obtaining the skills and talents needed by the organization—and of assuring that those skills and talents represent organization-specific knowledge and capabilities, levels of leadership excellence, and career commitment to the organization and its goals—is to focus on what happens to employees after they arrive. When human resources programs are integrated with overall organizational goals, moreover, they develop and promote not only "the best and the brightest" but those who are "right" according to organizational needs.

Identifying Variance and Closing Demand-Supply Gaps

In the systematic model proposed, the identification of variance between the demand created by strategic and operational plans and the availability of human resources as generated by personnel planning and development is an ongoing process, an activity that can take place at any number of system interfaces. In testing the viability of a preliminary strategy, for example, planners can draw on operational guidelines for human resources requirements to implement that strategy, compare these requirements with human resources availability forecasts, and identify any variance that should be considered—along with its cost implications—before the strategy becomes part of corporate plans.

With the comprehensive planning system in place, however, the process of identifying and dealing with the forecast variances between supply and availability—shown in outline form in Figure 1-7—becomes systematic. The objectives of strategic plans and operational requirements for achieving those objectives call for certain numbers and types of human resources—by skill codes, departments, locations, or other classifications—at different points of time in

Figure 1-7. **Simplified schematic of variance management within the basic model.**

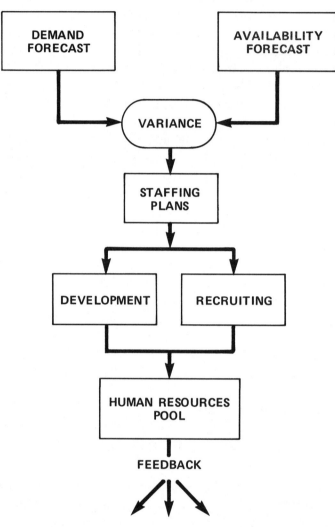

the planning cycle. Availability forecasts, based on human resources development programs, attrition rates, and other relevant data, can be produced in matching classifications and similarly projected to different points in time.

A comparison of these two types of forecasts produces variance projections—the gaps representing surpluses or shortages of people to meet organizational objectives. These gaps guide decision makers in forming new or revised staffing plans, which may call for different development programs, revised recruiting procedures or levels, or—in extreme cases—revision of corporate strategic plans. Operational interventions are also possible to close variance gaps—such as the introduction of laborsaving technology.

Guiding Principles Inherent in the Overall Human Resources Planning System

This book describes a model for planning human resources that is uniquely *comprehensive*, strategically *flexible*, systematically *integrated*, and eminently capable of gaining the support and commitment of top management because of perspectives and development techniques that make the human resources planning function more *credible* within the organization.

The model has been successfully applied, and could be successfully applied to any kind of organization, because these features are not by-products or accidental results of the planning approach. Rather, these characteristics are guiding principles in the development of an effective approach to strategic human resources planning and are built-in guarantees that the system will accomplish its ultimate goal: to provide the information needed to identify human resources demand; its availability; the "variance," or gap, between these forecasts; and the means of making the best choices for how to close this gap.

The strategic human resources planning system depicted in the generic model is deliberately and essentially:

- *Comprehensive*, incorporating business objectives and organizational conditions—both strengths and weaknesses as well as operational factors analysis, environmental change, and existing human resources policies and programs that will be shaped by strategic and operational plans. The development of the planning system requires the cooperation and participation of all parts of the organization and the collection of data from sources that are normally considered far afield from human resources concerns. There are ways of gaining this support and participation, explored at appropriate places in this book, but the most important reason why management will adopt a comprehensive approach such as this is that it will be perceived as a "business" system rather than merely a human resources planning system: Its benefits, and the critical planning direction it provides, accrue to the organization as a whole, not merely to the human resources department. (Thus, although we normally assume the need for a range of human resources programs to improve the availability of the skills and talents needed by tomorrow's organization, a comprehensive analysis of certain *other* organizations might indeed indicate the need for retrenchment and the phasing out of most existing human resources programs.)
- *Flexible*, because once the factors affecting supply and availability have been identified and quantified, planners can understand and adapt to the effects of change—different strategies, changing environmental conditions, new technology affecting operations, and workforce changes reflected in employee movement and development. An understanding of the relationships of change in the organization permits "what-if" mod-

eling of various alternative strategies, operational methods, and human resources activities or programs.

- *Integrated*, through information system technology that permits planners to more accurately assess strategic and operational demand, evaluate the impacts of human resources programs and policies, and make decisions and recommendations within the overall framework of corporate and business objectives. Thus, not only are human resources programs such as succession planning and career development complementary, but each owes its design objectives to the demands of long-range strategic and short-term operational goals.

- *Credible*—a stature attained by human resources planning because it responds to overall organizational needs. Nothing is assumed or taken for granted by the developers of a comprehensive, integrated system such as this: Determinations based on data and analysis, through the use of organizational diagnosis or other techniques, are an integral part of system development. The human resources planning system becomes credible, in short, because it is driven by the demands of the organization as a whole—not by the priorities of any department or function.

2

Concepts of HR Planning and Their Evolution in the United States

In a sense, integrated human resources planning such as that proposed here has no "history." This kind of systematic, integrated planning is in its infancy as a total system and could not have been born before today's convergence of newly sophisticated planning concepts for complex organizations and the information systems needed to integrate these concepts in a decision-making process.

In the free-world economies, neither government nor private-sector organizations have seen fit to attempt to incorporate today's planning concepts with the factors that influence human resources demand and availability across the entire organization and to do so in a way that identifies the difference, or variance, between supply and demand. The apparent complexities of the process, in the absence of a continuing "system" that gathers data from the many organizational sources involved and permits planners to analyze and model these data to evaluate the impacts of change, are necessarily daunting.

The planning concepts and the technology to implement them have arrived in the 1980s, however. It is only their effective integration that is completely new, although the microprocessor revolution beginning in the late 1970s has made the processing technology available for the first time to many organizations previously unable to afford computer costs.

The concepts that are merged in the integrated human resources planning system are shown in the simplified schematic in Figure 2-1. This shows that, in its most general terms, the human resources planning system aims at identifying the variance between demand forecasts and availability forecasts, so that management can intervene in any of the variables that affect these forecasts to assure the adequate supply of human resources in the quantity and quality needed in the years ahead.

Each of the planning concepts incorporated in the model has a history of

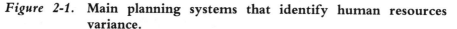

Figure 2-1. **Main planning systems that identify human resources variance.**

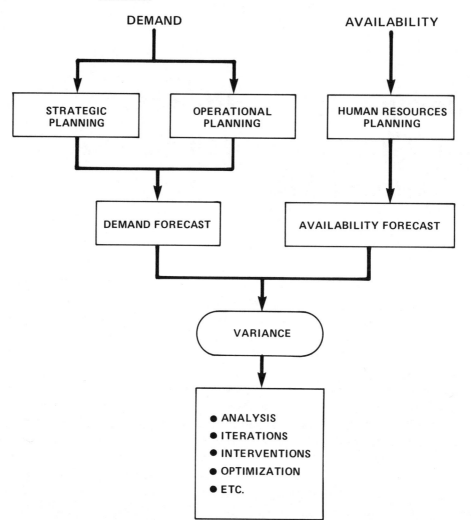

its own, or at least somewhat different sets of antecedents in its evolution to today's state of sophistication:

- *Strategic planning*, or long-range business planning based on environmental change and organizational capabilities in new environments, can be traced to every decision involving a new organizational direction based on changing times—Henry Ford's decision to offer standard Model Ts in one color (black) and pay Ford workers an unprecedented $5 per day to make them, for example. Strategic planning became formalized in U.S. concerns in the 1960s, suffered a relapse as the environment became less predictable, and is now enjoying a resurgence—although marked by a

new wave of controversy over its "place" in the organization, at staff or
line levels.

- *Operational planning,* or planning based on the actualities of the work itself,
  has its antecedents in the United States in the scientific management theories of Frederick W. Taylor and has evolved through modeling techniques developed in the postwar operational research era to today's highly
  sophisticated planning, scheduling, and cost-assignment systems.

- *Human resources planning,* traditionally called manpower planning, has
  had a checkered history conditioned by changing labor markets, technological impacts, scientific management, the human relations movement, and in the United States, sporadic government interventions of
  little lasting consequence. Today, human resources planning is recognized as including programmatic interventions that "proactively" shape
  availability—such as career development, succession planning, and appraisal systems for performance and potential.

The Meaning of "Availability" and Its Planning Significance

Historically, organizations that have attempted any significant degree of human
resources planning at all have focused most of their attention on the "demand"
side of the schematic shown in Figure 2-1. Strategic planning, whether rudi-
mentary or elaborate, has provided overall guidelines for the future direction of
the organization in a changing environment; operational planning, with its
short-term focus on the actual requirements of existing work, has simply been
an outgrowth of the need to continue operation and to improve efficiency
through the day-to-day allocation of human resources as well as the other resources that are necessary to production or to the provision of services.

Availability forecasting has only in recent years come to be understood as
a result of internal human resources development programs. In the past, "availability" of human resources has usually meant some vaguely defined external
population—low-cost labor in an underdeveloped nation, skilled factory workers in an industrial city, or millions of young men of draft age. With the Industrial
Revolution, this concept of "availability" presented planners with no particular
sense of urgency: Most jobs could be handled by interchangeable workers, with
minimal on-the-job training, and the supply of human resources to meet strategic
and operational planning needs seemed inexhaustible.

A fundamentally different meaning of the term *availability* has come to the
fore in the last few decades, as organizations have matured, become more technically and managerially specialized, and come to require increasingly cost-effective and productive managers and workers. Moreover, this new meaning of
human resources availability planning—which focuses attention inward on existing human resources and their development—provides the basic framework

or perspective from which human resources planners can actively shape the future organization to meet the requirements of strategic plans.

It is not presumptuous for human resources planners to attempt to "shape the organization" through programs of career development, the appraisal of performance and potential, succession planning, and other human resources development and planning programs. Rather, when human resources planning is understood as the primary source of the "availability" of people needed to meet the short- and long-term "demands" of operational and strategic planning, it becomes clear that nothing short of a systematic, integrated planning system will succeed in creating tomorrow's organization.

Put another way, companies with massive turnover rates and no particular job requirements to speak of can continue to view human resources availability in the old-fashioned way, as a product of external labor markets. If all that is needed is "warm bodies," and requirements are not likely to change in the next five to ten years, human resources availability depends on census data, labor-pool analysis, and wage and salary surveys to guide compensation policies. If most employees, including managers, will not be with the organization several years from now, there is obviously no point in long-term training and development programs.

Increasingly, however, the human resources demands of modern organizations require more than warm bodies. From the organization-specific skills and commitment of support workers to the positions of leadership at the upper levels of the organization, job requirements are more specialized than ever before. Even the military, traditionally a place where turnover has been virtually institutionalized except for a core of key officers and noncommissioned officers, is now seeking ways of creating more "career soldiers" with the skills and talents needed to operate and maintain multibillion-dollar investments in defense technology.

The general trend that Eli Ginzberg has called "the professionalization of the workforce"[1] and that others see as the growth of "knowledge workers" is cumulative evidence of changing human resources requirements in thousands of different organizations. Technological change, the demands of modern management, and the maturation of increasingly specialized jobs in more sophisticated Information Age industries have all accelerated the growth in the importance of skilled, knowledgeable, committed employees and managers.

Matching People and Jobs: Historical Antecedents

A concept central to the idea of human resources planning is that people have identifiable differences that are relevant to job performance. From the time of the pyramids, when some slaves were assigned to carry water and others helped push building blocks, employers have been attempting to put "the right people in the right jobs" based on observable or measurable differences among people.

At different times in the history of organized work, different aspects of the worker-work relationship have held the attention of employers. In the heyday of scientific management, for example, in the first two or three decades of this century, the work itself was the focus of all attention. The "right" workers were simply those who could go through the prescribed motions, at rates of speed determined by output requirements, and who were as monotonously consistent as the machines, desks, and countertops at which they worked.

Administrative science, emerging about 1915, applied notions of "innate suitability" to organizational functions; the human relations movement, starting in the 1930s, explored worker motivation; and the history of employee testing to help match people and jobs has led a course of its own down the years. Each of these "threads" has contributed to today's view of job matching as a human resources planning function.

Scientific Management

More than any other single source, most of the perspectives of Frederick Winslow Taylor (1856–1915), called the father of scientific management, fundamentally shaped American employers' views on human resources, the employment exchange, and labor relations generally in the twentieth century. Using the principles of scientific management, jobs could be classified by analyzing their component parts. The tasks involved in any job—Taylor studied shops and offices as well as factories—could be closely analyzed and specified, using time-motion studies and other scientific management tools, which meant that it was possible to define the characteristics of employees needed to perform these tasks.

Taylor advocated the scientific selection of workers—based, in part, on what today would be considered psychological testing—as well as training and development to improve productivity and cost-effectiveness.

The entire focus of scientific management was on jobs rather than people. Analysis of tasks, and ways of facilitating or speeding the completion of tasks through analysis by "efficiency experts," provided the criteria for human resources selection and development. The underlying assumption was that workers would do only what they were made to do or motivated to do by the pay system—which should be tied directly to task completion—and it was management's responsibility to find the most efficient ways of performing tasks and make certain that employees follow procedures.

Whatever the drawbacks of scientific management—and its wide adoption may have been the central cause of an almost century-long labor-management adversarial relationship—the movement's views on the importance of job analysis have had a lasting effect on human resources management and planning. The formal description of a given job, its requirements and compensation, is the basic foundation block of all human resources planning activities.

Administrative Science

The chief contribution of the administrative science movement, led by French industrialist Henri Fayol in the early decades of the century, was to legitimatize Personnel as a staff function. The acquisition and development of the different kinds of people needed to operate and manage the organization was too important a job to be left to chance or the vagaries of shifting fortunes, personal viewpoints, and individual ambitions. Organizations needed certain identifiable skills and talents, and the best way to satisfy these needs was through an administrative, centralized personnel function.[2]

Administrative science was based on a top-down view of the organization—as opposed to Taylor's bottom-up analysis of work beginning with its component tasks. Fayol first classified the various activities of an industrial enterprise into six groups: technical, commercial, financial, security, accounting, and managerial. Within each activity, he then identified the kinds of knowledge and skills necessary to complete typical functions. Managerial functions, for example, included planning, organization, command, coordination, and control. Many contemporary management theorists have retained Fayol's classification system with only minor changes.

Administrative science concerned itself chiefly with organizational structure rather than with performance techniques or specific procedures. Its contribution to human resources planning was considerable, however. It showed a need for a centralized, planning-oriented personnel function at the highest levels of management in large organizations, to identify and provide people needed to meet organizational requirements.

The Human Relations Movement

The human relations movement—which generally is considered to have started in 1924 with the work of Elton Mayo, Fritz Roethlisberger, W. J. Dickson, and others involved with the Western Electric Hawthorne Works—shifted the focus somewhat from jobs to people. Improved efficiency and productivity were not merely an issue of job design or structural organization but a matter of motivation, job satisfaction, and interest in the work itself. Job dissatisfaction, which human relationists linked to performance, could arise from factors having nothing to do with the job itself, such as company policies, supervision, interpersonal relationships, and job security.[3]

Later, others such as Frederick Herzberg said that these "dissatisfiers" had nothing to do with productivity: An unhappy worker could be as productive as the most willing employee. Instead, in his view, workers motivated by the work itself—a sense of accomplishment, chances for advancement, and so on—were those whose productivity improved.[4]

Whatever the relationship between satisfaction and productivity—and the debate continued under the general rubric of quality of work life programs—the 1930s and early 1940s saw a major shift in thinking about "the right employee for the right job," a new focus on employee needs as a factor in improved efficiency.

In order to put human relations ideas into practice—through job design that at least partially considered the needs of workers, less authoritarian supervision, improved conditions, job enrichment, and so on—in the unionized sector of the labor force, labor-management cooperation was essential. World War II was both a boon to the human relations movement and its eventual undoing, in this respect. During the war, labor-management cooperative committees sprang up in thousands of U.S. factories. As the economy improved, and a reduced war effort diminished the need for cooperative programs (which were usually established under government prodding), companies came to view these committees as incursions into managerial control. Labor, for its part, was glad to have increased wages instead of a voice in working conditions. By the late 1970s, some of these ideas had returned to unionized environments in the United States, especially in industries such as steel and autos where foreign competition had resulted in layoffs and the need for laborsaving technology.

For workers and managers generally, the heritage of the human relations movement has been a broad range of human resources programs aimed at improving employee morale, motivation, and knowledge about the organization and their work. Most of these activities, as noted by Szilagyi and Wallace,[5] have come under the planning and direction of the personnel department:

- Participative management, the range of activities from quality circles to suggestion-box mechanisms that allow employees to participate in the decisions that affect their working lives
- Job redesign, often aimed at presenting workers with more challenging or rewarding work by expanding responsibilities or more clearly putting the job into perspective as part of the overall organizational purpose
- Communications improvements, opening new avenues of two-way communication between supervisors and employees, between top management and employees, and within work groups where teamwork is essential

Today, behavioral scientists play a major role in such human resources functions as employee selection procedures, evaluation, organizational development (which looks at the "psychology" of the organization as well as of the individuals within it), training, and job design. Theories about why people work (such as Maslow's needs hierarchy) and what motivates employees to work harder (such as B. F. Skinner's operant conditioning theories) are applied to different kinds of employees in different situations. And while a universally applicable theory has yet to be developed, the perception that human resources planning includes questions such as motivation and individual response is firmly entrenched.

Personnel Testing

As might be expected given its nature, the use of testing as a planning instrument—to set minimum levels of competence for a job, screen applicants, categorize large groups (such as military recruits) for job assignment, or in some other way attempt to match people and jobs through preemployment evaluation—has a long and controversial history. Since the turn of the century, psychologists, work analysts, professional groups, and others have been developing one kind or another of testing approach designed for different objectives. As early as 1910, Hugo Munsterberg developed a test to select personnel for the job of motorman on the Boston Elevated Railway and tried to relate scores achieved on this test to later success on the job.[6]

Over the years, the issue that has caused the greatest controversy about testing has been predictive validity: How accurately does a test measure a person's performance in the future?[7] Where a test focuses on job-related knowledge or skills, such as a bar exam or a typing test, this is clearly not an issue. But where the test is expected to ascertain an individual's aptitude to become a lawyer or psychological suitability to sit in the typing pool all day, test validity enters less clearly charted waters. And to the extent that the test will *prevent* some individuals from studying law or being hired as trainee typists, such predictive tests become increasingly susceptible to controversy—or even litigation. For years, some employers have assumed that IQ tests provided a useful evaluation of general intellectual capabilities, for example, and could predict learning ability. More recently, these types of tests have come under fire as being culturally biased, favoring those with certain types of background and experiences, and inadequate as a test of "innate" intelligence or learning ability.

Despite the reputation of the military establishment as a notoriously thoughtless employer—everyone who has ever worn any country's uniform knows of occasional mismatches such as car mechanics who become medics, professors who are employed as clerk typists, and ill-suited individuals who are elevated to the position of platoon leader merely because they attended college—personnel testing for occupational classification received its first major application in the military. Early in World War I, it became clear that a standard instrument was needed to evaluate large numbers of recruits quickly, to weed out those patently unfit for service and classify others according to general capabilities and, in some cases, suitability for positions of responsibility.

Arthur Otis, who had been working on group tests of intelligence, turned over his findings to the American Psychological Association, empowered by the armed forces to investigate testing procedures. In 1917, the Otis test, with few revisions, was put into use as the Army Alpha Test.

The Alpha Test, still employed in a revised form in the military, was based on some 13 different varieties of questions, all combining to yield a single score. Arithmetic, reasoning, verbal ability, and general information are tested. The test has been considered highly successful for its limited purposes—notwithstanding the legendary administrative mistakes, such as those noted above, that mismatch people and jobs in the military. A companion test, the Beta Test for non-English-speaking and illiterate recruits, was developed to test spatial and other nonverbal relationships. Although the Beta Test became obsolete as the military came to require English literacy of recruits, it set the stage for the nonverbal tests in use today.

In the postwar era of the 1950s and 1960s, educators and industrial psychologists developed and used a wide range of tests intended to predict occupational attitudes or identify characteristics of behavior that were considered suitable (or unsuitable) in certain occupations. Personality tests such as the Bernreuter Personality Inventory, Edwards Personal Preference Schedule, and Minnesota Multiphasic Personality Inventory came into wide use among school counselors as well as employers. Presumably, such tests identify individual traits and needs—whether a person would rather do research or selling, for example—that can be associated with successful job performance.

Beyond assessing technical competence or job-required knowledge, testing has at times become a human resources planning tool in the hands of employers seeking "our kind of people" to join or manage the organization. Tests can be designed to evaluate personality traits such as respect for authority or gregariousness; to assess values considered important by the organization; or even to rate environmental factors considered keys to future performance. Unless such tests are clearly job-related, however, and can be backed by validation that shows a necessary relationship between test scores and actual performance, they are not only of limited value to the organization but may cause EEO problems, as well.

Human Resources Planning and Public Policy in the United States

The concept of human resources planning as a legitimate concern of public policy in the United States came to the fore with World War II, with the induction of 8 million Americans into the armed forces, subsequent personnel shortages, and escalating demands for workers to meet war production goals. Virtually overnight, past assumptions about the endless availability of human resources in the external labor market were reversed.

At the government level, the Federal Office of Production Management presided over the gradual shift from civilian to defense production until 1942. In January of that year, President Roosevelt created a new agency, the War Production Board, to oversee an accelerated defense effort. Production programs competed with one another for machine tools, scarce materials, and skilled workers. At the end of 1942, the War Manpower Commission was granted operating authority to supervise the mobilization of men and women for both military and civilian jobs and to make optimal use of "manpower" (increasingly women, in fact) for munitions plants, shipyards, aircraft plants, and factories engaged in the production of military materiel.

Toward the end of World War II, as larger firms engaged in war production looked ahead, the idea of "master planning" or postwar planning gained increasing attention. Management realized that the end of hostilities would require a shift to consumer products, and the long-range planning this entailed included human resources planning.

Oddly enough, the war may have "primed" American industrialists and government leaders to undertake human resources planning in both the public and private sector, but the most conspicuous example of such planning occurred under the Marshall Plan in Europe rather than in the United States. In America, the postwar boom capitalized on advanced production methods developed during the war, a previously pent-up consumer buying spree, and government programs for returning veterans—most notably the G.I. Bill, which sent millions of young men to college at government expense, just at a time when the economy was ready to absorb millions of college graduates in more specialized management jobs. As a result, when government defense procurement declined from $83 billion to $31 billion between 1945 and 1946, the gross national product slipped only slightly and was soon headed toward record levels in the United States.

In the West European countries, however, the end of hostilities saw a different picture. Widespread shortages of food, medical supplies, and clothing, together with decimated production facilities and a disastrous year for crops in 1947, created widespread suffering. The continuing crisis was addressed by General George Marshall in a Harvard University commencement speech (June 5, 1947), in which he called on the United States for "friendly aid in the *drafting of a European program*" for recovery (emphasis added).

The Marshall Plan that followed—a four-year, $12 billion program that by 1951 had raised industrial output by some 40 percent over prewar levels—was in large part a human resources planning program. Its implementation required the identification of people with the skills and knowledge needed in such fields as scheduling, procurement, transportation, warehousing, and the reconstruction of industrial capacity—all according to a planned sequence. In short, the Marshall Plan involved the "drafting of a European program" to employ the right people at the right time in the right locations.

Human Resources Planning and Technology

The next significant appearance of the idea of human resources planning as public policy emerged with the unexpectedly high unemployment rates of the late 1950s and early 1960s in the United States. At the time, many policymakers were convinced that automation was creating permanent, structural unemployment among displaced workers, often mature men whose skills were made obsolete by new laborsaving technologies.

In response to these fears, Congress passed the Manpower Development and Training Act (MDTA) of 1964, legislation that "marked the beginning point of a serious widespread interest in manpower planning at the national, regional, industrial, and firm levels."[8] The MDTA drew its authority from the Employment Act of 1946, which gave the federal government responsibility for maintaining full employment, promoting productivity, and assuring economic growth. The specific aims of the MDTA were training and retraining of displaced workers and improved job mobility and worker versatility to take advantage of opportunities in an uneven labor market.

Within a very few years, however, most of the original "targets" of the MDTA had found jobs in an expanding economy. By the late 1960s, the "structurally unemployed" were seen to be largely disadvantaged minorities, youth, and later women—groups that became the focus of job training and public service programs that succeeded the MTDA, including the Comprehensive Employment Training Act (CETA).

At about the same time that Americans were becoming concerned about the job displacement of factory workers caused by automation, international developments were causing an important shift in government policy toward higher education, science, and the role of government in shaping scientific human resources. When the Soviet Union launched *Sputnik* in 1957, scientific education and research became a political issue almost overnight in the United States, and an unprecedented flow of government aid to schools, high-tech employers, and space contractors quickly followed.

Environmental Impacts on Human Resources Planning

From the 1970s through today, human resources planning has concerned itself with a broad range of environmental factors with more or less immediate impact on the realization of actual organization-specific human resources goals. The view that planning for change in external labor markets, changing employee attitudes, new values of "new breed" workers, and other broad sociological, political, and economic change can lead to effective human resources plans may be valid in theory; in fact, as discussed in Chapter 4, strategic planning is based on an analysis of factors such as these, aimed at a determination of which environmental changes will affect the organization in the years ahead. In our view, the proper focus of human resources planning is inward. Without a comprehensive grasp of organizational objectives, operational needs, and existing human resources and their development needs, no amount of analysis of general environmental trends can have much meaning to human resources planners.

A chief cause of the interest in environmental analysis in the 1970s was government regulation, especially the Civil Rights Act and subsequent laws mandating EEO activities and record keeping for most employers. Government regulation—including OSHA, ERISA, the Equal Pay Act, and the Age Discrimination in Employment Act—wrought huge changes in corporate personnel policies and their costs. The record-keeping and reporting requirements of EEO regulations alone helped spur the introduction of human resource information systems in America (see Chapter 3), and for the first time, companies and public employers that had thought they were in "unregulated industries" found that government agencies could make costly demands on managerial time and personnel activities.

Whatever else employers thought of the new wave of regulation, most agreed on one thing: It could have been planned for. In retrospect, companies that spent millions "reacting" to laws and lawsuits—such as firms ordered to institute costly affirmative action programs—felt that they should have seen it coming. Political shifts, the growth of women in the labor force, the civil rights movement—these and other environmental trends could have been seen working toward EEO legislation.

Thus, having seen the impact of environmental change on corporate personnel practices and costs, human resources planners began looking at a host of other political, social, and economic factors that might have impacts. Today, some of the major trends that may (or may not) affect human resources planning include:

- The shifting age distribution of the workforce, as "baby-boom" workers age to create a "middle-age bulge" in the labor force of the 1990s, relatively fewer teenagers enter the labor force, and the retired population begins escalating in about the year 2010
- More women in the labor force, especially college-educated women seeking managerial and professional careers
- Inflationary pressures, which—combined with rising salaries for an increasingly "educated" workforce—call for more creative compensation systems
- Technological change, which—although of uncertain consequence in terms of overall employment levels—will make many jobs obsolete and require entirely new kinds of skills and managerial abilities in other areas

Further examples of these kinds of external environmental factors—a "taxonomy" of typical issue areas—are shown in Chapter 4, Figure 4-2.

Persistent Perceptions and Today's Requirements

Historically, the origins of the kind of integrated human resources planning and development system that is the basis for this book lie in a simpler time, when organizations were smaller, objectives clearer, and job requirements more specifically related to objectives. In the days before the Industrial Revolution, for example, the proprietor of a tailor shop had no trouble keeping the interrelationships of strategic, operational, and human resources plans in his head, and the importance of developing the right human resources to reach objectives— the apprentices and craftsmen to make the clothes dictated by fashion and the shop's production goals—was obvious.

As organizations have grown and become more complex, the critical relationship between people and organizational goals has become less obvious to proprietors and managers. The organization's objectives may not be mere production goals, for example; return on investment, market share, short-term profitability, asset growth, cost reduction, new technology, or a range of other aims may be driving organizational plans. At the same time, human resources needs have changed: Production lines on which people are often interchangeable parts have replaced the artisan class, the rise of the managerial class has created changing human resources needs, and expanding functions in the organization—marketing, distribution, finance, legal, research, transportation, clerical, security, and any number of other activities needed to maintain the multifaceted organization of today—have further clouded the relationship between people employed and organizational goals.

The syndrome under which increasingly large and complex organizations "take on a life of their own," with only the most tenuous resemblance to original objectives, is not being disparaged here. The world is more complex, undoubtedly; but the human mind has not reached the limits of its comprehension of complexity, by any means. Rather, the point being made is that the role of human resources in most organizations today is just as important as it was in the time of small tailor shops—but a great deal harder to understand and "keep in one's head." Hence, the need for systems. Data gathering and processing systems permit the analysis of the factors involved in strategic plans, operational plans, and human resources plans and show how these factors are interrelated, allowing managers to assess future human resources needs and manage the development of human resources in ways that achieve organizational ends.

In the past, the development of this kind of systematic approach to human resources planning has been delayed by these kinds of top management viewpoints and biases:

- The continuing misconception, extant since the Industrial Revolution, that human resources are "available" in virtually unlimited supply and can be bought on short notice, when needed, at costs corresponding to their contribution to the organization.
- A traditional reluctance to invest in in-house development of human resources because of the expense and time involved. Even today, when most organizations have established a training and development function, this function is among the first casualties of recessionary periods or temporary business downturns. Top management often sees training and development as more of a frill than a necessity.
- The relatively low status of the human resources function—compared with finance, operations, or marketing, for example. Staff human resources managers have only in recent years begun to reach the top planning levels in most U.S. firms, a result of climbing personnel costs and the need for increased productivity, technically competent employees, and improved management.
- Resistance to information technology by human resources professionals themselves. Such resistance has been a "real" cause of top management's guarded confidence in the personnel function. Too often, human resources professionals grounded in humanistic ideals view computeriza-

tion generally as antithetical to individualism, freedom of choice, and the creative expression of distinctly "human" characteristics. There can be more than a modicum of truth in these perceptions when computerized information systems are improperly designed: for example, when a performance appraisal system looks at a manager's results only and produces an unqualified rating from 1 to 5. In actuality, however, computerization of data makes possible *more* attention to individual characteristics and performance criteria, not less, because it relieves people of repetitive clerical tasks so that they can spend more time on what's important.

■ The methodology of human resources planning is perceived as "soft" in comparison to financial or operational planning, an intrinsic handicap of a function dealing with people rather than dollars, machines, or raw materials. Although much remains to be understood about such issues as the appraisal of potential (how to identify the leaders of tomorrow, for example), the modern tools of human resources planning and development, when applied in the context of organizational goals and operational needs, are at least as scientific as econometric analysis—and far more capable of "creating" the organization of the future.

Craft has summarized the general perceptions regarding human resources planning that remain widespread among top managers—most of which, it will be seen, are addressed by the systematic approach proposed in this book. In his view, the HR planning function is seen to suffer from:

■ An inadequate theoretical framework
■ Little integration of the quantitative and the qualitative
■ Excessive emphasis on demand forecasting and little attention to availability forecasting
■ Inadequate use of behavioral intervening factors
■ Emphasis on short-range projections
■ Questionable forecasting data
■ Unrealistic expectations of forecasting
■ Inadequate emphasis on evaluation and consequent lack of commitment to implement plans and programs indicated by evaluation[9]

The framework proposed for our integrated human resources planning and development system is nothing less than the framework of strategic and operational plans—where the organization intends to be on the long-range planning horizon and how it intends to get there.

3

The Technology of Planning: Today's Human Resource Information Systems

Human resource information system (HRIS) technology is often the modus operandi, especially in large or complex organizations, of a successfully integrated, flexible human resources planning system. The advent of these computerized personnel information systems presents planners with the tools needed to efficiently examine what in some organizations might be an otherwise mind-boggling volume of data about the organization, its work, and its workers—as well as their interrelationships and the impacts of change created by planned strategies.

Computerized personnel information systems of one sort or another are now in place in most U.S. companies of more than a few hundred employees. Some are simply payroll systems, used to assure the accurate and prompt issuance of checks, but an increasing number partake of the characteristics of a true HRIS. Using microcomputer-based systems that sometimes incorporate payroll functions, the new wave of HRIS users includes organizations primarily concerned with more efficient benefits administration, employers that need data to comply with government regulatory requirements, and organizations seeking a range of decision-making support data to increase productivity, reduce costs, and optimize operations. In many cases, the microprocessor revolution, which has spawned the personal computer, has also brought human resources planning within the reach of smaller organizations previously unable to afford the technology.

Objectives, Background, and Definitions

Most of these and other HRIS applications include some form of "planning," if only planning for next year's budget. Systems that permit quick analysis of changes in measurable variables—such as the cost of adding a new employee benefit or of training six new technicians—are essentially planning tools.

Today, many larger organizations are using an HRIS in the growing field of human resources planning (née manpower planning), but few have found ways of integrating this planning with strategic business planning and operational planning. The needs of the overall system, as discussed in Chapter 1, underscore the importance of an automated information system that permits up-to-date data collection, enables planners to look at data in many ways, and provides common definitions of information across departments. These needs, or "specifications," of an integrated human resources planning system include, for example:

- Information about related business, operational, and human resources factors, such as the effects of interest rates and productivity on the purchase of new laborsaving equipment
- The ability to perform contingency, or "what-if," analyses based on changes in either demand forecasts or availability and rapidly update projections as new information comes in
- Timely and accurate reporting capabilities that can give managers the information they need to develop appropriate strategies and the most effective programs and policies to achieve them
- Measurement capabilities that allow managers to assess the effectiveness of such human resources programs as management development, performance evaluation, appraisal of potential, succession planning, and others in attaining corporate business objectives

Clearly, this means a mechanized personnel information system. At every stage in the strategic planning process, from diagnosis of organizational strengths and weaknesses and financial considerations through operational analysis and the development of human resources availability, there is a need for information that is complete, up-to-date, consistently defined, and capable of being manipulated by planners seeking answers to "what-if" hypotheses.

Planners use the HRIS and the employee data base in ways that are both general (or cumulative of corporate personnel data) and specific (or related to specific human resources functions). General planning data, such as the display of organizational employees shown in Figure 3-1, help managers develop and analyze long-range strategic perspectives on organizational needs and goals. The more specific applications of HRIS technology to personnel functions, as discussed under "Applications of an HRIS" below, answer planning questions as they relate to specific functions: How much will benefits cost three years from now? Who is available to move into the job of financial vice-president? How many mechanical engineers will be needed to offset turnover at a given location during the next five years?

One critical reason for having an HRIS, of course, is that all information analysis—whether for general strategic planning purposes or for functional pro-

Figure 3-1.   **Company population breakdown—by job function.**

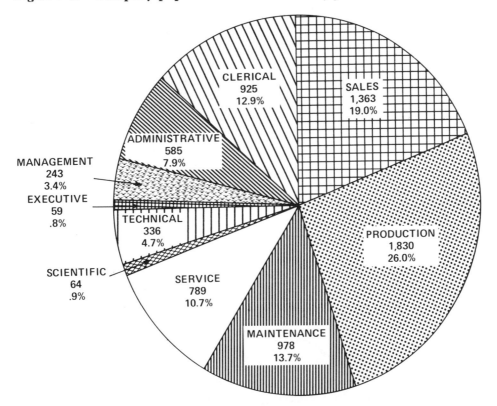

grams—uses the same information. Jobs and skills classifications are defined in the same way; people's skills are quantified to a large extent; and the measurements used are consistent throughout the organization. When a change is made to the data base—whether it's a single new employee or a pay raise for an entire class of employees—the change is made once for all, and the new data are available to all HRIS users.

Most important from the strategic human resources planner's viewpoint, the ability of today's computer system to digest and process voluminous amounts of data—from external environmental trends affecting human resources to personnel demand forecasts for scheduled and potential operations—permits the systematic analysis of all factors affecting the availability and demand requirements of human resources in the years ahead. The outcome of this process, discussed in detail in Part IV of this book, is a human resources variance forecast, such as the one depicted in Figure 3-2. Behind this apparently simple chart lie many hours of data collection, analysis, program development and evaluation, and computation of the impacts of change on human resources availability and demand.

The need for an automated data system is also apparent in the construction of forecasting "models"—the simulations of reality that relate planning factors

Figure 3-2. **Human resources variance forecast.**

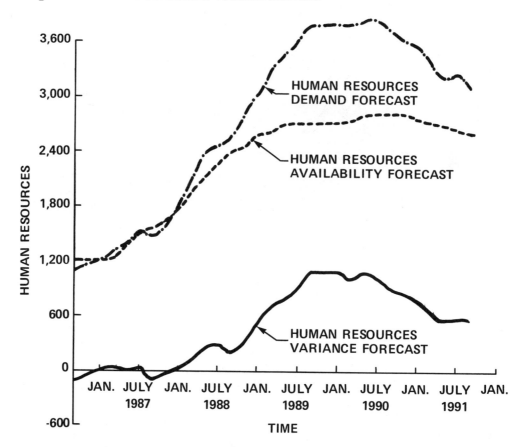

to one another in equations that represent relationships in the real world; dozens or even hundreds of variously interdependent factors must often be included. Model testing, and the manipulation of model variables "to see what would happen" if a planning variable were changed, can entail a seemingly endless number of chain reactions, different kinds and ratios of dependencies, and new data for each interrelated factor. This work is simply not feasible without the power of computerized information systems.

A brief review of the history of computers and the reasons for their somewhat tardy arrival on the personnel management scene helps put today's human resource information systems in perspective. That perspective includes this important principle: Computers are nothing more than management tools; it is the data, and how managers analyze the data made available by this technology, that count.

History and Evolution of Computers in Personnel

Charles Babbage (1792–1871) is generally credited with the invention of the first true computer, a device that could do more than simple mathematics. A colorful nineteenth-century Englishman, Babbage conceived a machine that could calculate logarithms and other functions swiftly and precisely. Babbage's dream machines—they were never completely built, for want of precision tooling—were extensive systems of gears and cogs.

But one Babbage concept had the main parts of a modern computer: a logic center able to manipulate data according to programmed rules; a memory for storing information; a control mechanism for effecting instructions; and finally, input and output devices. One of his notions, the use of punched cards to feed instructions to the machine, was put to use by the U.S. Bureau of the Census in 1890 and by an office-machines company that later became International Business Machines.

The punched card system used in the 1890 census, actually invented by Herman Hollerith in the late 1880s, permitted mechanical sorting, listing, and summarization of data. When the first electronic accounting machinery (EAM) cards were developed for use with the earliest electronic digital computers in the 1940s, the 80-column cards were used by some payroll departments to store a necessarily limited amount of information about employees.

The EAM equipment of the 1940s made it possible to process punched cards electronically, but these operations were limited to executing a fixed set of instructions that were actually wired into a control panel. Wires were plugged into the panel or board much like an old-fashioned telephone switchboard, and new instructions for the EAM meant changing the configuration of plugs in the board. The extremely small card-storage space of 80 columns limited the amount of information retained; at most, a card used for payroll or personnel data kept basic information such as name, Social Security number, salary data, sex, birth date, and a few company codes.

As noted by Walker, the use of computers in personnel has generally lagged behind applications in finance, engineering, and other business functions.[1] A large part of the reason for the relative slowness of their adoption in human resources is attributed to the dynamics of personnel data—people moving in and out of the employee population, changing jobs in the organization, being promoted, learning new skills, and having an almost limitless array of changes occur that affect their relationships to jobs, benefits, pay, and other costs associated with employment.

While the 80-column cards were still being used in the 1950s and early 1960s, the costs of maintaining personnel records that went beyond basic information were prohibitive. Then, with the development of more powerful equipment such as the IBM 360 line in the 1960s, the advent of management information systems (MISs) designed to incorporate the total data of the organization into one system further showed the distinctive complexity of personnel information.

While the use of computers was spreading to inventory control, accounts receivable, and other areas, most companies felt that the effort involved in collecting and maintaining personnel records—beyond payroll-type data—was too expensive to justify a "stand-alone" personnel information system. There was no "bottom-line payoff" to computerizing personnel data. Exceptions to this general state of affairs included a few government contractors using skills inventory systems to help estimate and bid defense contracts as early as the 1950s and, later on, a few larger banks and insurance companies that had both the computer facilities and the high labor costs that made it worthwhile to mechanize personnel data.

All of this changed quickly in the 1970s, spurred by the information requirements of government regulation, tumbling computer costs, and the growth of time-sharing for companies without computers. For employers of more than a thousand or so people, the costs of complying with government reporting requirements under the equal opportunity laws, ERISA, OSHA, and other legislation suddenly made computerized personnel systems "economically feasible." Especially in EEO cases, employers were appearing before government agencies and courts with nothing but good intentions in hand: They had not deliberately discriminated in employment practices, in most cases, but they had no statistical data to support those practices, the "effects" of which were often discriminatory to women or minorities.

To fulfill government reporting requirements and protect themselves from costly settlements, companies began developing stand-alone personnel information systems that carried data on applicants, pay characteristics and changes, and compensation and benefits, as well as data describing job functions. As time went on, it became increasingly clear that the same kind of data needed to comply with or assure equity under the equal pay laws could be used by compensation professionals to better analyze and plan compensation, that job analysis data could be incorporated into the system to improve performance evaluation programs, and so on.

Once the personnel department had its own system, with basic personnel data on work and workers collected and processed according to uniform procedures for the entire organization, the various functions of personnel—compensation administration, EEO, training, and so forth—were able to draw on these data, add elements specific to their function, and create the "modules" discussed under "Applications of an HRIS" below. As hardware and software costs have continued to come down in the microprocessor era of the 1980s, the capabilities of computerized human resource information systems have increasingly been used to analyze the costs and benefits of specific human resources programs and to plan for organizational and human resources change.

Basic Concepts of an HRIS

Human resource information systems are inherently planning systems, because they provide the kinds of information, and illustrate the cause-effect relationships among data, that are needed to plan change. No two systems are exactly alike if they have been developed as they should be, on the basis of the specifics of organizational human resources and the needs of individual companies.

As Walker points out, however, there are at least five basic concepts that all personnel systems have in common: The complete HRIS definitionally includes a data base, data entry methods, data retrieval techniques, provisions for data quality, and an administrative function or department often called the human resources information center (HRIC).[2]

The Data Base. The number and kinds of different "data elements" in the data base—from Social Security numbers to performance appraisal ratings—essentially define the scope and capabilities of the HRIS. These elements—covering both organizational information (such as job codes and job descriptions) and employee data (such as age, race, salary history, and sex)—can number in the hundreds; a typical fully developed HRIS may have 400 to 500 elements in the central data base and 100 more in code-related "tables," which carry detailed companywide data on types of employees, such as all employees at a given location or in a certain salary range.

The needs analysis that is the essential first step in HRIS development—the process of determining the personnel objectives of the system, its reports, desired retrieval capabilities, and human resources programs served by the system—will determine what should be in the data base. Because an input method must be devised for each element, as well as editing procedures, processing steps, and types of reports or methods of displaying the element, there are economic limits to the number of elements that can be included in the system. The kinds of information that *could* be included in the data base about people and jobs are virtually limitless—from school grades to medical histories—so the data base must be carefully limited to the kinds of information that will serve the purposes of the HRIS, as determined by the needs analysis.

Data Entry. Each item of information in the data base has to come from somewhere, and methods must be devised to link this "origination point" with the HRIS in a way that permits the supplying of data that are accurate, timely, and revised as often as necessary. Some data come from the company or a specific department, such as job location or the characteristics of a benefit plan; other information comes from supervisors; and some comes directly from employees, such as home addresses, career planning preferences, or skills inventory information.

Data that originate with the employer can often be kept in separate tables that carry information on groups of employees, types of jobs, benefits or compensation packages, or other arrays of data common to all jobs or employees within a certain category.

Data that come in about employees are often entered and kept up-to-date by the use of a "turnaround document," a report first filled out by the employee; entered into the HRIS, which prints out the report; and returned to the employee's management for verification—and perhaps an annual review.

An "ideal" form of turnaround document is a comprehensive document sometimes known as a payroll change report or personnel action form. Whether viewed as a "personnel" form or a "payroll" form, this turnaround document is used to make changes to both systems or to make all changes in an integrated payroll-personnel system.

For example, when a promotion has been approved, the form is filled out and signed, sent to data processing, and returned to supervisors and perhaps to the employee involved. Once verified, it is returned to the systems administrator and is used to update all relevant data elements in both personnel and payroll files. Thus, the single change not only results in a different salary rate but updates such files as job function codes, employee level, pension data, and a range of others that may include parking privileges.

Data Retrieval. The data resident in the HRIS should be available for retrieval in whatever formats and to whatever extent the needs analysis indicates. Different modules (see "Applications of an HRIS" below) or personnel functions will require different ways of looking at information, and each must be accounted for in the system's design.

The technology of data retrieval has made enormous strides in recent years, in large part aided by the advent of microcomputers. In many cases, data have become so "available" to a broader range of managers and clerical people throughout the office that the human resources information center administrators responsible for retrieval (see below) are more concerned with limiting access to sensitive data than with providing further access.

Retrieval means more than mere "access," however. The methodologies should be in place to permit users of the HRIS to produce fixed reports—such as EEO-1 reports or head counts by function—as well as reports devised to analyze specific kinds of data. The versatility of today's systems, including some microcomputer-based systems, permits users to generate a wide range of "ad hoc" or tailor-made reports and obtain information in formats that show a diverse array of relationships, historical data, and "what-if" outcomes of change in any data base element.

Ordinarily, the fewer "fixed" reports that are produced regularly—in relation to ad hoc reports—the more effectively the HRIS is being utilized. Fixed reports have a way of outliving their original purposes and can grow in number over the years to reach a point where information overload becomes an issue among organization managers.

Data Quality. Systematically or through administrative procedures, the HRIS must include provisions for data quality: the accuracy and timeliness of data and how they are measured and sustained. The concept of accuracy in a fully developed, multipurpose, elaborate HRIS with many data elements is, in a sense, a philosophical issue. Accuracy standards, which should be set for every data element, do not always have to be 100 percent: This goal may be unnecessarily expensive to attain.

Payroll information—how much a person is paid, for example—should of course be 100 percent accurate, and efforts to assure this will never be too expensive. For other kinds of data—such as where college degrees were earned—the accuracy goal may be 90 percent, eliminating the need for rigid editing requirements for this element. The needs analysis, again, will guide standards of accuracy and timeliness. In some organizations, education and training data are just as critical as payroll information, for instance.

Timeliness also affects data quality. If a given report is accurate "as far as it goes" but does not include the latest pay period or some other important data not yet available, data quality suffers.

Periodically, HRIS administrators test the accuracy of the data base through samples and audits of information of various kinds, compared to data from the originators or from input documents. Timeliness is also reviewed, usually in response to a user department's request for some more up-to-date information.

The Human Resources Information Center. Most medium- to large-scale HRIS installations—with many personnel users and a complex data base covering many kinds of information, retrieval methods, and capabilities—set up an administrative function made up of data systems people who know about human resources needs or vice versa. Often called a human resources information center (HRIC), this organization performs functions that are indispensable to effective personnel system use—from technological research to data base security and privacy controls.

The HRIC is essentially an administrative organization that sees to it that data are being correctly entered, establishes editing runs, and enforces the accuracy and timeliness standards determined by management.

In addition, however—and this is why personnel expertise should be resident in the HRIC—this organization is responsible for all kinds of access to the data base. In addition to conducting retrievals for "clients" in various personnel functions, the HRIC may also help users develop reports of their own. This requires not only an understanding of what's in the data base and how it can be retrieved but some appreciation of the needs of the users. In certain cases, for example, a department may request a "new" report when an available fixed report will suffice. Or users may not realize that the data base contains more useful data than they had thought: They can get data that show where a person's pay stands in an overall pay bracket or range, for example, in addition to just the amount of the person's current salary.

Data base security, which is the protection of this valuable resource from unwarranted use or intrusion by "hackers," and data base privacy, a broader issue involving personal rights and corporate policies, are also within the purview of the HRIC. Increasingly, especially with the proliferation of microcomputer use, human resources systems have security and privacy provisions "built in" to their software. Only certain departments can see certain data, for example; only users with a security clearance above a certain level can view certain data (and a higher level is needed to print out those data). In even the most security-conscious systems, however, there remains a need for an administrative function to assign access codes, monitor usage, and regularly change codes to assure that data are secure. Privacy issues, a growing concern among Americans in the Information Age, are usually dealt with through company policies implemented by the HRIC. What kinds of information should be stored in the data base? (Medical history? Disabilities? Home ownership?) Who can access personnel data? (Top managers only? Just those with a "need to know"? Anyone with a micro?)

Some of these privacy issues can be addressed through systematic procedures, using different access codes or codes that apply only to certain kinds of data. For example, only salary administrators may be allowed to see pay data.

Other privacy issues depend on organizational policies: Do we allow employees to see their entire record, or everything except certain evaluations? What kinds of information do we give out over the phone, under court order, or not at all? Often, the HRIC may be responsible for obtaining signed releases from employees who may wish credit checks to be honored or job information to be made available.

Finally, the HRIC is the logical organization to suggest and develop "enhancements" to the HRIS, to satisfy new needs that arise or to take advantage of the latest technology. This latter function underscores the importance of having a research and development capability in the modern HRIS, to keep abreast of rapidly changing developments in the costs, capabilities, and improved features of computer hardware and software becoming available today.

System Design

The above "basic concepts" of the true HRIS tell nothing about personnel system design—the structure of the data base, its file arrangement, or what kinds of computers go where in the organization, all of which are considerations that will depend on corporate resources and the requirements uncovered in the needs analysis.

Design is, or should be, a mirror of organizational needs and capabilities. If the need is for extensive demographic data to monitor an affirmative action plan, this will influence design; if the company owns a mainframe computer that is being underutilized, this will be a design factor. Microcomputers have opened the way for a broad new range of systems configurations, including distributed points of input and retrieval, and even distributed data bases (the compensation department, for example, can have its own data base, using only basic data from the main personnel system).

In other organizations, the advent of desktop computers for every manager may be awaiting the development of more "easy to use" systems. Most critically, however, design depends on what the HRIS will be expected to do, as discussed in the section below on "Applications of an HRIS."

One type of HRIS configuration is shown in Figure 3-3. In this illustration, users make inquiries or submit data on forms to a human resources information center, which enters that data in the appropriate HRIS modules' data bases.

Data enter each module in collection formats determined in advance; processing occurs and reports are issued according to the functional needs of each module; and at the same time, a central human resources data base is maintained (and accessed) by the separate modules.

Within this overall scheme, a number of different hardware configurations are possible: The HRIC could operate a huge, mainframe computer and deal

Figure 3-3. HRIS "hardware network."

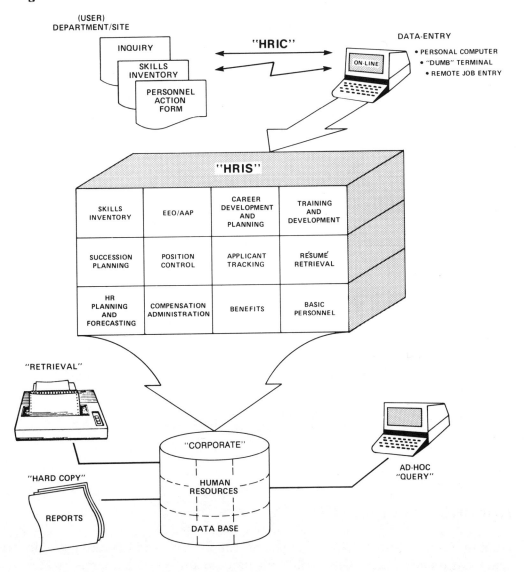

with manually prepared input through a staff of systems programmers; data could be entered directly into computers located in functional departments (each with its own module); or input could occur in some combination. Increasingly, the spread of low-cost microcomputer technology has led to the distribution of both the input function and the data bases. Each function can usually draw on the central human resources data base for basic personnel information and create its own function-specific data base accessed locally. When the functionally separate micros are "on-line," a change made locally automatically changes the central data base; in other systems, new data are periodically sent to the central location for updating.

Figure 3-4. **HRIS "application network."**

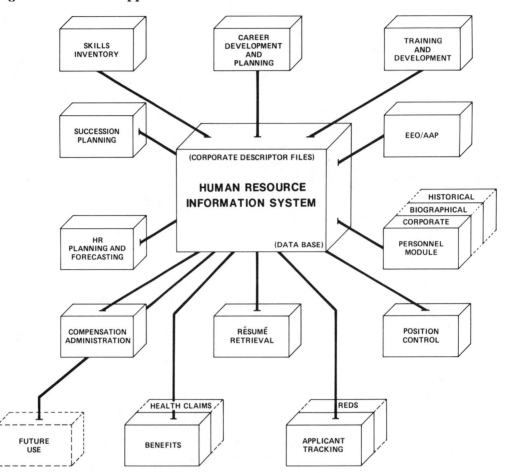

Applications of an HRIS

Human resource information systems are usually built and operated as a linked array of functional modules, each with its own purposes in human resources management and its own distinctive characteristics. Figure 3-4 shows a dozen such modules, each designed for specific departmental or functional applications, in a fully developed HRIS. In the pages that follow in this chapter, each of these modules is briefly described from a personnel user's perspective: The kinds of information available in each functional module—especially human resources planning information—are exemplified, and the general features of each are listed.

In developing an HRIS, Walker points out that the most effective approach is to start with two or three modules, get those operational, and add needed modules like rooms of a house built to meet expanding requirements. Walker also lists certain criteria that define a module:

1. The purpose of the module is directed to one specific function of personnel.
2. The module has its own input forms or screens.
3. There are some internal transformations that happen to the data. . . .
4. There are some reports or analyses that are particular to that user.
5. There may be some data elements that are unique to that user.[3]

Basic Personnel Module

The basic personnel module is usually the first or among the first modules created in HRIS development and brings with it the administrative procedures, retrieval methodologies, coding conventions, and basic employee data base on the population covered by the system. That population may include only active employees, all who have ever worked for the organization, or some limited-scope variation—such as all full-time regular employees in the past five years.

The basic personnel module provides a cornerstone of fundamental information, including name, Social Security number, service entry date, age, race, sex, job classification, location, salary comparison data, and other basic information consistent with corporate needs. It is used to support head-count statistics, turnover analysis, salary administration, appraisal reviews, EEO reporting, and possibly payroll functions (in an integrated payroll-personnel system).

The kinds of business planning questions answered by the basic personnel module include:

- How many employees in the marketing department have ten or more years of company service, backgrounds in chemical engineering, and work on the East Coast?
- How many employees in the $20,000–$28,000 salary range left the company in each of the last five years?
    Who are they, and why did they leave?
    Which departments did they come from?
- Which employees have received an above-average performance rating for two or more consecutive rating periods since 1983?

Because the basic personnel module is usually the first part of the HRIS to be developed, the kinds of data it keeps and the types of reports it generates will usually reflect the organization's first priorities or main reason for having an automated personnel system. Thus, in one company, the basic module may have the capability of turning out all EEO reports and monitoring an affirmative action plan, while in another, this module carries all compensation information.

Typically, this module contains basic information that is collected and edited once for all other modules: A change in an employee's address, for example, is made once in the basic personnel module. To make such changes and review data in this module, the system usually produces an employee profile of basic information, sent periodically to each employee as a turnaround document. The

Figure 3-5. **HRIS basic personnel module features.**

- SERVICE RECORD ADMINISTRATION
- FORCE PLANNING STATISTICS
- PERSONNEL DIRECTORY INFORMATION
- LENGTH-OF-SERVICE STUDIES
- EEO/AAP ADMINISTRATION
- LITIGATION SUPPORT
- DISPARATE IMPACT
- STANDARDIZED CODE CONTROL
- LABOR RELATIONS INFORMATION
- EMPLOYEE PROFILE PRODUCTION
- TURNOVER ANALYSIS
- TURNAROUND DOCUMENTS
- HISTORICAL STUDIES
- AUDIT FUNCTIONS
- INTERNAL/EXTERNAL PLACEMENTS

employee reviews the data, makes any corrections or changes, and returns the profile to the information center.

Some of the features likely to characterize a basic personnel module today are shown in Figure 3-5.

Wage and Salary Administration

Whatever the relationship of the HRIS to the organization's payroll system, there is usually a need for a separate module to track, analyze, and plan compensation. The complexities of compensation administration in companies with a range of different salaries, wage rates, incentive plans, performance-based pay systems, pretax benefits, noncash compensation, stock plans, and other compensation methods that vary in both dollar amounts and time intervals make computerization of data a virtual necessity.

Because of "the time cost of money," or interest rates, there is an added reason in an inflationary economy to devise a means of more accurately planning compensation. Funds held by the organization in short-term accounts to pay salaries over the next year or two may be excessive, for example, if merely "estimated" on the basis of broad projections of past trends. A compensation planning model that takes into account the voluminous actual data in an HRIS—

Figure 3-6. **HRIS wage and salary administration module features.**

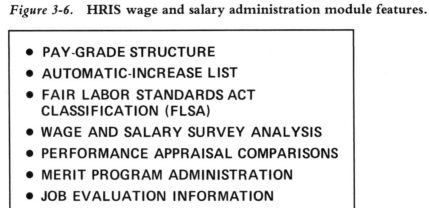

- PAY-GRADE STRUCTURE
- AUTOMATIC-INCREASE LIST
- FAIR LABOR STANDARDS ACT CLASSIFICATION (FLSA)
- WAGE AND SALARY SURVEY ANALYSIS
- PERFORMANCE APPRAISAL COMPARISONS
- MERIT PROGRAM ADMINISTRATION
- JOB EVALUATION INFORMATION
- SALARY BUDGET ANALYSIS AND ADMINISTRATION

raise amounts, intervals between raises, and actual regular and merit increases of existing employees—can drastically reduce the margin of error in estimating future payroll costs, permitting the organization to take full advantage of investment funds.

Some typical compensation questions that an HRIS helps answer include:

- What is the average salary by job classification?

    What is the quintile bracket by classification?

    How do recent performance appraisals relate to salaries?
- What is the annual salary budget by division?

    What is the current expenditure on salaries for each division in comparison to its annual budget?

    What variations from budget exist, including name of employee, division, salary increase, and reason?
- When was the last wage or salary increase for all employees in the benefits section?

    What is the breakdown by amounts and performance appraisal ratings?

    When are the next forecast data due?

Access to readily obtainable reports on wage and salary data in the organization will provide compensation professionals with the wide range of analytical decision-making information required to effectively administer pay programs. Depending on the reports designed, analysts can examine pay to assure adherence to company guidelines concerning merit pay, track performance with salary increases, and track pay by skill level, job family, demographic characteristics (age, race, sex), or other variables in the data base.

The features or kinds of data and capabilities made available by wage and salary modules are summarized in Figure 3-6.

Benefits Module

The diversity of benefits plans offered to employees in the modern organization—especially the growing use of flexible, or "cafeteria-style," plans that permit employees to choose specific benefits to match their preferences or needs—can make the benefits module the single most important reason for having an HRIS. Information about dozens of specific benefits—from pensions to vacation time—can be collected more efficiently, maintained centrally, made available for management analysis of costs and usage, and communicated to employees at costs incomparably lower than would be possible without automated systems. And the rising costs of benefits—which now account for 30 to 40 percent of all employment costs in the average U.S. company—underscore the critical importance of an ability to analyze and manage these expenses.

The growth of flexible plans that in effect create "tailor-made" benefits packages for each employee would probably not have occurred in the absence of automated systems. Flexible plans normally start with a set of "core" benefits, such as life insurance, and then allow the employee to select from a menu including different pension contributions, health insurance of different types (such as dental plans or spousal benefits) at different costs, time-off variations, child care, deferred savings accounts, stock options, and a host of other possibilities. The popularity of such programs is firmly based in changing worker demographics: Benefits plans originally designed for a man with a wife and children at home now apply to only about 15 percent of the U.S. workforce. Employees in two-career families may not need duplicative health insurance, for example.

To provide all employees, or all of a certain class of employees, with a benefits package costing the company the same amount, however—especially when some costs such as medical coverage fluctuate at different rates than others—flexible plans require vast amounts of computations, current analysis, and record keeping. Moreover, they can be effective only if employees are fully informed, a communications effort that might be prohibitively expensive without the aid of mechanized reports.

Some of the key questions typically answered by a benefits module include:

- Which benefits are available to whom?
- How much has Ernie Moore contributed to his pension fund?
- At present participation rates and allowing for planned change, how much will dental plan benefits cost the company five years from now?
- Which benefits should be phased out because they are not sufficiently used? Which added or repriced?

Benefits modules can also provide employees with regular statements of "where they stand" with regard to retirement investment, accrued leave time, or other specific data. Some companies have initiated "bonus" programs to control costs. If an employee does not use medical insurance benefits during the

Figure 3-7. **HRIS benefits module features.**

- **EMPLOYEE BENEFITS STATEMENTS, PROOF LISTINGS**

- **"CAFETERIA-STYLE" BENEFITS AND HEALTH-CARE PACKAGES**

- **BENEFITS TRACKING, INCLUDING MAJOR MEDICAL, HOSPITAL, DENTAL, DRUG, SURGICAL, PROFIT-SHARING, STOCK, LIFE, LONG-TERM DISABILITY, SUPPLEMENTAL LIFE, INSURANCES**

- **USER-DEFINED: PENSION PROJECTIONS AT NORMAL, EARLY, AND LATE RETIREMENT; CONTINUOUS, CREDITED SERVICE CALCULATIONS; SOCIAL SECURITY PRIMARY INSURANCE; AND FAMILY MAXIMUM BENEFIT AMOUNT PROJECTIONS**

- **EMPLOYER AND EMPLOYEE BENEFIT COST ANALYSIS BY COMPANY**

- **ACCRUING OF VACATION TIME AND SICK LEAVE**

- **RETAINMENT OF VESTED TERMINATED EMPLOYEES' DATA AND/OR BENEFICIARY**

- **ERISA VESTING SCHEDULES**

- **HISTORICAL RECORD REPORTS RELATING TO COMPENSATION, BREAKS IN SERVICE, BENEFIT ELIGIBILITY, AND ERISA**

- **GENERATION OF ANNUAL REPORTS**

year, for example, he or she receives a credit toward other benefits or other compensation. Figure 3-7 lists the range of possible features of a fully developed benefits module.

Self-Funded Health Insurance Subsystem. For companies that have opted to deal with rising medical coverage costs by establishing their own, self-funded insurance programs, a health claims module is a virtual necessity. As an adjunct to the benefits module or a separate subsystem, this module provides the information needed to offer employees a comprehensive and versatile health-care program, track costs, and at the same time avoid the overhead costs of an outside insurance carrier. Although such programs require the establishment of a financially sound reserve fund—and no such program should be contemplated without current, qualified legal advice—properly controlled and administered funds can both improve employee benefits and reduce overall costs.

A health claims module that permits such effective administration typically provides the features listed in Figure 3-8.

Clearly, the advantages of having a self-funded program—including the ability to measure the cost-effectiveness of various kinds of treatment and care, govern cash flow more rigorously, and provide more effective care for employ-

Figure 3-8. **HRIS health claims module features.**

- **ELIMINATES INCORRECT PAYMENTS AND COSTLY OVERSIGHTS**

- **ELIMINATES DUPLICATE THIRD-PARTY PAYMENTS**

- **PERMITS CONTROL AND RETRIEVAL OF MEDICAL OR DENTAL PLAN OVERPAYMENTS**

- **MONITORS VOLUNTARY EMPLOYMENT BENEFICIARY ASSOCIATION (VEBAS) BY COMPANY**

- **ENSURES ACCURATE AND EXPEDITIOUS CLAIM PROCESSING**

- **REDUCES COSTLY REPROGRAMMING COSTS WHEN ADJUSTING COVERAGE**

- **REDUCES TURNAROUND TIME, WHICH IMPROVES EMPLOYEE MORALE**

- **PERMITS COMPUTER-ADJUDICATED EMPLOYEE CLAIMS PROCESSING**

- **FACILITATES GENERATION OF COST SAVINGS AND ANALYSIS REPORTS**

- **ALLOWS TAILORED BREAKDOWN OF FINANCIAL DATA ASSOCIATED WITH COMPANY HEALTH-CARE PROGRAMS**

- **PERMITS GENERATION OF SURVEY ANALYSIS REPORTS**

ees—cannot be taken for granted. The data made available by this module are essential to achieving the advantages of self-funded medical coverage.

Training and Development

The central reason for developing an HRIS training module is to obtain the information needed to improve the effectiveness of training and development versus costs. In organizations with a major training investment, with courses going on in many locations, covering numerous subjects, and with different purposes or objectives, the complexities of cost-benefit analysis may require automated information systems help. For example, these kinds of questions can be addressed by an HRIS training and development module:

- What are the total costs of an in-house training program—instructors, facilities, materials, time, and so forth—on a per-student basis, compared with an externally available course?
- Who is scheduled to take the class on management development in the current year, by name, skill level, and location?

- What have been the dropout rates of a certain training course over the past five years, and what variables have occurred in that training over that time?
- Where are the trainees of yesteryear? That is, how do graduates of one course (or location, instructor, and so on) compare with those of others, in terms of later performance appraisals or other measurements?

The training module can carry information of value both to training development and administration managers and to employees themselves. The kinds of data needed by the training department include course schedules, enrollments, sites, recommended training for skill levels, a catalog, identification of employees who need training, and course evaluation.

Individual records generated by the module can include educational achievements and degrees, certifications, courses taken in-house and outside, results of courses, tuition reimbursements, and training recommendations for career development. This and other information can be provided to employees as part of the career development program.

In practice, many companies utilize an employee turnaround document such as a skills inventory form, which lists all credentials and specific skills possessed by the individual. With this, employees and their supervisors can use the training module catalog to decide on potential training and set up schedules for the coming year.

Figure 3-9 shows some of the features of a typical training and development module.

Figure 3-9. **HRIS training and development module features.**

- **EASY TRACKING OF COURSE ENROLLMENT, SCHEDULING, AND LOCATION SELECTION**
- **DEVELOPMENT OF RECOMMENDED TRAINING COURSES BY GRADE/SKILL/MANAGEMENT LEVEL**
- **DEVELOPMENT OF SHORT- OR LONG-RANGE TRAINING PROGRAMS IN RESPONSE TO IDENTIFIED SHORTCOMINGS IN THE ORGANIZATION**
- **MORE EFFECTIVE COMPARISON AND EVALUATION OF TRAINING PROGRAMS (BOTH INTERNAL AND EXTERNAL)**
- **INTERFACE WITH SUCCESSION PLANNING, EEO/AA AND CAREER DEVELOPMENT MODULES**

Career Development and Planning

The importance of career planning and career development to the future availability of human resources needed by the organization—as discussed in Chapter 8—may require the creation of a career development module as a sub-system of the HRIS. And although the emphasis in career planning is always on individual aspirations and preferences, the stakes involved in assuring human resources development to meet organizational needs—to match individual goals with corporate goals—are too high to ignore the need for analysis, management, and planning.

A career development module provides the information needed to answer questions such as these:

- What vacancies exist or are approaching for supervisors?
     What are their requirements?
     What will be their salaries?
- Who is available within this career path—on the basis of career plans and qualifications—by name and salary?
- What positions are open to Mary Wilcox?
- Are we meeting our affirmative action plan goals?

One of the key advantages of a mechanized career development information system, as discussed in Chapters 8 and 9, is that it permits the up-to-date and economically feasible reporting of opportunities to employees. Conceivably, an employee could come to a career planning office alone—without a supervisor in attendance—and access the career planning module to obtain printouts of job openings, locations, salary ranges, qualifications for the specific jobs, or even dates when jobs may become vacant. Not all companies can feasibly provide such "open access" to employees, and some might limit these data to selected employees or certain jobs. But if, on the basis of corporate strategic plans, the system could tell employees where the greatest number of upper-level management positions will be available in the years ahead—where to look for a "fast track" to a better job—then the employee could plot an appropriate career plan. Also, if the system provides information on the areas where the organization expects slower growth or will be cutting back, the employee will be able to alter his or her existing career development plan.

Some of the features that a career planning module can provide are depicted in Figure 3-10.

Skills Inventory Module

Because of the importance of the skills profile or skills inventory data to other programs such as training and career planning—and because skills inventories are inherently complex and detailed in many organizations—a separate

Figure 3-10. **HRIS career development/planning module features.**

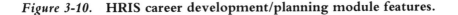

- ● FACILITATES EMPLOYEE SEARCH TO FILL VACANT POSITIONS
- ● PROVIDES EMPLOYEE RECORD OF SUCCESSION PLANNING, TRAINING, AND DEVELOPMENT
- ● ENABLES TRACKING OF COMPANY EMPLOYEES TO PROMOTE DEVELOPMENT
- ● FACILITATES IDENTIFICATION AND ANALYSIS OF REQUIRED INFORMATION FOR CAREER COUNSELING
- ● PROVIDES COMPUTER-ASSISTED CAREER GUIDANCE SERVICE
- ● ENABLES A MORE INFORMATIVE OUTPLACEMENT AND RETIREMENT PLANNING NETWORK
- ● ENABLES SURVEY ANALYSIS OF JOB SKILLS, SELF-ASSESSMENT, CAREER ASPIRATIONS, AND CURRENT JOB UTILIZATION WITHIN THE COMPANY
- ● PROVIDES FOR MORE UNIFORM SELECTION STANDARDS

module for collecting, storing, and maintaining records of individual qualifications and experience may be desirable.

The skills inventory has many uses in the human resources department, but some of the specific planning questions it can help answer include:

- ■ Do we have enough people with the specific skills needed to accomplish next year's production goals?
- ■ Do we have the human resources to bid on a certain project requiring known levels of skills and management personnel?
- ■ How many (and who specifically) have licenses of a certain type to practice in this state?
- ■ If we were to move into another market area or product line, do we have people (and where are they) with experience in this area?

The skills inventory, often a turnaround document that can be periodically reviewed and updated by employees, carries detailed information on educational achievements, training, and skills experience. Some skills inventories are extremely detailed and require careful and sometimes time-consuming effort by the individual originating the data and his or her supervisor. On the plus side, most employees are vitally interested in listing all of their qualifications if that may lead to job improvement.

Figure 3-11. **HRIS skills inventory module features.**

> - **PROVIDES SKILLS PROFILE INFORMATION FOR CONTRACT BIDS**
> - **PROCESSES QUERIES TO FILL INTERNAL VACANCIES BY SKILLS QUALIFICATION AND EXPERIENCE**
> - **PROVIDES VITAL RECORDS AND INFORMATION DURING DISCRIMINATION CASES**
> - **PROVIDES AUDIT REPORTS FOR JOB REVIEW AND STATUS**
> - **PROVIDES AUDIT REPORTS OF SKILLS**

The skills inventory, a vital tool in human resources planning and career development, can provide the features listed in Figure 3-11.

Succession Planning

A fully developed succession planning system such as the program described in Chapter 8, an essential consideration in assuring long-range stability in the management of the organization, may require a succession planning module. This module focuses on the collection and maintenance of data that underlie succession charts—the qualifications, tenure, and other recorded evaluations and criteria of those in line to move into key positions in the firm.

In addition, as discussed in Chapter 8, succession planners can use the HRIS to develop the succession charts themselves, update all changes automatically, and search the data base for new candidates in cases of unplanned vacancies. Also, the automated system is normally linked with the training and development department, so that a continuing effort may be made to assure the readiness of potential successors: The module permits analysis that pinpoints training or development needs, which can be forwarded to the development function as well as to the individual.

Some typical questions answered by the succession module:

- Who exactly is qualified for consideration in filling the position of vice-president of human resources in the event it is vacated?
- If John Kline is moved up, who is available to fill his position (and the replacement's position)?
- What are the effects of the new strategic human resources plan—or any new strategy—on training and development requirements, and in turn, what are the effects of new requirements on succession charts?

Figure 3-12.   **HRIS succession planning module features.**

- **IDENTIFIES QUALIFIED REPLACEMENTS TO FILL MANAGERIAL POSITIONS AT ALL PRESCRIBED LEVELS**

- **IDENTIFIES GAPS IN MANAGERIAL POSITIONS SO THAT INTERVENTION STRATEGIES CAN BE DEVELOPED**

- **DESIGNATES SUCCESSORS AND BACKUP CANDIDATES FOR ALL KEY POSITIONS**

- **IDENTIFIES MANAGERS IN LINE WITH BUSINESS GOALS BY UTILIZING DATA ON POTENTIAL AND READINESS FOR PROMOTION**

- **AUTOMATICALLY GENERATES NEW OR UPDATED REPLACEMENT CHARTS**

Automation of the succession planning function, as discussed in Chapter 8, permits the inclusion of vast amounts of data, evaluations, criteria, and detailed qualifications in the management of succession planning. Further, changes in the succession charts can be quickly analyzed for their impacts across and down the company. The general features of a succession planning module are shown in Figure 3-12.

EEO/AAP Module

This module, designed to track and report equal employment opportunity data and the progress of the organization toward the goals and objectives of any affirmative action plan, has often provided the justification for the expense and time involved in HRIS development. Many computerized personnel systems started in the early 1970s primarily as a means of efficiently complying with the reporting requirements of the EEO laws, including Title VII of the Civil Rights Act of 1964 (as amended in 1972), the Equal Pay Act of 1963, laws applicable to federal contractors, and regulations outlining the need for affirmative action plans.

This module tracks applicants and new employees by race and sex, job function, pay, training, and other conditions of employment, from benefits to transfer and promotion, and permits managers to analyze the impacts of employment practices on minorities in relation to all employees.

Regulations applicable to employers whose employment practices may have resulted in de facto discrimination—usually determined by an analysis of "relevant labor pools" compared to race/sex profiles of company employees—require the establishment of AAPs, with a series of goals and timetables for correcting imbalances between available minorities and employees. Courts and administrative agencies have decreed that AAPs must cover virtually all job functions, levels of employment, and employment-related practices—a requirement that involves huge amounts of record keeping and vast reporting capabilities.

In addition, employers seeking protection from EEO litigation that might allege discrimination several years in the past need accurate records on what has happened in previous years: Complete data on promotions, qualifications, and the treatment of all similarly situated employees are often the basis of a successful defense of previous practices.

In addition to its EEO reporting and AAP tracking capabilities, this module can provide answers to such questions as these:

- Are the women and minorities in our company achieving middle management executive positions?

    What are their numbers and percentages in these positions, in each of the last five years?

    How many are leaving these positions, and why?

- Which women and minorities received promotions in each of the last three years, into which positions and at what salaries?

- What percentage of job applicants, by department, are women and minorities compared to the overall percentages employed and hired in those departments?

The general features of an EEO/AAP module are shown in Figure 3-13.

Applicant Tracking

Applicant tracking can be a vital human resources function for several reasons: A company may be in a nonhiring phase at the moment but be anticipating large employment needs in the near future; competition for certain skills or credentials may be intense, and the company is not getting its share; high turnover rates among newer employees may indicate some undiscovered problem; EEO requirements may not otherwise be accounted for in the company; or applicants may simply be "important" to the organization, either because so many must be hired or because their skills are so vital.

The applicant module carries data on the individual—name, address, experience, skills, age, and so on—as well as the results of personnel department activity such as tests, reference checks, interview results, and any job offers. In addition, information such as the names of interviewers, dates, how the applicant heard about the job, and other data that may be relevant to organizational needs can be included. In some organizations, for example, a goal of applicant tracking may be to determine which interviewers or recruiters are responsible for hiring the most successful employees—or those who become turnover statistics.

Figure 3-13. **HRIS equal employment opportunity and affirmative action program module features.**

- PROVIDES FEDERAL EMPLOYEE REPORTS MANDATED BY LAW REFLECTING VITAL JOB STATISTICS ON FEMALES AND OTHER MINORITIES (EEO-1 AND EEO-4)

- PROVIDES SUPPORT DATA FOR LITIGATION

- ALLOWS FOR SPECIFIC PINPOINTING OF AREAS OF EMPLOYMENT UNDERUTILIZATION

- PROVIDES FOR THE ESTABLISHMENT OF LONG- OR SHORT-RANGE RECRUITMENT OBJECTIVES IN COMPLIANCE WITH FEDERAL AND COMPANY GUIDELINES

- PROVIDES FOR SURVEY ANALYSIS OF CURRENT EMPLOYMENT DEMOGRAPHICS

- AUGMENTS DESIGNATED CORPORATE STAFF TO AID IN THE DEVELOPMENT AND ADMINISTRATION OF AFFIRMATIVE ACTION AND EQUAL EMPLOYMENT OPPORTUNITY PROGRAMS

- ALLOWS FOR PROPER INTERFACE OF EEO/AA PROGRAMS WITH WAGE/SALARY TRACKING, TRAINING AND DEVELOPMENT, MANAGEMENT SUCCESSION PLANNING, AND CAREER DEVELOPMENT MODULES

Typical questions answered by this module include:

- How do different employment offices or recruiters compare in applicant-hire ratios?
- What training needs are identified at this stage?
- What are the characteristics of applicants who decline job offers? Why do they decline?
- Who are our most effective recruiters?

Applicant tracking modules may also be required to keep records and complete EEO-1 reports on women and minorities applying for jobs—in the absence of an EEO module or similar system—and typically have the features shown in Figure 3-14.

Automated Applicant Letters. By linking the applicant module with word processing capabilities, organizations sending large numbers of standard letters to applicants can further partake of the "office of the future" advantages of HRIS applications. Each letter can carry individual information from the applicant module data base—name, address, test scores, and so on—as well as one of

Figure 3-14. **HRIS applicant tracking module features.**

- RECRUITER ANALYSIS
- AGENCY TRACKING AND FEE STUDIES
- REQUISITION CONTROL
- SOURCE-OF-EMPLOYMENT STUDIES
- DECLINATION ANALYSIS
- APPLICANT-HIRE COMPARISON ANALYSIS
- RECORDING OF APPLICANT EVALUATION REPORTS
- SALARY OFFER STUDIES

several standard responses to the application: Call us for a further appointment, apply again after a certain date, we have nothing for you at this time, or we are pleased to offer you a position.

In one system, known as the rapid employment data system (REDS), employment office personnel can select from a menu of approved paragraphs covering different kinds of applicants and responses. Other systems are even more automatic: All applicants who receive certain test scores, for example, can be sent a certain kind of letter. The score, coded into the system, triggers the standard letter.

Résumé Retrieval System. For some organizations, perhaps employers of seasonal workers or project-basis employers that have widely fluctuating needs for additional staff, a résumé retrieval system that operates as a subsystem of the applicant tracking module may be essential. This system simply mechanizes the evaluation, classification, and identification of résumés that may be needed later.

In addition, the system could include the résumés of internal staff, through an interface with the skills inventory system, so that when a certain skill or managerial competence is needed, individuals can be quickly identified and résumés included in proposals. The design of the résumé retrieval system will depend on the kinds of requirements planned for or likely to occur: Specific skills experience, location, overseas preference, professional licenses, and other data relevant to anticipated needs should be included.

Position Control Module

The position control module is designed to collect, organize, and report data on jobs rather than people. At any given time, the organization has a specific number of authorized jobs with specific responsibilities (determined usually by job evaluation), salary ranges, departmental relationships, and other character-

Figure 3-15. **HRIS position control module features.**

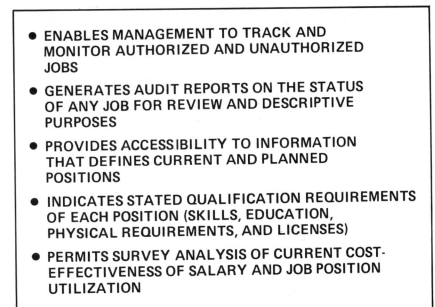

- ● ENABLES MANAGEMENT TO TRACK AND MONITOR AUTHORIZED AND UNAUTHORIZED JOBS
- ● GENERATES AUDIT REPORTS ON THE STATUS OF ANY JOB FOR REVIEW AND DESCRIPTIVE PURPOSES
- ● PROVIDES ACCESSIBILITY TO INFORMATION THAT DEFINES CURRENT AND PLANNED POSITIONS
- ● INDICATES STATED QUALIFICATION REQUIREMENTS OF EACH POSITION (SKILLS, EDUCATION, PHYSICAL REQUIREMENTS, AND LICENSES)
- ● PERMITS SURVEY ANALYSIS OF CURRENT COST-EFFECTIVENESS OF SALARY AND JOB POSITION UTILIZATION

istics. The position control module is based on a coded representation of each job and carries its characteristics, its incumbents, and other data necessary to control unwarranted or unplanned employment patterns.

For example, the position control module answers such questions as:

- ■ What positions are authorized in the finance department in salary brackets 15 and 16?
  Are they occupied, and by whom?
  How does this compare with actual head counts?
- ■ Which positions are vacant in the company, by department and other classifications?
- ■ What are the salary ranges and other characteristics of positions experiencing above-average turnover?
- ■ Is there an actual, approved, and authorized position, current or planned, for new employee John Smith?

The position control module can carry an elaborate and highly detailed data base on jobs and their incumbents and may serve as the framework for human resources planning, succession planning, training development, budgetary control, and recruitment initiation. It may, for example, include extensive job description elements, status codes, educational qualifications, spans of control, career path data, and other information that puts the position into perspective from an organizational planning viewpoint.

Interfaced with other modules, the position control subsystem can provide job vacancy information to applicant tracking or career planning modules, for example. Position requirements can be examined in light of affirmative action plan goals and timetables, as well. Most important, the position control module permits human resources planners and managers to oversee and control employment activity in far-flung or diversified organizations, where supervisors have the autonomy to add employees but may lack the overall planning perspective necessary to orderly growth. The main features of the module are listed in Figure 3-15.

The Human Resources Planning Module of an HRIS

Obviously, each of the potential functional modules of an HRIS described above involves or permits some form of human resources planning. The data and their relationships permit the modeling of future compensation costs, benefits expenses, succession plans, career development and training needs, and a host of other specific plans based on existing factors and strategic plans.

The integration of all of this functional planning with other human resources plans and with overall corporate strategic planning can be accomplished by human resources planners using an HR planning module. This module presents planners with the information needed to envisage and manage "the big picture" of human resources availability in the organization, a subject explored in greater detail in Chapter 9, and to assure the coordination of human resources programs of all kinds with overall strategic plans and objectives.

The kinds of reports and data generated by the human resources planning module may be broad compilations, such as those shown graphically in Figures 3-16 through 3-18, or they may be highly specific, such as the attrition report shown in Table 3-1.

As discussed in other sections of this book, human resources planning, to

(Text continues on page 63.)

Table 3-1. Attrition rates (January–October 1986).

	Summary							
Departments	*B*	*E*	*T*	*A*	*Rate*	*Turnover*	*Rate*	*Total Rate*
Executive	27	26	1	26.5	3.8%	2	7.5%	11.3%
Legal	20	17	3	18.5	16.2%	–	–	16.2%
Finance	149	151	10	150	6.7%	6	4.0%	10.7%
Human resources	521	466	100	493.5	20.3%	29	5.9%	26.1%
Business development	136	139	20	137.5	14.5%	11	8.0%	22.5%
Manufacturing	290	386	54	338	16.0%	16	4.7%	20.7%
Plant services	115	113	11	114	9.6%	11	9.6%	19.2%

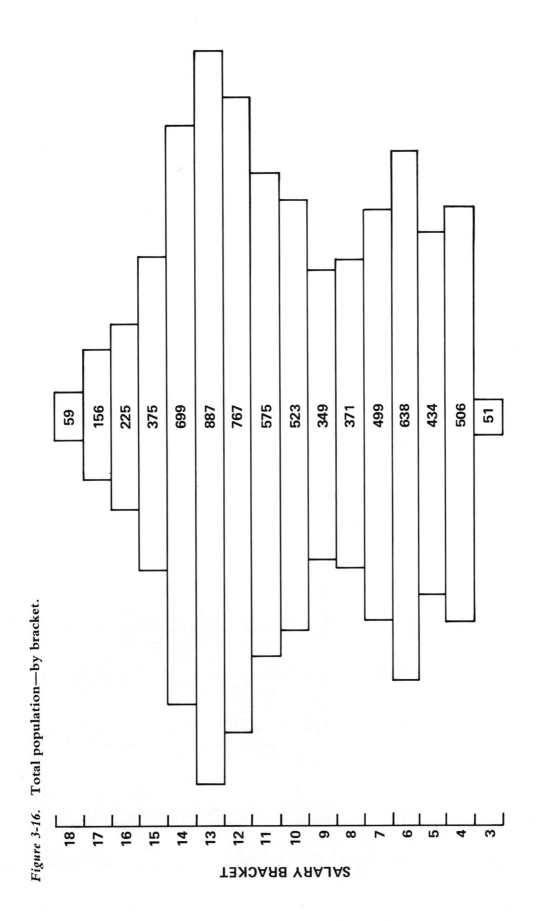

Figure 3-16. Total population—by bracket.

Figure 3-17.   Total population—by length of service.

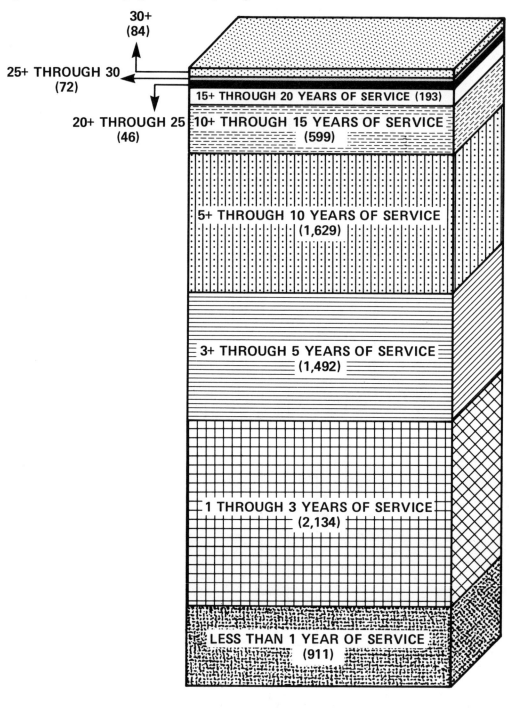

30+
(84)

25+ THROUGH 30
(72)

15+ THROUGH 20 YEARS OF SERVICE (193)

20+ THROUGH 25
(46)

10+ THROUGH 15 YEARS OF SERVICE
(599)

5+ THROUGH 10 YEARS OF SERVICE
(1,629)

3+ THROUGH 5 YEARS OF SERVICE
(1,492)

1 THROUGH 3 YEARS OF SERVICE
(2,134)

LESS THAN 1 YEAR OF SERVICE
(911)

Figure 3-18.   **College degrees report.**

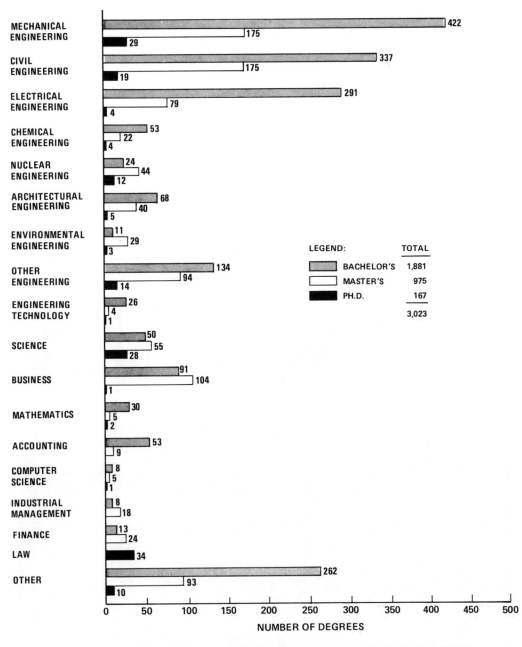

NOTE: EACH EMPLOYEE IS COUNTED AT THE LEVEL AND DISCIPLINE OF THE HIGHEST
DEGREE ATTAINED ONLY.

Figure 3-19. Actual and projected nationwide engineering and engineering technologies degrees.

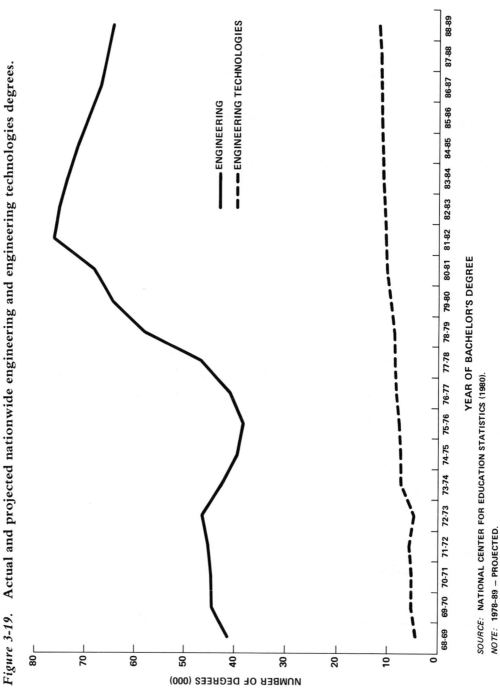

ENGINEERING

ENGINEERING TECHNOLOGIES

NUMBER OF DEGREES (000)

YEAR OF BACHELOR'S DEGREE

SOURCE: NATIONAL CENTER FOR EDUCATION STATISTICS (1980).

NOTE: 1978-89 — PROJECTED.

Figure 3-20. **HR planning module features.**

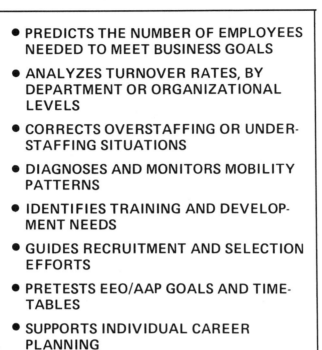

- PREDICTS THE NUMBER OF EMPLOYEES NEEDED TO MEET BUSINESS GOALS
- ANALYZES TURNOVER RATES, BY DEPARTMENT OR ORGANIZATIONAL LEVELS
- CORRECTS OVERSTAFFING OR UNDER-STAFFING SITUATIONS
- DIAGNOSES AND MONITORS MOBILITY PATTERNS
- IDENTIFIES TRAINING AND DEVELOP-MENT NEEDS
- GUIDES RECRUITMENT AND SELECTION EFFORTS
- PRETESTS EEO/AAP GOALS AND TIME-TABLES
- SUPPORTS INDIVIDUAL CAREER PLANNING

be truly systematic and comprehensive, must deal with the personnel demand requirements that derive from strategic and operational planning as well as the availability forecasts arising from human resources programs and existing personnel. The HR planning module of an HRIS focuses primarily on the availability side of this continuum: Who are the people we have now? What are their characteristics (skills, qualifications, personal data, compensation, and so on)? And what are the impacts of human resources programs—from recruitment to pension planning—on these human resources?

In addition, the human resources planning module may carry data linking today's human resources with future needs: staffing packages for projects that are in the future, for example, or data on the quantity and quality of human resources needed to enter a different market. If the human resources planning function is the primary locus of strategic planning in the organization, all "demand-side" strategic and operational factors affecting human resources must be part of the same system, at least conceptually (see Part IV of this book).

External data on labor force availability may also be part of this module, depending on organizational needs and—again—the locus of strategic planning. Figure 3-19 shows projected engineering degrees in the United States, for example.

Some of the general features and capabilities of a human resources planning module are shown in Figure 3-20.

PART II

The Demand Side: Strategic and Operational Planning

The three chapters in Part II explore the bases for demand forecasting, the kinds of information needed to analyze the human resources requirements of the organization in the years ahead. Existing means of ascertaining these kinds of information must be understood by the planner, and in some cases—more likely to occur in the area of strategic planning—the planner will face the even more challenging task of organizing the information-gathering effort needed to determine long-range human resources demand requirements. Either way, whether data and strategic objectives are readily available or must be probed for and extracted through new analytical techniques, the systematic inclusion of these demand factors is essential to realistic human resources planning.

Chapters 4 and 5 deal with overall, or corporate, strategic planning and the development of strategies—ways of reaching long-term objectives—through an iterative "testing" process that uses planning information generated by operational demand forecasts and human resources availability planning, covered later in this book. Chapter 6 deals with the short-term perspective—the operational planning that determines the quantity and types of personnel required to carry out the organization's work, now and in the near future. Thus, the sequence of chapters does not necessarily represent a chronological order of system development: All information gathering, and the development of systems and programs to analyze and act upon information, should proceed concurrently.

Contributors to the Planning Process

Throughout the rest of this book, the term *planner* will be repeatedly used. It is important to clarify at the outset that by *planner*, we do not refer exclusively to corporate staff planning professionals. Strategic planning is by no means restricted to the realm of "experts" who develop brilliant strategic plans that will then be implemented by line managers. On the contrary, contemporary practice demands active participation and often leadership by operating unit heads, with professional planning staff acting in a support role.

A typical arrangement for planning is patterned after the prescription of Peter Lorange and Richard F. Vancil. An organization subscribing to this approach might establish three levels of planning teams:

1. A corporate strategic group (CSG) comprised of the top officers of the organization, such as the chairperson, CEO, operating division heads, and top staff heads. This group would be responsible for reviewing the overall business portfolio for the organization and for monitoring the performance of planning and implementation activities associated with these programs. The CSG also serves as the review and approval function for new business opportunity areas to be considered for addition to the corporate portfolio.
2. A business family strategic planning team, generally led by the head of a group of related businesses, concerned with achieving optimum synergy among the products or services of this group and with determining the most effective range of products or services.
3. A business element strategic team, whose task is the development of clear competitive strategies for a particular product or market niche.[1]

It is important to recognize that team members, regardless of the level, are line and staff managers with established responsibilities. They are appointed by management as participants in the planning process for one of two reasons: They have certain experience or expertise, and/or they will be expected to implement the strategy once it is defined. To a certain extent, this approach acknowledges past failures in strategic planning, where plans were developed by corporate staff without due consideration for effective implementation.

The best way to manage the strategic process is to make "planners" out of everyone who will be involved in the development and implementation of the strategy and to achieve a balance between managers and specialists who gather data, analyze them, and synthesize them in usable form—and operating managers who must employ the data to formulate and implement strategies.

4

Strategic Planning: The Critical Framework

Involvement of human resources professionals in the strategic planning process is absolutely critical to the success of this effort. Strategic planning in the United States has traditionally been the responsibility of corporate planning, or some other high executive council, a turf the human resources function is reluctant to presume upon. The overall strategic plan, consisting of the future organization's position in a new environment and how it expects to get to that position, is often "handed down from above," with little or no input from personnel people.

Such an approach reflects an inadequate or misunderstood definition of the meaning of strategic planning. The strategist's role in the organization is, first and foremost, to understand the identity of the organization; its corporate mission, policies, and objectives; and how existing operations and planned work affect human resources demand. As discussed in the introduction to Part II, the best way to accomplish effective strategic planning is to make "planners" out of everyone who will be involved in both the development and the implementation of strategies, including operational managers.

In some organizations, perhaps, corporate planning may be sophisticated enough to include all departments and functions in the planning process—from the initial evaluation of internal conditions through environmental scanning and the development of scenarios that will provide the basis for strategies enabling the firm to deal with the future. Even in these organizations, however, the integration of all planning information needed for the development of imaginative, creative scenarios for future conditions is often incomplete.

The challenge for human resources planners is to be truly "strategic," to plan in terms of the total organization's resources, its changing capabilities and markets, and the factors in the external environment that will impact on future operations—including the availability of and demand for human resources.

In this chapter, the sections of the model shown in Figure 4-1 are discussed, from the data-gathering processes that lead to an understanding of the internal and external factors defining the future to integration of that information. Some

Figure 4-1. **Detailed outline of internal and environmental aspects of the strategic planning process.**

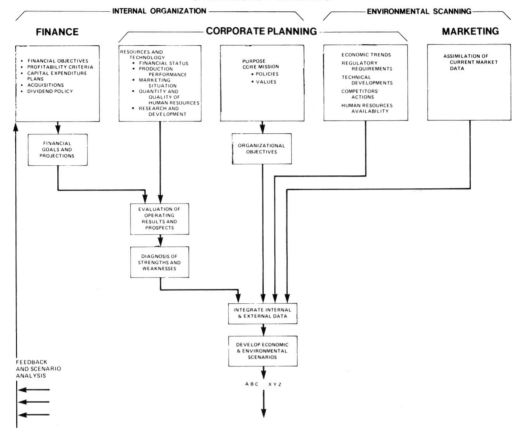

of this information may be difficult to obtain, some will require creative and carefully executed management procedures (such as the determination of the company's core mission), and some may turn out to be irrelevant to the overall planning process. None can be safely ignored.

The purpose of this phase of the strategic planning process is to obtain the information needed to create scenarios of conditions in the future that the organization may have to deal with—the subject of Chapter 5. For these scenarios to be anything more than speculation, the information on which they are based must include:

- *Internal factors*—financial assumptions, resources and technology, and a clear perception of organizational mission
- *External factors*—the conditions of change and developments in the environment that will bear on the organization's future

The Internal Organization: Evaluation of Organizational Goals, Objectives, Assets, and Liabilities

An essential requirement for the organization embarking on strategic planning is a clear understanding of its own internal processes—how it works and why. This is derived from a thorough analysis of the organization's past and present record, as well as its "strengths and weaknesses," an organizational diagnosis that helps explain the company's past behavior and present capabilities.

Different organizations are dominated by their own unique histories; objectives; current policies; and kinds of financial, marketing, or other constraints and opportunities. For virtually all companies, however, an analysis of internal goals and capabilities should include factors that fall within three categories, shown in the Figure 4-1 model as follows:

- *Finance*—the basic financial criteria such as return on investment, profit objectives that the organization must achieve, and the pivotal economic factors influencing such goals
- *Resources and technology*—corporate planning's view of the internal factors driving past and present performance and future capabilities, from financial considerations through technology and human resources, which together with financial goals, lead to the evaluation and the diagnosis of strengths and weaknesses
- *Core mission*—the appraisal and analysis of the organization's reason for being, designed to lead to a clear, universally understood statement of the organization's objectives for the future

Each of these kinds of internal analysis leads to specific types of planning information, later combined with external and marketing data, required to develop scenarios that will be the basis for planning strategies.

This internal evaluation proceeds concurrently, so it does not matter where data gathering starts. Also, some organizations will already have a wealth of data in certain areas and less or none in others. The purpose of the discussion below is not to provide an in-depth treatment of the factors involved in the internal evaluation process; rather, its purpose is to provide a brief overview that will help clarify the terms used and assure that no important ingredient of this analysis is overlooked or insufficiently considered.

Finance and Financial Goals and Projections

The traditional point of departure for strategic planning in profit-making enterprises has been the development of financial criteria reflecting bottom-line results. Because management's performance is usually measured by profits, it is not surprising that financial results are the leading indicators of effectiveness, often to the exclusion of every other factor.

This pressure to produce is not necessarily compatible with strategic planning for the long-range viability of the organization. For example, stockholders and the financial community closely monitor a public company's quarterly results and exhibit little enthusiasm for major capital expenditures—such as plant renovation or research—that could enhance future operations or ability to compete. If such expenditures reduce current dividends, the battle lines are drawn. Thus, it is not surprising that managers seeking high marks from shareholders focus on short-term financial results most of the time.

Most organizations therefore begin both the annual and long-range planning processes the same way: by focusing on the return on investment (ROI) and profit margin that they wish to attain. In some cases, the ROI will be a "given," as it is for regulated utilities in the United States; at other times, when the organization is a subsidiary or controlled by a conglomerate, ROI and profit margins are dictated by the parent organization.

Financial assumptions to be gathered in the model also include a range of other costs of doing business and factors relating to those costs, such as inflation. Overhead costs, both fixed and variable, must be understood in relation to the organizational needs they support—facilities, management, research, and the development of human resources, among others.

Financial Goals and Projections. Generally, these assumptions lead to preliminary decisions about resource allocation that will fundamentally influence the nature of strategic plans. As difficult as the information-gathering process may at first appear to nonfinancial planners, the importance of understanding the organization's financial policies—the goals of the organization's financial management plan and their implications—cannot be overstated. Often, strategies necessary for successful change may be impossible to implement because of financial policies needed to fund them—financial policies that are often based on entirely different goals and criteria.

Goals of Financial Management. Although the goals and priorities of financial management differ among organizations, in general the main goals are profitability, liquidity, and solvency.

Profitability goals are to earn the highest return possible for resources used or capital employed, consistent with management's desire and ability to bear risk. Liquidity goals are to have sufficient cash to meet short-term needs. Solvency goals involve having sufficient cash and cash sources available at times when long-term obligations and claims such as bonds and pensions become due.

Financial management encompasses such questions as:

- Scorekeeping: How well are we doing?
- Attention directing: Which problems need to be examined?
- Problem solving: Which is the best way of getting something done?

The types of decisions that come under the heading of financial management include: new investments, R&D expenditures, account balances, replacement decisions, cash flows, mergers and acquisitions, and resource allocation.

The major dilemma is one of enjoying increased profitability while reducing risk. The concepts of profitability and risk are diametrically opposed.

Financial Statement Analysis. This is the process of understanding and interpreting the financial and nonfinancial condition of an organization. It is useful in identifying the strengths and weaknesses of a firm and aids in the development of future strategic plans. Generally, financial statement analysis consists of three types:

- Common size analysis
- Ratio analysis
- Percentage change analysis

In each case, ratios or percentages are developed that are usually compared to some standard (such as the budget, last year's results, industry norms, or competition) as follows:

- Comparison of company data
    - To industry norms
    - To last year
    - To the budget
- Comparison of company data to data on competitors
- Comparison of industry data to data on other industries

Common Size Analysis. This analysis expresses each expense on the income statement as a percentage of total revenues and each asset, liability, or equity account on the balance sheet as a percentage of total assets.

Ratio Analysis. This analysis utilizes the data from all four financial statements and provides a broader perspective on the firm's financial condition. Typically, ratio analysis helps answer four key questions:

- How profitable is the organization?
- Can the organization meet its short-term obligations?
- To what extent is the firm financed by debt?
- Is management utilizing its assets effectively?

Percentage Change Analysis. This analysis allows one to track changes in income statement or balance sheet accounts from one reporting period to the next. It is useful in diagnosing key problem areas relative to specific accounts.

Resources and Technology, Including Human Resources

The next major step in the internal evaluation stage of strategic planning is an examination of the organization's resources and technology. This should include:

- Financial status, which may dictate the level of resources available for strategies (see the discussion in the preceding subsection)
- Production performance, or how well the organization is doing its work
- Marketing situation, including analysis of both customers and competitors
- Quantity and quality of human resources—the skills and talents that now exist in the organization and their ability to adapt to future needs
- Research and development considerations, including new and developing technologies that could drastically change the organization's "resources and technology" capabilities, costs, and markets

The current financial status of the organization, based on data normally supplied by corporate planning, may be the single most important "resource" factor to evaluate. If, for example, changing technology requires a vast investment for capital improvement and funding is unavailable or unobtainable because of a weak financial situation, this is a critical consideration in the assessment of current capabilities.

Performance, customarily measured in terms of productivity, is a demanding subject of analysis in most organizations. Care should be taken not to confuse performance with profitability—a financial factor—because an organization may be making money while productivity declines or while its share of a rapidly expanding market is shrinking.

Throughout this phase of the internal evaluation process, classified above in functional areas from finance to R&D, run two major themes of particular relevance to most organizations involved in strategic planning for a different business in the years ahead. They are (1) technological developments, which may be in the process of changing everything about the organization from the productivity of workers to existing products and markets, and (2) the quantity and quality of human resources, both as they exist in the company today and with regard to their adaptability to the future. Each of these areas deserves special attention before the planner proceeds to an evaluation of operating results and prospects and a subsequent diagnosis of strengths and weaknesses.

Technological Developments. Even for organizations that may be "at the leading edge" in their fields, keeping pace with technological change is of critical importance. The pace of technological change in today's Information Age is such that no organization can afford complacency, lest it lose its place on the leading edge, and eventually its markets or profitability, to more innovative firms.

In recent decades, examples abound of companies that failed to maintain their technological leadership and paid dearly for "business as usual." National Cash Register, for one, had to write off a $139 million loss in the early 1970s because it was unsuccessful in shifting from electromechanical to electronic designs.[1] Similarly, companies including General Electric, Sylvania, and RCA experienced significant financial losses by staying with vacuum-tube technology at a time when transistors were revolutionizing the electronics industry.

Being aware of technological developments, and assessing their impacts or viability in the long run, does not necessarily dictate a corporate strategy. Some organizations may not feel threatened by an upstart producing a technologically advanced product at a higher market price and may decide their best strategy is to hold their price advantage. They may be right; or they may be right up to a certain point in time—a point that should be strategically planned for in advance.

Also, strategies for adapting to or pioneering technological change may vary. Some developments may become available through royalty arrangements; others might be acquired through patent purchases or a buyout of the company itself.

Market conditions can also affect decisions about technology. In some cases, holding on to an obsolete technology can be appropriate if the organization is clear about its objectives. For example, hi-fi buffs who consider themselves "audio purists" continue to buy expensive stereo equipment that uses vacuum tubes. General Electric, one of the few companies that has kept on making vacuum tubes, initially lost money by continuing to manufacture the tubes but eventually turned this part of its business around. As time passed tube production became a "cash cow" for GE, compared with the more contemporary solid-state technology requiring investment capital.

Whatever the strategy adopted in response to technological change, the implications of such decisions can have enormous impacts on the existing organization. Huge R&D expenses and capital investment may be required; specially skilled personnel for jobs that did not previously exist may be needed; new forms of organization may be required; and the entire focus of the firm— its reason for being—may be shifted. In some cases, technological change may require closing obsolete plants and underutilized facilities and laying off a significant part of the existing workforce. In addition, technological change is one of the factors impinging on the analysis of the organization's human resources: Do we have the people needed to compete in the new technological environment?

Quality and Quantity of Human Resources. The internal availability of human resources within the organization—their numbers, skills, qualifications, learning ability, potential, and other characteristics relevant to business operations—is a critical factor often ignored in preliminary strategic planning. Typically, it is assumed that "we have plenty of time to get the people," develop needed managers and workers, train specialists, or fulfill other human resources requirements of the overall strategic plan.

Especially in high-tech industries, however, weak or nonexistent information about the ability of the internal workforce to carry out the strategic plan can have serious consequences. For one thing, personnel costs now account for nearly 50 percent of all operating costs in the average U.S. firm, and any significant escalation in these costs—for added training or for pay and benefits to lure experienced people from other firms—can have major impacts on the financial strength of the organization.

Changing skills requirements and the advance of technology are among the factors causing many companies to reevaluate past assumptions about human resources availability. Large engineering and construction firms, for example, have traditionally maintained lean organizations. As new projects increased demand for people, pirating became the rule instead of in-house development. But as a nationwide expansion of energy projects, coupled with the relative lag of supply from schools, tightened this market, these firms began experiencing a general scarcity of knowledgeable engineers.

The impact of technology can have opposite effects, of course. If large numbers of existing employees are likely to be displaced by technology or changing operations, the organization should begin planning for reductions in force. Strategies for dealing with redundant employees range from abrupt plant closing and massive layoffs to long-range retraining, relocation, early retirement, and similarly gradual measures. For the company to have a choice of which techniques to use to reduce staff levels, however, strategic planning must provide an assessment of what technological change will do to existing and future employment levels in the organization: Which jobs will become obsolete, and how soon?

Even where force reductions are indicated, however, the strategic business plan will point the way to a future in which new skills, managerial talents, and professional specialties are required. This stage of the planning process must examine the existing levels of expertise within the organization to fill these new positions and evaluate the staff's ability to grow and meet future needs.

The internal human resources evaluation required at this stage will use information generated by human resources planners in the internal availability analysis. As discussed in Part III of this book, these data come from human resources programs, including performance appraisal, evaluation of potential, career management, and management succession. Each of these critical programs provides both general and detailed information about the quantity and quality of human resources available from within the organization.

Evaluation of Operating Results and Prospects

When all of the preliminary information has been gathered and organized from finance and corporate planning about the organization's financial goals and basic capabilities, an evaluation can be made of where the company stands today. In most cases, this evaluation is premised on a continuation of programs and policies already in place. Later on, of course, when the other elements of the strategic planning process have been analyzed and developed, appropriate strategies or interventions that may significantly change organizational structure, resource allocation, and a broad range of policies and programs may be introduced.

No approach to planning can succeed without a clear view of the existing situation, however, including transitional or currently changing factors such as the impact of new technology. This basic evaluation of existing resources, financial goals and projections, and immediate prospects forms a baseline for evaluating the current strengths and weaknesses as an organization, which together with a sharpened view of organizational objectives gained from core mission analysis and information on the external environment, forms the starting point for the development of scenarios depicting different organizational futures.

In this discussion—although not necessarily in practice—the evaluation of the organization's strengths and weaknesses is separated from analysis of the core mission. The processes used to determine these important ingredients of strategic planning may be the same, however: interviews, questionnaires, meetings of key personnel, records review, and other techniques may accumulate both kinds of information. The "strengths and weaknesses," though, focus on the relatively "hard" data of existing resources, capabilities, and prospects. The core mission—knowable to planners through the techniques of organizational diagnosis, as well—is based on hard data, too, but it also includes perceptions of organizational leaders: such factors as "what the company stands for" and where it's headed in the years to come.

Diagnosis of Strengths and Weaknesses

Organizational diagnosis, the approach to determining strengths and weaknesses that is recommended as most effective in the strategic planning process, is a powerful and appropriate intervention. It is also one of the most difficult ideas to sell to management.

Properly conducted, organizational diagnosis examines the organization to its fundamental core, the way a lengthy and thorough medical examination might cover the physical and mental makeup of an individual—from the day of birth throughout life to the present moment.

Most managers, and especially American managers, are not that introspective. Their strength typically comes from the fact that they are "doers" rather than thinkers, concerned primarily with what can be done today and tomorrow. Further, the organizational diagnosis process is designed to uncover "weaknesses" realistically, which may include revelations about managers whose policies led to the problems.

As developed by Harry Levinson, the diagnostic procedure examines the organization from the day of its establishment and traces its development through the years.[2] It identifies the various challenges and crises with which the company has dealt and correlates past coping behavior with present practice and processes. Past behavior may or may not be appropriate in the present environment, of course, which forces an explanation for current organizational behavior.

Working from this historical perspective, the diagnostic model permits an analysis of current functioning—providing a framework for analysis of the strengths and weaknesses that will affect the organization's ability to meet present and future challenges.

One Approach to Self-Analysis. One way to overcome management resistance to the self-analysis required in the organizational development approach to both determining strengths and weaknesses and ascertaining the organization's core mission is to make managers part of the process.

In an approach that was successful at one company, for example, the top 12 officers were designated as an organizational development council. The facilitator explained to the council the concepts of organizational development and presented its members with a choice of diagnostic models. The council then selected a suitable model and authorized a study.

To minimize resistance within the ranks, an informal poll was conducted that asked people who they thought had power and influence in the organization. This led to an initial list of nominees, who were asked directly whether they agreed that they had influence. Eventually, this process verified a final list of 24 managers who apparently had the power to help or hinder the diagnostic process. All of these managers were made members of the organizational diagnosis team and participated in the development and analysis of a massive internal review completed 14 months later.[3]

Concurrent Strategies to Achieve Change. In some cases, the organizational diagnosis process is also used because of or in conjunction with plans to revise organizational structure. For example, if the organization is planning to change from a hierarchical to a matrix management approach, such a radical restructuring will affect most of the company's norms, behavior, and management processes. Plans must be made in order to manage the transition period between the present organization and the matrix, with key people identified and new responsibilities detailed. Negative reactions and functional roadblocks to the changes must be anticipated in advance, and resources to effect the changes must be assigned. Under such conditions, the benefits both of thorough self-analysis of the organization's current strengths and weaknesses and of clarification of its overall goals by analysis of the core mission are especially evident.*

Defining the Organization's Core Mission

The core mission of an organization, as defined by Beckhard and Harris,[4] is nothing less than its *raison d'être*, its reason for being. Its explicit definition and recognition as a guiding force in strategic planning is important because decisions based on departmental or parochial "goals and objectives" may be at variance with the core mission of the organization as a whole. When all planning and decision making, including resource allocation, is based on the same core mission, the organization is less likely to suffer from conflicting policies or programs out of step with the overall strategic plan.

Goals and objectives are not necessarily the same as—or always consistent with—the core mission. Goals are often functional or departmental, or based on a relatively narrow view of the organization's future. One group in the com-

---

* A comprehensive book describing new techniques and applications of organizational diagnosis, by Andrew O. Manzini, is scheduled for publication by AMACOM in late 1987.

pany may be making decisions as though the future lies in domestic products, for example, while another group sees the future in international operations. Such situations present great potential for wasted effort, inefficiently deployed resources, and a lack of cooperation.

The core mission should be as explicit and sharply defined as possible, but it is more important that it reflect the reality of what the organization is trying to accomplish in the long-range future. For example, the O. M. Scott Company[5] reportedly spent a year deciding between two core missions: The first was "to make fertilizers"; the second was "to keep lawns green." It finally decided to adopt the second as a core mission, a decision that led to investment in facilities to produce a variety of implements and chemicals "to keep lawns green." Such product diversification would not have been consistent with fertilizer production alone, the company's traditional business.

In wealthy organizations—or those possessing an uncommon abundance of resources—it is possible to have multiple core missions, because they can all be achieved. Theoretically, the simple expedient of spending more and more money can solve the problems that emerge from unclear or multiple missions. In reality, however, even the most prosperous organizations reach times when they must make a decision to allot priorities to different core missions.

The behavior of managers and others in leadership positions is significantly affected by their perceptions of the core mission. Assuming that managers allocate resources and make other major decisions on the basis of their understanding of the mission, any differences in their perceptions will have serious implications for the organization.

Despite its importance, a clearly written, unequivocal core mission statement does not exist in many firms or has not yet been effectively communicated internally. For strategic planning to proceed with a clear purpose, it may be necessary for the human resources planner (or a consultant) to work with top management to develop a meaningful statement.

Developing the Core Mission Statement. In the absence of a clear core mission statement, planners can undertake its development and articulation in a number of ways. One way is to simply ask the CEO and hope he or she has a sharply focused (and of course, correct) answer. A more effective approach, because it helps create the involvement of top management that is needed in strategic planning, is to interview each of the top executives of the company.

The interviewer can start with a preamble paraphrasing the O. M. Scott Company experience. Each executive is then asked for a definition of the organization's core mission. In all likelihood, the most common response will be that the mission of the company is to make money. The interviewer cannot disagree with this but should press on.

The interviewer should point out that the definition of a core mission is that it provides a sense of *how* the organization makes money. What kind of business are we in? What is our reason for being? While it is obviously an "objective" of a company to make as much money as it legally can, the interviewer should stress the difference between objectives and the overall core mission.

Organizations in "planned economy" or Socialist countries may have objectives other than profit, of course, which have profound impacts on their core mission. The provision of jobs may supersede profits as a goal. For such companies to remain viable—providing employment whether profits justify job security or not—governments usually intervene in other ways, as well, through tariff barriers or the creation of statewide monopolies.

When the interviewer has collected all of the core mission statements from executives, it will usually be apparent that significant differences prevail in how managers see their company's reason for being. These differences need to be discussed and reconciled, but this is potentially a highly valuable and fruitful process. An open, constructive discussion of different opinions can lead to a better definition of the core mission, one that is finally supported by a consensus of top managers.

The chief human resources official in a large organization can be the ideal catalyst in managing the discussion needed to reconcile divergent views about the core mission. Personnel executives normally have the human relations skills that are needed for this process. More important, leading a successful core mission development process should enhance the position of human resources in the organization and reinforce the credibility of the head of human resources as a strategic planner concerned with overall organizational direction and goals.

From Mission to Organizational Objectives. The clear statement of an unequivocal core mission invariably leads to a sharper definition and more cohesive picture of organizational objectives, a critical ingredient in the development of strategic planning scenarios, examined in Chapter 5. Objectives, in the strategic sense, are those things that management wishes to achieve, such as:

- Growth by certain percentages at certain points in time
- Meeting of specified profit targets
- Entry into new markets
- Increased employee population
- Introduction of new products

As can be seen, most objectives are profit-oriented, or can be viewed as "subobjectives" of goals related to bottom-line results. Also, objectives are normally quantified—dollar amounts, percentages, calendar dates, and so on—and provide management with performance standards and a means of measuring progress toward goals.

Ideally, the definition of objectives emerges from the specific realities of the organization. Such goals should be less a "wish list" than a clear appraisal of obtainable benchmarks, based on such factors as:

- The capabilities of internal resources, strengths, and weaknesses as derived from analysis of the financial, performance, technology, and human resources capabilities of the company

- The value system of top management, including perceptions of the overall core mission and attitudes toward its successful accomplishment
- The realities of the external environment, as discussed in the next section, which include market pressures, regulatory requirements, demographic change, economic factors, and other external changes

It is also important to realize that organizational objectives are not necessarily identical with official statements. Lofty ideals such as fair employment or job security, concern for stockholders, or contributions to the quality of civilization do not necessarily translate into operational objectives as expressed through actual behavior.

Genuine objectives nearly always focus on the survival of the organization, improvement of its market position, and the constant and relentless pursuit of profitability. In the course of events, it is likely that the achievement of these true objectives results in the accomplishment of idealized goals: Employment is provided, shares appreciate, taxes are collected, and useful products or services are made available to more people.

The External Environment: Assessing the Impact of Change on the Organization

In an ideal business world, long-range plans could be based on inward analysis alone: We should do what we are best able to do, what makes the greatest profit, or what we can do with our new technology and resources at hand. If the world remained the same, or changed in readily predictable ways with obvious effects on the organization, strategic planners could ignore the troublesome, difficult, largely uncontrollable external environment—the totality of outside factors that may or may not affect the future organization.

In strategic planning, environmental scanners are the "historians of the future." Their task is essentially twofold: to identify change and to isolate and track those changes that will have impacts on the organization. Depending on the organization, the kinds of change that could have impacts range from natural resource reserves in a foreign nation (and that nation's political climate) to the regional fertility rate among 20- to 24-year-old women. Some are fairly easily projected—such as demographic age distribution based on a population that has already been born; and some defy easy analysis because they depend on a complex of other factors—such as political attitudes toward government-supported day care. Almost all are beyond the control of the organization, and some will have profound effects on strategic plans.

As shown earlier in the flow diagram of the model (Figure 4-1), corporate planning is responsible for identifying and evaluating the factors in the external environment that will affect the organization in the years ahead. These factors include:

- Economic trends, such as projected inflation rates, raw material costs, energy costs, productivity rates, interest rates, and other domestic or international economic factors impacting on the organization
- Regulatory requirements, including government regulation that applies to specific industries, laws affecting the treatment of workers by all employers, and government programs affecting the quality and quantity of the labor force generally
- Technical developments, such as the impact of new products and services; technology affecting employment, jobs, and markets; and new skills requirements
- Competitors' actions, including international competitors, new companies, diversifying organizations, and firms exiting the marketplace
- Human resources availability, involving the future supply of the skills and talents in the external labor market

At the same time, the marketing organization is usually responsible for preparing an analysis of where the company stands in the marketplace today, shown in the Figure 4-1 flow diagram as "assimilation of current market data," including trends and developments in the external environment affecting markets.

As discussed in the sections that follow, the nomenclature and analytical framework for examining the external environment can vary enormously. Terms should be consistent, however, and the outline for examining environmental conditions must be relevant to the organization's strategic planning needs.

Frequently, the question that arises in companies undertaking environmental scanning for the first time is more basic: Who does it? In one sense, this is academic. The important thing is that someone do it, so that the long-range plan reflects the realities of changing business conditions in the environment of the future.

Ideally, the human resources planner should be a participant in the environmental scanning process, providing research guidelines and assessing the priorities of data and trends relating specifically to human resources. Corporate planning and marketing planning organizations should have the perspective and capabilities necessary to structure the overall scanning process. Responsibility for the initial framework, including determining which aspects of the environment deserve the most attention because they are most critical to the organization's future, might thus repose with the corporate and marketing planners, although input from other staff managers and operational planners is essential. The strategic planning process should highlight the key environmental trends affecting business plans, so that these factors can be integrated with internal data to develop scenarios upon which alternative strategic plans will be based.

Thus, the overall perspective for environmental scanning should be corporate, although participation by departments with specific kinds of expertise—legal, financial, human resources, and line organizations and subsidiaries—is essential.

Data Collection Framework and Procedures

In environmental scanning, planners assume the heady role of predicting what the future world will look like—the conditions that will prevail in government, society, the economy, and their business five, ten, or more years into the future. Uncertainties abound, of course, from the pace of technological change to the possibility of wars and natural disasters. But the planning process requires a realization that the future will come whether we do anything about it or not and that certain environmental conditions will change between now and the planning horizon.

Moreover, some of these environmental changes will have enormous impacts on the future organization, its markets, costs of doing business, labor force requirements, and other opportunities and constraints. Consider the following examples:

- Organizations dependent on an assured supply of raw materials must continuously monitor changes in the availability, the price and delivery schedules, and possibly the capabilities of major suppliers—in addition, in some cases, to monitoring political developments in nations that dominate supply.
- Businesses in heavily regulated industries—such as petrochemicals, nuclear power, or pharmaceuticals—must keep abreast of regulatory agency trends, impending legislation, and shifting public attitudes that in time may be converted to regulatory actions or new laws.
- Consumer products firms—or for that matter, any company dependent on consumer buying patterns—must generate demographic projections, economic data such as income distribution and interest rates, and a wealth of specific information to assess the future market for their goods or services.
- Industries at the leading edge of technological change—either because they produce Information Age goods or services or because they are using a changing technology—must project the impacts of technical developments on markets, competition, investment needs, the labor force, and other conditions of doing business in the years ahead.

Countless other examples would only serve to confirm the fact that the list of potential "issues" or external environmental factors affecting the business may indeed be daunting: Books on "megatrends" in the economy and society may be merely the starting point, as planners seek to account for a myriad of variables—and their interconnected relationships—that may influence the future environment.

For example, assume that a key factor in your company's future planning is the average retirement age of workers: Will the decades-long trend toward earlier retirement continue in the late 1980s and 1990s, will it slow, or will it reverse itself, as some predict? The factors that impinge on this issue in the United States include potential legislation raising the retirement age for full Social Security benefits; inflation rates that could inhibit earlier retirement; the employment situation for older Americans; the health of private pension funds; regulatory and judicial activity based on the Age Discrimination in Employment Act; changing worktime patterns in industry (such as more part-time work and job sharing); the health of older workers; and the retirement patterns of women in the workforce, which may differ from past patterns for men. And in addition to these and possibly other "macro" factors affecting all workers, each organization will have specific factors related to the kinds of work performed (and the impact of technology), benefits plans, region, and the present age structure of the workforce.

To get some idea of how much an environmental factor such as the retirement age can change, consider that in the early postwar years, nearly half of all American men aged 63 to 68 worked; by the mid-1980s, only about one-fifth of the men in that age group are in the labor force.

Thus, the complexity and range of potential environmental issues affecting long-range planning can be overwhelming if undertaken from scratch, without the framework provided by corporate and marketing planners. Some ways to develop such a framework and procedures for managing the scanning activity are suggested below, followed by a discussion of the human resources department's specific responsibilities in assuring that personnel aspects of the environment are accounted for in the overall process.

Starting the Environmental Scan. The process of creating an environmental scanning system is funnel-shaped: At first, all external information, trends, conditions, and assumptions about the future that *might* affect the organization are gathered; evaluation within the organization will narrow the range and number of items that bear analysis and tracking so that the issues considered are those with genuine relevance.

The kinds or categories of external factors, as suggested earlier in this chapter, might include economic trends, regulatory requirements, technology, competition, and human resources availability. But these categories are hardly sacrosanct. Depending on the type of business the organization is in and on organizational objectives, an environmental category might be "government action" instead of "regulatory requirements," for example.

Although nomenclature is unimportant, the specific factors that will eventually become part of the strategic planning process can affect the organization's future profoundly. The process of identifying, evaluating, and tracking these key issues begins, as noted above, with the broadest possible listing and definition of environmental issues that may have impacts on the organization, to assure that no significant trend is overlooked.

For example, under the category of government action or regulatory requirements, possibly the following kinds of issues might first be identified and defined:

- Corporate and business taxes
- Income tax laws
- Social Security changes
- Medical cost containment
- Alternate-workhour legislation
- Job training
- Public service employment
- Pension regulation
- Public works
- Equal employment
- Age discrimination
- NLRB trends
- Plant closings legislation
- OSHA and industry-specific regulation
- Immigration law
- Medicare/Medicaid
- Disability/workers' compensation
- Research and development spending
- Comparable worth
- Minimum wage
- Quality of work life programs
- Unemployment compensation
- Privacy legislation
- Antitrust
- Housing
- Education
- Child care
- Welfare
- Defense spending
- Industrial policy
- Trade legislation
- Industry regulation/deregulation

This list is by no means complete, and within many of the items listed is a broad range of specific issues, trends, and coming developments that the planner will need to spell out, define, and analyze. While most apply to federal government activity, many involve state and local laws and regulations, as well—enacted in some cases "in advance" of potential laws at the federal level. (For example, five U.S. states now have some form of plant closings legislation, with such requirements as prenotification, justification of the move, and the provision of retraining and employment opportunities for displaced workers. The movement in Congress for a national law gains impetus every time that a company abruptly closes its doors and moves to Alabama or Taiwan.)

The overriding objective of the initial environmental scan is to be comprehensive—to leave nothing out in terms of the economy, demographic and workforce change, the political arena, or technological change that could affect the environment in which the organization operates now and in the years ahead. To the extent that resources permit, the initial scanning process can also be more detailed than indicated above. For example, the "alternate-workhour legislation" category could itemize recent trends and proposed legislation affecting flexible hours, job sharing, part-time employment, compressed workweeks, and the reduction of the typical 40-hour workweek under the Fair Labor Standards Act. (In California, for instance, certain employers may qualify for a program that allows workers on four-day-workweek schedules to be compensated for the fifth day from the unemployment compensation fund.)

For most organizations, however, the range and complexity of environmental issues that could affect the future business are too great to permit detailed analysis at this point. The next step, then, is to reduce the scope of the environmental scanning process to focus on those issues most relevant to the organization's future.

Focusing on Relevant Issues. Procedures for evaluating and assessing the importance of environmental trends and factors will vary according to management structure, planning organizations, and operational characteristics. Participants in this process might include all line managers in every department, or a central planning staff at corporate headquarters, or both.

Whatever technique is used—memo distribution, meetings, questionnaires, or combined methods—the process should be "circular" rather than strictly top-down or bottom-up. A plant manager in southern California has better insights into the labor market effects of changing immigration laws than a New York headquarters planner, as a rule; a chemical company's research department has a clearer perception of what technological change will mean to the firm's product line than its personnel department; and so on.

Corporate planning organizations, with the perspective of the long-range strategic plan for where the company is headed, are in the best position both to begin the reiterative process of issue identification and "prioritization" and to finally develop a "short list" of issues relevant to the overall strategic plan. The process should be ongoing, however, as new developments or trends come to the attention of both staff and line managers involved in the process.

Each department or function in the organization will have special expertise in selecting and evaluating the environmental issues of most importance to the firm. In the process of putting the broad environmental scan through the "funnel" of relevance to the company, these functions are in the best position to assess each issue, provide data or position papers explaining its implications, and in some cases, provide the "probability" estimates that will go into the development of strategic planning scenarios. The finance department will have inputs on interest rates, inflation, and some tax law trends; the research group will isolate and explain technological change and projected developments; public affairs people will evaluate legislation and other government activity; and marketing will have data on such issues as income distribution trends, migration patterns, and competitors' moves. The human resources department, as discussed in greater detail below, will bring to bear personnel objectives in its analysis of the demographic, governmental, economic, and technological changes likely to affect the quantity and quality of human resources available to the organization—and the overall environment in which workers work—in the years ahead.

Through a circular, reiterative process of evaluation and expert assessment, the original comprehensive list of environmental factors affecting the organization's future should be distilled to a detailed list of "critical issues," each accompanied by an assessment of the implications of change on the organization's plans and objectives.

As suggested earlier, the continuing evaluation of the external environment should take place simultaneously with the internal examination of the organization's goals and objectives. Doing both tasks at the same time will focus attention on the environmental factors most important to the organization, minimizing time spent gathering and analyzing superfluous information. For example, if the internal evaluation reveals that the organization is discontinuing a line of products aimed at 16- to 24-year-olds to focus on older consumers, or that technology will reduce its labor requirements for entry-level young people, the environmental "issue" of there being fewer young people in the U.S. population of the 1990s is not necessarily critical. (Because of "baby-bust" demographic trends, the share of the U.S. labor force made up of 16- to 24-year-olds will go from 24 percent in 1975 to 17 percent in 1995, declining in absolute numbers by over 2.5 million between 1985 and 1995.)

Finally, it should be clear that while the "funnel" process does reduce the environmental scan to essential issues, it is also likely to result in the addition of environmental factors that may have been overlooked. Plants located in one part of the country or world may be facing an entirely different labor market situation than others, for example; or departmental people with a closer view of their own needs may be aware of the significance of a trend that had not seemed important to corporate planners.

The process of examining environmental trends from a functional or departmental perspective is considered in the following section on the human resources environment. The same kind of process should be taking place in all other departments of the organization—finance, marketing, production, distribution, or other segments with planning input—if environmental scanning is to be comprehensive and complete.

The External Human Resources Environment

No matter how well an organization generates needed human resources through internal development, conditions in the overall environment, industry, or location can have drastic impacts on the future availability, competence, expectations, and costs of employees needed to staff the company in the years ahead. Even in "no-growth" employment situations, where the organization expects to operate with a sharply reduced workforce in the future, a view of the future environment is essential. If robots are going to replace most production workers, for example, how can the company be sure of an adequate supply of technicians to run and maintain the robots, and at what costs? How will layoffs affect labor relations, employee morale, and the ability of managers to manage? Is government intervention possible or a consumer backlash against the company's products? If attrition and turnover are expected to reduce employment levels to the desired size, how can the organization be sure that "the best and the brightest" don't leave first? Will the company end up with a cadre of senior managers unable to find jobs elsewhere and time servers waiting for their pensions?

More typically, organizations expect to add human resources between the present and the long-range planning horizon. The people needed in the future will come both from the existing organization—through internal development programs discussed in Part III of this book—and from external supplies of entry-level workers, college graduates, industry competitors, and other sources.

In addition to concerns about the availability of the human resources needed for the future organization, however, human resources planners must consider a broad range of factors relating to the cost, performance, and capabilities of the future labor force—which will be working in an environment unlike today's in many important respects. These conditions of the external environment—including demographic and workforce trends, government regulation of human resources, economic change, and technology affecting jobs—must be included in the environmental scanning process from a personnel department perspective and analyzed for relevance to the organization's long-range human resources plans. Further, most of the environmental factors to be discussed in the next section have direct planning relevance within the personnel department, because most of them affect the future costs of benefits plans, compensation strategies, productivity improvement, and other human resources programs and policies.

External Availability of Human Resources. Few organizations will be able to meet all of their future human resources needs through internal development. Growth, movement into new fields, replacement of workers lost through attrition, and especially in technologically advancing organizations, the need for new people with specialized and up-to-date educational qualifications will usually require some recruitment from the external labor market. Environmental scanning must take into account any projected change in that market that will have an impact on the organization's ability to obtain the people needed in the years ahead. Some examples are:

- The likelihood of fewer skilled craftspersons and factory workers in the future because of demographic trends (fewer teenagers), increased college enrollments, reduced job prospects in certain basic industries (such as steel, autos, rubber), and other environmental changes, including changing social attitudes about the desirability of blue collar careers
- A possible shortfall of electrical engineers and computer scientists, especially those having advanced degrees, because of educational trends

(fewer graduate students, faculty losses, reduced federal aid to education) and increased demand by industry and government

- A shortage of computer repair mechanics, an existing reality that is likely to worsen in the absence of expenditures for job training (although technological advances may send computer mechanics the way of keypunch operators, a declining profession)
- Shortages of unskilled entry-level labor in certain of the burgeoning service industries—such as fast-food retailing—because of environmental change that includes "baby-bust" demographics and, possibly, government restrictions on immigration

While these are among the most likely kinds of general labor market changes expected in the United States in the next decade or so, they are by no means the only or the most important impacts of environmental change on human resources availability.

As discussed earlier, under "Data Collection Framework and Procedures," the initial effort in the environmental scanning process should be to cast as wide a net as possible: The number and variety of external factors that may have an impact on human resources availability is potentially enormous, as indicated in Figure 4-2.

In practice, of course, the human resources planner has the advantage of a perspective based on the organization's existing human resources characteristics and the requirements of the long-range strategic plan. Knowledge of existing skills and talents needed to perform work, the organization's benefits and compensation programs, the demographic characteristics of the existing workforce, and other data based on the internal evaluation discussed at the start of this chapter will help focus attention on those external factors affecting the path to a future human resources environment. But the task of selecting and analyzing the factors relevant to human resources availability is never simple and bears constant reevaluation in light of changing conditions.

For example, the availability of engineers in general and specifically engineers with energy industry experience has been the subject of periodic controversy in the United States. During the 1976–81 period, the widespread perception was that a severe shortage loomed on the horizon, attributable to these factors:

- A boom in high-technology industries
- High activity in the energy/power field
- Anticipated federal government investment in synfuels R&D programs

The demands of industry not only appeared likely to tighten the market for engineering graduates but were inhibiting engineering school growth by seducing university professors with more attractive salaries. In addition, high salaries available to B.S. engineers discouraged many from pursuing advanced degrees, further decreasing the number of candidates for professorships. Al-

Figure 4-2. **Factors in the external environment that could affect human resources availability.**

POPULATION AND LABOR FORCE:

- LONG-TERM AGING OF AMERICA
- FEWER YOUTH THROUGH THE 1990s
- MIDDLE-AGE BULGE
- RETIREMENT TRENDS
- WOMEN WORKERS
- IMMIGRATION
- MIGRATION PATTERNS
- EDUCATION OF WORKERS
- TRAINING/SKILLS
- MARITAL STATUS
- HOUSEHOLDS
- MINORITIES
- LABOR UNIONS

THE ECONOMY:

- INFLATION IMPACTS
- COMPENSATION TRENDS
- BENEFITS COSTS
- PRODUCTIVITY
- WAGE AGREEMENTS
- CAPITAL INVESTMENT
- TECHNOLOGY
- INTEREST RATES
- ENERGY
- UNEMPLOYMENT

GOVERNMENT:

- SOCIAL SECURITY
- PENSION REGULATION
- EEO
- OSHA
- FLSA
- MINIMUM WAGE
- WELFARE
- EDUCATION
- ALTERNATE WORKHOURS
- PUBLIC EMPLOYMENT
- JOB TRAINING
- UNEMPLOYMENT COMPENSATION
- PLANT CLOSING LAWS
- JUDICIAL TRENDS
- HEALTH CARE
- TAX LEGISLATION/RULINGS

SOCIAL ATTITUDES:

- JOB SATISFACTION
- WORKER "RIGHTS"
- WORK/LEISURE TRADE-OFF
- CONSUMERISM
- RELOCATION
- CHILD CARE
- DISCRIMINATION

EXTERNAL ENVIRONMENTAL FACTORS AFFECTING THE AVAILABILITY OF HUMAN RESOURCES REQUIRE CLASSIFICATION, OR A "TAXONOMY" SUCH AS THE ABOVE OUTLINE, TO PERMIT DISCUSSION, RESEARCH, AND ANALYSIS FOR RELEVANCE TO THE ORGANIZATION'S HUMAN RESOURCES PLAN. IN THE ENVIRONMENTAL SCANNING PROCESS, THESE ISSUES ARE NARROWED DOWN AND MORE SPECIFICALLY DEFINED, ADDITIONAL FACTORS MAY BE ADDED, RELATIONSHIPS ARE ASSESSED, AND A FINAL LIST OF "CRITICAL" ISSUES AFFECTING HUMAN RESOURCES AVAILABILITY IS DRAWN UP.

though the number of engineering graduates increased during the 1977–81 period, master's degrees decreased proportionally, and the number of Ph.D.'s in engineering fields actually decreased, in absolute numbers, by 12 percent.

Another contributing environmental factor expected to worsen the imbalance between supply and demand for engineers, in addition to the synfuels program, was the anticipated increase in defense spending sought by the Pentagon. Highly cyclical, the defense industry is given to sudden, large-scale demands for technical personnel. To obtain the human resources they need, defense contractors lure engineers from the private sector with inflated salaries made possible by the luxury of cost-plus contracts. Compensation in the private sector is limited by the needs of long-term growth and competitive costs.

Still another factor expected to reduce engineering human resources supplies in the burgeoning high-tech economy was the growing number of engineers who leave their discipline for management and sales positions, reportedly because of earnings limitations in the engineering profession.

All of the foregoing factors combined to create legitimate fears about the environment's ability to produce enough engineers, especially in the energy industry, to meet demands. As it turned out, however, this gloomy picture has not been the whole story. Through the first half of the 1980s, at least, other factors have intervened to ameliorate the effects of these environmental changes.

For example, a faltering economy in the early 1980s and the government's de-emphasis of the synfuels program reduced both the real and projected demand for engineers. Even with the expected increase in demand by the defense industry, it now appears that the shortage of engineers applies only to certain disciplines—for instance, computer design, medical electronics, bioengineering, and word processing equipment.

Also on the bright side of the engineering employment picture are such factors as:

- Increasing enrollment of women and minority group members in engineering programs
- Grants from industry and some state governments to supplement faculty salaries and obtain up-to-date laboratory equipment and technical facilities

For some engineering-dependent firms, another avenue of relief from impending shortages may be available: the use of foreign engineering companies to do engineering and design work to U.S. specifications, under subcontracts.

Obviously, the environmental factors that can have an effect on the quality and quantity of human resources available in the future are not always strictly quantifiable. Some data are more certain than other important variables: We can know the age composition of the working-age population ten years from now, for example, because of past birthrates; but the number of 22-year-old engineering graduates who will decide to remain in school to pursue different kinds of advanced engineering degrees depends on less "knowable" factors—including future government aid availability, industry demands, the economy, the perceived value of an advanced degree, education resources, and factors specific to various engineering disciplines, such as advances in data processing technology or health-care legislation.

When the environmental factor is critical to the organization's future human resources, however, the planning process must be most analytical of information that is least reliable.

Marketing Data

Depending on the nature of the organization, the data-gathering process shown in the Figure 4-1 model as "assimilation of current market data" can be the most important process in establishing the objectives and direction of strategic planning. In companies where this is the case—consumer products firms that rely on high sales volumes in extremely competitive markets—marketing planning is usually well advanced.

For example, when a company is spending millions of dollars on advertising and merchandising techniques to reach a large segment of the public, market research is usually well developed. Sales and distribution data show what is happening to each product from week to week, and analysis of the market tracks competitors' sales and overall market shares and penetration.

A company that knows its products are purchased mainly by 34- to 45-year-old women living in major metropolitan areas, for example, will in all likelihood have demographic data on this market throughout its distribution area—if only to assure that the millions spent on advertising are spent effectively.

Marketing objectives can in some cases be the key component of an organization's core mission, as well. If marketing planning indicates that a competitor's new product is likely to largely usurp the market position of your own best-selling item, a new analysis of the firm's reason for being may be in order.

Such new developments are usually part of a fully developed marketing organization's evaluation of the direction of the external market, shown in the Figure 4-1 model as "current market data." Their position in the model suggests that market trends must be considered in the development of scenarios for the future organization, the possible environments in which a changed organization will operate.

In consumer organizations that pay a great deal of attention to their markets, the assimilation of current market data and trends may be the easiest part of the strategic planner's information-gathering effort. Market research is often far more advanced than organizational analysis in consumer products companies, for example. In many firms, the environmental data sought by the human resources planner to evaluate the future availability of people—such as trends among working women, income distribution, retirement patterns, and education—will already be coming into the company, via the market research department responsible for tracking a changing market.

The kinds of marketing information to be included in environmental scanning will differ among companies, according to existing markets, products and services, and plans to enter or create new markets. For a typical consumer products company marketing nationally, however, areas of research and evaluation might include:

- Income data and trends
- Spending characteristics and patterns
- Population or demographic trends, such as:
    age distribution trends
    sex, race, birth rate, marital status, if applicable
    labor force participation and trends
- Inflation and interest rates
- Migration and immigration trends
- Societal attitude changes in such areas as:
    leisure-time habits
    readership or viewing habits
    product or service preferences
    perceptions of value
- Competitors' experience and plans
- Technology affecting marketing
- Government activity affecting marketing, such as:
    trade policy
    industry-specific regulation
    media regulation
    fair trade laws and other state/local legislation
    new tax policies or income distribution
    changes in government spending affecting markets
- General economic indications

Keep in mind that, as the model in Figure 4-1 indicates, marketing information requires a perspective distinct from other external data affecting corporate operations, such as human resources availability. The same kinds of data may be relevant to each but may in fact have far different implications.

Integrating Internal and External Data

Once all of the preliminary information has been obtained, planners are in a position to integrate the relevant internal and external data and prepare an evaluation of what the organization has done and what it is capable of doing in a changing environment. At this time, the focus is on the status quo: data and information about what is and will be the organization's position without interventions in present procedures and plans. Later on, alternatives to this status quo will be explored.

The process of determining which data are "relevant" to the organization—especially in the external environmental sphere less familiar to most managers—may be one of the most challenging tasks faced by the planner at this stage. The processes for collecting data discussed in the sections of this chapter on the internal organization and the external environment have been heavily weighted toward "management participation" at all levels; we have sought to underscore the importance of gaining the involvement and insight of the most influential managers in the firm—especially in the definition of the core mission. If the reasons for this approach have not become evident by now, planners will meet them full force at this stage of the strategic planning process.

If the strategic planning analysis of the internal organization and the external environment has been worth the effort, a somewhat "new" perspective on where the company is today is likely to emerge. Factors that have not been sufficiently considered may shed new light on the organization's ability to continue in its present posture. Analysis may show that while sales and profits have been rising, market share has not. There may be a surplus of inventory, a shortage of mechanics, or any number of "weaknesses" as well as unexpected strengths uncovered by the information-gathering processes.

Management resistance to "new" information or ideas is often in direct proportion to the extent that these data or ideas vary from the managers' own perceptions. Although the processes described earlier go a long way toward determining key individuals and even creating management consensus, the evaluation of "where we are" based on the integration of data is not likely to satisfy all managers—especially if the news is bad.

It has been pointed out that managers typically work through four stages in their psychological perceptions of unwelcome change:

1. *Denial.* The first reaction to unexpected or threatening data or conclusions is to deny that they are valid or that such change is important to the organization.
2. *Defense.* When it is shown that new information is irrefutable and that it will indeed force change in the way the organization operates, managers are likely to express annoyance and engage in a defense of present practices.
3. *Depression.* When managers have exhausted their resources to deny or defend, they will drift into a depression regarding the issue and its impact—a depression in which they have no motivating convictions about the response required by the change.
4. *Acceptance.* Finally, managers not only become resigned to the change but join the adaptation process, enabling a coordinated effort to deal effectively with the changed situation.[6]

Many other factors come into play in the difficult process of integrating data and convincing top management of their reality—all assuming the data are in fact irrefutable—but the planner who is aware of the need for top management's support will develop techniques appropriate to organization-specific requirements. In some companies, the only person who must be convinced is the CEO.

Top management's perceptions of the environmental factors affecting the business represent a special challenge. Everyone who reads a newspaper or watches television has preconceptions about "where we're headed" as a nation and as an economy—often heavily influenced by his or her political beliefs. Moreover, environmental data are often subject to varying interpretations or conclusions: Does the minimum wage, for example, bring more young people into the labor market, or does it serve to increase teenage unemployment?

Environmental issues and their impacts on the organization—even if determined through the broad-based reiterative processes described in the preceding section—may require a certain amount of additional "selling" to management, especially in organizations that have traditionally reacted to environmental change rather than planning for it. Such firms are likely to include those that are:

- Long-established and have been steadily meeting their goals in growing markets, such as the major U.S. auto companies before the late 1970s
- Historically entrenched in relation to government, such as firms in industries that have long been regulated or historically unregulated, where the political environment is often taken for granted
- Dominant in their market, with little or no concern for competition
- Reliant on relatively few customers and oblivious to the environmental forces that may be changing their customers' businesses
- Supplied by a historically abundant flow of resources—including an apparently limitless supply of human resources—and therefore unconcerned about environmental change that could affect this availability

The integration of data regarding environmental factors and simultaneously gathered data regarding internal factors leads to the basis or starting point for preliminary views of the future organization—the organization's place in the world that lies on the long-range planning horizon. These views are the strategic planning scenarios discussed in Chapter 5.

5

Scenarios and Strategies

If handed a few million dollars and asked to start a business—any business—that would prosper ten years from now, most people would become instantaneous strategic planners. Some romantic individualists would set out to do what they always wanted to do and felt they could do best: perhaps open an art gallery. Others, maybe more businesslike and practical, would focus on "where the action will be" a decade hence: perhaps a chain of diet taco stands in the American Southwest.

The point is that both types of response, one inner-directed and the other grounded in perceptions of change in the external world, are strategic. The first—based on individual goals, mission, and aptitudes—is analogous to plans based only on analysis of the internal organization, as discussed in the preceding chapter. The second approach begins with the kind of scanning of the external environment explored in the preceding chapter and proceeds to the subject of this chapter, the development of likely scenarios and strategies to succeed in the world that looms on the planning horizon ahead.

In the real world, of course, the two ways of selecting a strategy for future prosperity are in fact inseparable. For one thing, the future environment *includes* the planner's organization, and some dominant or innovative companies will in effect create the conditions in which they operate.

As a rule, strategic planning initially requires a view of the future environment, a scenario of relevant conditions on the planning horizon. Strategies to cope with change emerge from a fusion of "inner" and "outer" realities. Scenarios and strategies are not the same thing. A scenario is a documented narrative of anticipated conditions that the organization expects to deal with at some time in the future; a strategy is a way of dealing with a scenario. In our view of strategic human resources planning, however, scenarios and strategies to deal with them are interdependent from the outset: Even the preliminary selection of scenario-strategies is based on the interrelationships of environmental conditions, organizational objectives, and human resources demand and availability.

The purpose of this stage of the planning process is to identify the realm of the possible. Creativity, a different vision of the options, and broad perspectives should be brought to bear at this point. When likely scenarios have been stated as clearly as possible, the development of strategies to deal with them should proceed unfettered by the constraints of past practices, traditional goals, or—up to a point—the organization's ability to implement those strategies. The point at which strategies might be considered unfeasible because human resources are insufficient, however, is never "fixed" and immutable. A central purpose of a proactive strategic planning system is that it permits planners to create change as well as plan for it. The operational demand factors covered in Chapter 6 change for different strategies and are susceptible to management interventions, and the human resources availability factors examined in Part III are nothing less than the end result of strategy-based personnel programs and policies—from performance appraisal through succession planning.

In the preliminary stages of scenario and strategy selection and analysis, however, planners are urged to accept a relatively low "reality threshold." The realities forced upon the planner by operational demand and human resources availability may patently preclude the implementation of a given strategy. Preliminarily, that will become evident from the analysis covered under "Testing Hypothetical Strategies Against Human Resources" later in this chapter. In the ongoing strategic human resources planning system—when all parts are operating and with programs in place—the effects of different strategies will be more readily identifiable. Moreover, with the kind of data available in the recommended model, and with systematic analysis of these data, the final strategies will be nothing if not "realistic."

For now, however, the focus is on the possibilities rather than the limitations of strategic planning.

Planning for Uncertainty

The word *scenario*, first used in English in the nineteenth century[1] and popularized in Hollywood as an outline of proposed scenes for a movie, entered the general business lexicon in the 1960s from the language of political affairs, where it had come to mean "an account or synopsis of a projected course of action or events."[2]

For purposes of the present system, however, the meaning of the word *scenario* is somewhat more limited than its frequent usage today would indicate. Often, the term is employed to include organizational plans or alternative courses of action to deal with different "scripts" of the future environment: The scenario is both an outline of the future and a statement of the company's strategies for dealing with the future.

It is our view that strategies must be kept separate from scenarios at this stage, when the goal is to objectively identify the key environmental factors and the change in those factors. There are several reasons for this separation in the development of scenarios—the most important focusing on the need for flexibility in strategic planning—but "reason enough" may be the difficulty inherent in predicting future conditions and events in the world outside the organization. It has been pointed out, in fact, that the entire field of long-range business planning suffered a decade-long setback because of inaccurate or incomplete forecasts in the late 1960s and early 1970s.

As noted in one Conference Board publication, "corporate long-range planning developed and, in many companies, succeeded in the relative stability of the 1960s."[3] By 1966, one author was able to write that "A plethora of cookbooks on corporate planning has been published in the last two years [1964–66], and for those unable to digest a full book, a host of more specific 'recipes' appears monthly, if not weekly, in the business journals."[4]

The economic, social, and political stability of the 1960s began giving way later in the decade, of course, leaving strategic planning in disrepute. "In fact," say Chandler and Cockle, "during the 1960s considerable disservice was done to the science by the enthusiastic and excessive claims made for it" on the part of those who were later proved to have misjudged the future environment.[5]

Strategic planning has had a resurgence in recent years, but not because scenario development is any easier or because the world is any more stable or predictable. Managers, realizing that long-range plans must be made if their organizations are to be instrumental in shaping their own futures, have undertaken strategic planning out of necessity. In one group of companies studied in 1967 and again in 1977, for example, it was found that many "had redesigned their planning systems in the early 1970s, essentially making a fresh start at formal long range planning."[6]

More recently, the use of scenarios to depict a set of related external factors in the environment that will affect the organization has also had a resurgence, as a key component of strategic planning. Multiple scenario use "more than doubled" between 1977 and 1983 at leading U.S. industrial companies, one study found, although the authors note that "there appears to be no agreement on the meaning of the term 'scenario.'"[7]

The ways that scenarios can differ are as varied as the needs of specific organizations: Some will be elaborate constructions of mathematically demonstrable relationships, some more casual depictions of expected trends; some organizations will feel a need to develop multiple scenarios and assign degrees of probability such as "most likely" through "least likely," and others will simply try to focus on a series of different alternatives that each reflect about the same degree of probability. Elaborate computer modeling will be the basis for some but will merely provide backup data or documentation for others.

An even more fundamental way in which the idea of the scenario differs among organizations is whether or not the scenario or each of the multiple scenarios incorporates strategies. The point may appear to be academic, since scenarios and strategies go hand in hand, and any depiction of the future environment assumes that the organization will be part of that environment.

For purposes of retaining the flexibility made possible by the present strategic planning system, however, we recommend that the meaning of the term *scenario* be confined to the external environment at this stage. Further, we favor an "optimistic-pessimistic" classification range for multiple scenarios rather than measurement techniques that attempt to assign probabilistic values. The scenarios should all be likely to occur, but each will have different impacts on the organization—some as threats, others as opportunities, and many as simple "differences" that will call for new or altered strategies.

When the scenarios describing the sets of conditions in the external world have been finalized, planners can develop preliminary organizational strategies to deal with each scenario. At first, planners need not concern themselves with the identification of what it will take to interact with a given environment, leaving all options open in a climate conducive to creativity and innovative solutions. As discussed in a later section of this chapter, the range of strategies developed in the preliminary stage will be tested against resource availability before preliminary strategies are selected and analyzed, on the basis of operational demand forecasts and human resources availability. For now, however, planners should focus on the very difficult task of assessing the environmental factors relevant to the organization—to develop scenarios of anticipated external conditions—and creating a broad range of possible strategies to cope with such future conditions. The critical benefit of this approach lies in the need for flexibility. A strategy or course of action that "doesn't make sense" or appears unfeasible should not be discarded out of hand. It may not be possible to implement it with existing human resources, for example, but the interventions available to strategic human resources planners, discussed in Part III, may make it possible.

Development of Environmental and Economic Scenarios

Scenarios are developed on the basis of a distilled, highly parochial, or self-interested view of the data gathered in the environmental scanning process described in the preceeding chapter. As discussed there, the process of assessing the environment is ideally "funnel-shaped," beginning with consideration of the broadest possible number of factors and being narrowed—by managers familiar with organizational goals, financial targets, and the characteristics of human and other resources in the organization—to the most critical conditions or related sets of conditions in a changing world.

For some organizations, scenario development will necessarily be quantitative or more elaborate than the simple narrative style recommended here. Financial institutions, for example, must pay close attention to projected interest rates and utilize vast macroeconomic models to forecast this factor. The complexity and data sophistication of a scenario provide no guarantee of accuracy, of course,[8] but this is not the main reason we prefer simple narratives as scenarios. Scenarios must be readily grasped and understood by planners—no matter how extensive their documentation or supporting evidence—in order to portray a complex environment's actual impacts on the organization. The impacts, in the final analysis, are what matter—not the inches-thick printouts or charts covering the wall.

General to Specific Scenarios. One approach to scenario development that utilizes the funnel technique for environmental scanning is to proceed from the general to the specific. For example, in the political arena in the United States, a change of parties and policies in the administration of the federal government is often a general factor contributing to scenario development.

Prior to the 1980 presidential election, one firm developed two general scenarios, one for a Carter reelection and one for a Reagan victory. If Ronald Reagan were elected, the scenario assumed that:

- Federal regulations would be less restrictive.
- The role of the federal government in domestic affairs would be generally reduced.
- Most Reagan programs, probably about two-thirds, would be approved by Congress.
- Key regulatory agency appointees would support free enterprise and business philosophy.
- The inflation rate would decline to 6 percent by 1982.

This scenario was then further particularized to develop a more industry-specific version, with greater relevance to the organization, an engineering and construction services firm in the energy industry. Part of the more specific scenario assumed that:

- Funding for the synthetic fuels program would be reduced by the Reagan administration, in part because of the stabilization of oil prices.
- Projected revenue from synfuels plant design and construction would be less than anticipated.
- The future of the nuclear power station market would worsen, with the market shrinking because of rising costs, high interest rates, and the political implications of government support for the nuclear power program.
- When power-plant construction resumes, it will primarily involve plants of the coal-fired type.
- There will be a return to private-sector financing rather than federal government financing of such projects.

As history has shown, many parts of this scenario turned out to be substantially correct.

The environmental scanning process described in Chapter 4 will uncover a broad range of economic, political, social, and technological areas of potential change affecting the organization. As noted earlier, some of these changes will be predictable—such as the age composition of the population ten years from now—but most will carry one degree or another of uncertainty. It is this uncertainty that a flexible strategic planning system is designed to address, and in scenario development, this design means the use of multiple scenarios.

Multiple Scenarios. The critical issues affecting the organization's future cannot be ignored because "we just don't know" what will occur in the years ahead.

Strategic planning is a necessary activity, not in spite of uncertainty but because of uncertainty. The use of multiple scenarios, each describing a different set of possible conditions relevant to the organization, is the basis for a flexible planning system that will adapt to unknown or unforeseeable eventualities.

The narrative form recommended for scenarios, and shown in the examples of multiple scenarios below, does not preclude the use of extensive documentation and supporting data. Rather, the narrative form is ideally a précis, or summary, of the best available evidence, analysis, and informed correlation of data and projections. The scenarios themselves, however, should emerge as relatively straightforward statements of anticipated change, readily grasped by planners responsible for developing strategies to cope with each type of change.

For example, an organization vitally concerned with the market for synfuels plants might have at least three different scenarios depicting possible change in OPEC oil pricing policies and the availability of oil. The multiple scenarios might look like this:

Scenario 1: American industry and the federal government will continue to perceive the long-term domestic energy situation as essentially unstable, even though the current oversupply and reduced price of crude oil may suggest normalization. They will recognize that such oversupply is caused not only by the increasing availability of North Sea oil produced by Britain and Norway, but also by the temporary ineffectiveness of the OPEC cartel engineered by Saudi Arabia in its attempt to eliminate as many marginal competitors as possible, including the domestic United States oil industry. Saudi Arabia's aggressive pricing also has the added political incentive of preventing its arch-rival Iran from financing the Iranian war with Iraq through oil revenues, and of minimizing Iran's ability to export its revolutionary fervor to other moderate Arab states; however, it is expected that significant price increases will occur once such issues are resolved. The United States government's recognition of the Saudi's long-term strategy will lead to a proactive American response focused on continuing the development of energy reserves. Actions will include stockpiling of the Strategic Petroleum Reserve, direct coal substitution, the continuation of nuclear development, and unrestricted oil exploration in all potentially oil-bearing domestic locations. The economic price threshold of domestic oil production will be maintained through a variable import fee. Domestic oil drilling activity will result in major new oil and gas field discoveries, minimizing the need for either high oil imports or a crash synfuels program.

Comments: The likelihood of scenario 1's actually taking place is probably less than 10 percent because of a continuing lack of a domestic policy consensus and a questionable oil resource base.

Scenario 2: OPEC crude oil prices will move upward or downward gradually, in line with supply conditions, inflation, and international political considerations. In any case, the price of crude oil imported to the United States will deliberately be kept below that of synthetic crude produced from shale or coal. Even if Middle East tensions are taken into account, because of the refusal of North Sea producers to either join the OPEC cartel or curtail production, there will be no prolonged interruption of crude production overseas. Industry and government are aware that the world's oil supply from the Persian Gulf dropped from 37 percent in 1973 to 18 percent in 1986. Synfuels programs in the United States will be initiated for the long-range future to come on-line beyond the year 2000. Synfuels activity in the next decade will be limited to research and development.

Comments: This outlook is close to current government policy and might be considered a middle, or base, case for planning purposes. But there is probably less than a 40 percent chance that foreign political events in the next decade will be so kind to U.S. interests as to allow such orderly development.

Scenario 3: Political unrest in the Mideast as well as in Central and South America will result in takeovers in countries now considered to be "oil-pricing doves" and installation of governments unfriendly to the United States. This would be followed by the threat of or actual interruption of the flow of crude oil from these countries, most probably including Saudi Arabia. Such a denouement would force the United States to a decision: to engage in military action or to initiate crash programs for synfuels and shale oil production. Both approaches at once are probable. Assuming military action does not lead to a major war, the United States will finance the construction of coal and shale conversion plants using existing technology. Military intervention, if undertaken, will be successful and result in a temporary resumption of the oil supply, along with a price rollback that renders synfuels production uneconomic. Nevertheless, the synfuels plants will be completed and go on stream. A second generation of synfuels plants will be designed and built on a more orderly basis, using more advanced technology, to meet the energy needs of the decades after the year 2000.

Comments: Considering the current volatility of global geopolitics, there is a 50 percent chance that this scenario or a similar one could occur in the next ten years.

Again, scenarios such as these are outcomes or summaries of what may have been extensive data-gathering and analysis programs. For example, in the cases above, it is evident that at some earlier point, planners determined that several key environmental factors would shape all scenarios in this area. These included:

- Political climates, both domestic and in other nations
- Government funding for synfuels development
- Commercial synfuels plant awards
- The possibilities of war and revolution

Scenario Development Techniques. There are many ways of developing strategic planning scenarios, ranging from highly data-intensive modeling procedures to the apparently mystical insights of a philosopher-king in the CEO's chair. For companies not blessed with a soothsayer, however, the task of scenario development usually begins where the environmental scanning process leaves off. Although environmental scanning never "ends" in a changing world, at any point in time, this process should result in a clear set of critically relevant trends, assumptions, and facts about the external environment—including the uncertainties that necessitate scenario development.

One technique for scenario development, often used both to achieve management consensus and involvement in the process and to obtain the organization-specific insights of practicing managers, is the Delphi method, named for the ancient Greek town and its famous oracle. The Delphic Oracle ascended Mt. Parnassus periodically, listened to the gods, and came down with accurate predictions, according to mythology. The Delphi method in strategic planning treats all of a selected group of key managers as though they were isolated oracles, and the "gods" that inform their predictions are the end results of environmental scanning plus their knowledge of the company and managerial intuition.

The selection of a panel of key managers to develop scenarios may be crucial to the process: In some organizations, key people may include line managers and others far from the corporate boardroom as well as executives from all major departments. The "right" mix for a Delphi panel will probably include both the most influential managers and the most knowledgeable, and may also include outside subject matter experts with special insights into critical environmental factors. Generally, the Delphi panel should be composed of those with the best understanding of the organization, its industry, and its environment—managers who probably have the other all-important qualities, credibility and influence.

In the Delphi process, each manager develops one or more scenarios separately, on the basis of the same environmental data and assumptions, bringing to bear his or her own perceptions of the importance of these data to the company. Each may also be asked to estimate probability, if scenarios are being rated on a scale of likelihood. This separation of effort promotes candor and creativity in scenario development.

These initial analyses are usually collected by a review committee created for this purpose, which begins the process of clarification and distillation. A list of questions on specific issues may be developed and each oracle-manager asked to respond. Depending on time and resources, the review group can engage in a continuing refinement of the most widely supported scenarios, until finally the number of scenarios has been distilled to a manageable quantity and their key elements refined.

Another way to produce scenarios is to conduct a full-fledged organizational diagnosis (OD)—the technique recommended in Chapter 4 to examine strengths and weaknesses as well as develop a statement of the organization's core mission—but this procedure is even more time-consuming than the most elaborate Delphi procedure, as a rule, and for this reason may be inappropriate as a means of getting preliminary scenarios "on the table" for early analysis. Later on, when all parts of the strategic planning system are in place and functioning, the use of OD techniques in scenario development may be easier to sell to top management.

Development of Preliminary Strategies

Strategies are the means by which organizations will achieve their ends, and preliminary strategies are the initial outlines of specific plans of actions that will accomplish organizational goals in different environments. At this stage in planning, each scenario is closely examined for its distinctive conditions affecting the organization's ability to achieve its goals, and a separate strategy is developed for each scenario that will best enable the organization to deal with those conditions.

Preliminary strategies may be broad and speculative or specific and conservative, depending on the nature of organizational goals and environmental conditions. In general, however, the planner at this juncture should probably be more concerned with expanding the horizons of the possible, reaching for more creative or innovative strategies, than confined to "business as usual" projections. The purpose of preliminary strategy development is to bring to light plans that match the scenarios of the future, the actions the organization might take to cope with, and preferably prosper in, the environment to come. Initially, the approach is inclusive: All strategies that might work to achieve objectives in each scenario should be considered. When an ideal or optimal strategy for each scenario has been determined, each strategy can be tested for feasibility of implementation. The testing process, as will be shown, permits the alteration and refinement of strategies that may not at first appear feasible.

Environmental scenarios may require a broad range of strategies that should be considered. For example, one scenario may posit that a competitor will bring a major new technology to fruition several years before you are able to do so, taking over a large share of your present customers and creating an even broader market for a new product based on this technology. If this is the case, your options include strategies based on:

- Active response, such as the purchase of the competing company, a crash R&D program to catch up to or surpass the new technology, or a venture into another line of business
- Passivity, such as waiting to see what effects the new product will have on sales
- Some middle ground, including increased effort to achieve the technological breakthrough, contingency plans for developing new products or services, and long-range plans for reductions in force among affected workers

If another scenario on the same subject says that the competitor will have the new product before you will but that it will cost too much for the market and will not be competitive for at least five years, an entirely different set of options may be open to managers.

The development of a preliminary strategy may be an elaborate process including detailed timetables and goals, or the strategy may simply be a new approach to labor relations, the broad outlines of which are to be filled in later. For example, one author suggests these basic ingredients of a strategy:

- Selecting market niches that offer an optimum match between market demand and company resources
- Selecting and enhancing the technologies needed to maximize production efficiency
- Expressing the strategy in terms of targets
- Specifying the sequence and timing of actions required by the strategy to meet these targets, in a manner that reflects organizational capabilities and external conditions[9]

While there is little to argue with in the textbook definition of a strategy, in the real world, organizations differ greatly in the ways they arrive at strategies for future action. As Glueck points out, some are strictly "programmed," reflecting stable environments or the expectation that little will change; others are flexible, such as the strategies based on different scenarios recommended here.[10]

Preliminary strategies may also be broad and thematic rather than specific and programmed on timetables. For example, Japanese industrial firms have significantly increased their profitability through a strategy of "doing more with less," or more work with fewer people, by productivity improvement. A case in point is Hitachi, a diversified consumer goods manufacturer, which tripled sales between 1972 and 1982 while reducing its workforce from 163,000 to 151,300 through retirements, transfers, and attrition. At Hitachi's Mito Works—where locomotives, elevators, and escalators are built—production tripled while the workforce required to meet this production was being cut in half.

By this time, it is no secret how the Japanese have managed to combine job-displacing technology with high worker morale and employee cooperation. Japanese workers are not fearful of automation, computer-controlled machine tools, or robots—because of job security and other quality of work life policies and programs that characterize major Japanese firms.

Ironically, both the production technologies used in Japanese factories and the Japanese approach to labor relations were largely influenced by U.S. companies and American behavioral scientists. Japanese firms sent teams of production people to study U.S. methods in the postwar years, and as McMillan has observed, their labor relations policies followed "the essence of the Deming/Duran philosophy."[11] Of course, cultural factors in Japan—paternalism, the enjoyment of teamwork, the strength of family ties and perceptions of employers as extensions of the family—made the adoption of these labor relations approaches more successful than they might have been in other countries.

Nonetheless, Japanese firms adopted the general strategy of involving workers in quality control and improved production at an early stage in their economic resurgence. Specific programs that filled in and implemented the overall strategy varied—although one form or another of job security characterizes all major Japanese industrial firms that have introduced laborsaving technology—and some programs grew naturally in this employee relations climate. The first formal quality circles, for example, were not created until 1964, although now there are some half-million QCs in Japan.

Today, U.S. and European manufacturers are looking to Japan for "new ideas" in labor relations, including quality circles and other techniques aimed at reducing adversarial relationships between workers and managers, promoting participative management, and engaging the entire workforce in the pursuit of improved productivity.

An example of the effect in the automobile industry of the new strategy—which seeks to humanize work through concern for workers—is found at the Ford truck plant in Louisville, Kentucky. There, production line workers are allowed to stop the line to align truck bodies on two pins, reducing the physical strain of forcing mating components into place, even though this stoppage reduces productivity—on paper. In fact, "slower is faster" in this case, an improvement attributed to worker involvement.

Contingency Strategies. Often, the development of strategies based on "what-if" scenarios includes a number of tentative or preparatory actions the organization can take if certain scenarios become reality. Depending on the extent of the threat (pessimistic scenario) or opportunity (optimistic) posed, the organization will allocate more or less resources to prepare for these contingencies. Probability must also be weighted before major investments are undertaken, but contingency strategies are often designed with limited objectives, to prevent "unpleasant surprises" and the worst of their effects or to give the organization a "head start" in dealing with a new market situation, technological change, skills shortage, or other development that cannot be strictly planned for.

For example, one engineering firm specializing in nuclear power plants some years back hypothesized the occurrence of a major malfunction at an existing nuclear facility. This apparently pessimistic scenario anticipated that the plant suffering such a malfunction would immediately need experienced technical staff to minimize further damage, prevent contamination of the environment, and eventually restore the plant to a safe operating condition.

It was further assumed that the demand for specialized engineering resources to handle this work on short notice could be met only by diverting such resources from existing nuclear power projects. In order to deal with this kind of scenario, the engineering firm identified a small, core group of specialists who could be assigned to such a task at a moment's notice, without severe interruptions to existing projects. The strategy included a means of augmenting this small group with additional engineers, using the human resources data bank, in any numbers and with any specialities that might be required.

When the Three Mile Island accident did occur, the Nuclear Regulatory Commission responded quickly to the demands of the press, politicians, and environmental groups and issued orders for design modifications and safety improvements not only at Three Mile Island but at all nuclear power plants operated by utilities. This retrofit work could of course be performed only by specialized firms, most of which were already committed to ongoing projects.

Having prepared for this contingency to some extent, the consulting engineering firm was better able than others to deploy its human resources skills. It had developed a scenario anticipating the emergency, coupled with a course of action or strategy to deal with it. The firm's core group was called in by the owners of the disabled Three Mile Island plant and quickly enhanced the company's reputation for quality retrofit work. Thus, a "pessimistic" scenario turned out to be an opportunity for this farseeing firm.

Results of Preliminary Scenarios. When fully developed, each scenario and its accompanying strategy will imply needs for certain levels of resources, including human resources. These implied projections can be quite specific, as shown in Table 5-1, indicating in this case the number of automotive tire production workers needed in one department (No. 320) over a five-year period. The forecast is further broken down by product type in this hypothetical example: Fundamentally different production processes are required to manufacture what are here called "standard-tread" automotive tires and radial-design tires.

In Table 5-1, the current forecast is based on the organization's strategy for the most likely scenario. Cases 1 and 2 posit scenarios in which the demand for standard tires would be greatly reduced, because of declining domestic automobile production resulting from economic and political factors (such as rising interest rates or the expiration of current trade agreements limiting foreign imports). Case 3 represents another highly likely scenario, one in which the company's market for radial tires improves dramatically—perhaps because of the success of its prime customer for radial tires, a car manufacturer with a new model that revolutionizes the industry.

This kind of detailed human resources forecast may or may not be part of the preliminary planning process, depending on the sophistication of existing planning methods and the capabilities of currently usable personnel information systems. Because such forecasts must be regularly updated on the basis of new data—the current forecast may become case 3—mechanized information systems are critical.

Testing Hypothetical Strategies Against Human Resources

As indicated earlier, the creative perspective considered necessary to the development of a full range of hypothetical strategies to deal with possible environmental scenarios should not at first be inhibited by real-world limitations of organizational capabilities. Initially, at least, preliminary hypothetical strategies should be based almost entirely on the optimization of organizational prosperity in a different external environment: If demographic trends indicate that a campus should be turned into a nursing home, this can be a preliminary strategy.

Table 5-1. Automotive tire production department No. 320 forecast.

Scenario options:

Case 1 — Standard-tread workload reduced to 25 percent of forecast
Case 2 — Standard-tread workload reduced to 50 percent of forecast
Case 3 — Standard-tread workload reduced to 50 percent of forecast and
 radial workload increased to 170 percent of forecast

	Sept. 1986	Oct. 1986	Nov. 1986	Dec. 1986	1987	1988	1989	1990
Standard-tread								
Current forecast	120	125	131	150	140	130	120	110
Case 1	30	31	33	38	35	33	30	28
Case 2	60	63	66	75	70	65	60	55
Case 3	60	63	66	75	70	65	60	55
Radial								
Current forecast	300	310	320	300	290	280	270	260
Case 1	300	310	320	300	290	280	270	260
Case 2	300	310	320	300	290	280	270	260
Case 3	510	527	544	510	493	476	459	442
Dept. 320 total								
Current forecast	420	435	451	450	430	410	390	370
Case 1	330	341	353	338	325	313	300	288
Case 2	360	373	386	375	360	345	330	315
Case 3	570	590	610	585	563	541	519	497

More realistically, however, there is a need for a preliminary stage that tests hypothetical strategies against organizational resources. At this early stage, the purpose of this testing is to eliminate from consideration those strategies that are simply not viable, that cannot be implemented by the organization as it now exists or as it could feasibly be reconstituted within the planning time frame. A chewing gum manufacturer cannot reasonably become a housing contractor, obviously, but does it have the resources to manufacture dental-care products?

The "resources" that should be considered in this preliminary testing of hypothetical strategies include financial, technological, physical plant, and other relevant assets and capabilities. The resource that is our focus, and is in fact often the most critical resource to be assessed, is people and their skills. For each strategy, certain quantities and qualities of human resources must either exist in the organization, be achievable through internal development, or be obtainable through reasonable external recruitment efforts. In short, the purpose of this stage of strategy testing is to test the viability of strategies against the availability of the human resources they will require.

The final objective in the development of long-range human resources strategies based on business plans is the selection of the most likely scenario and the strategy that most effectively deals with it. Before reaching this point, however, much planning information about the status quo of organizational human resources availability—data that are a product of the procedures described in Part III (as well as of operational demand for human resources, the subject of Chapter 6)—must be added to the model. At this point, however, the general viability of hypothetical strategies is being tested, on the assumption that no human resources management intervention will greatly alter the status quo and that operational demands are "givens" based on past experience or known human resources requirements.

With the focus on human resources, then, the preliminary steps for evaluating the viability of strategies are those shown in Figure 5-1, from "Demand Forecasting Options" through "Are Strategies Adequate?" This sequence permits the planner to take the next step—"Discard Nonfeasible Strategies"—which is the first step in narrowing the field to strategies that can viably deal with future needs and conditions.

Standard and Estimated Staffing Criteria

Staffing criteria are simply the numbers and skills of people needed to do specific kinds and amounts of work. But the degree of difficulty in determining such criteria varies enormously, from the staffing of a 24-hour tollbooth to the conversion of a power plant from coal to oil. Such staffing criteria are usually based on known needs—the past and current staffing requirements for producing so many automobiles, for operating each store, or for constructing an office building. Operations can be divided up in terms of such measures as unit labor costs, management spans of control, sales per call, and an almost unending gamut of techniques for relating human resources needs to given levels of production, services, construction, or any other form of organizational endeavor.

In strategic planning—and specifically in this preliminary stage of testing proposed strategies against the human resources that can be made available—the task of determining staffing needs may be much more difficult and much less certainly resolved. *Future* strategies are being tested, which may involve not simply "more of the same" product you know all about, but new products entirely or services not previously available anyplace. In addition, factors such as the introduction of technology have impacts that are not always easily ascertained; for example, most companies that introduced office automation in the 1970s expected "people savings" that never materialized. Change of any sort—in products, markets, methods of operation, and the external environment—means that projections of the human resources needed for a different future will in the final analysis be no more than estimates.

On the other hand, standard staffing tables such as the one in Table 5-2 can be developed with a great deal of specificity, based on managers' experience and analysis of anticipated needs. As shown here, this staffing package projects the number and types of skills needed to build a single plant; similar tables could be developed showing the staffing requirements for a production process geared to turn out a certain quantity or for the installation of a new computer system

Figure 5-1. **Preliminary evaluation of human resources strategies/forecasts.**

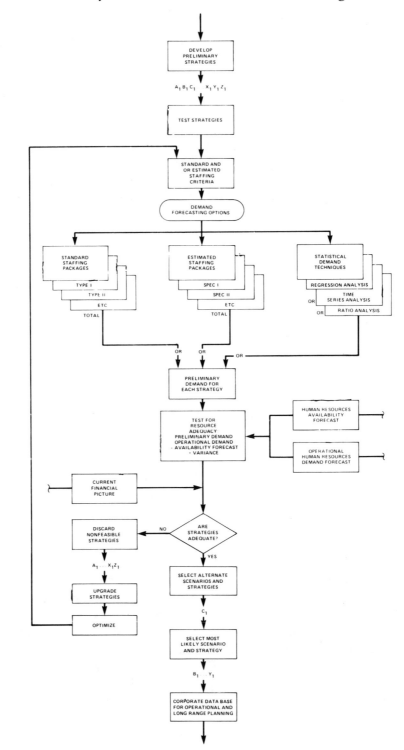

Table 5-2. Anticipated staffing levels for department No. 550—architectural, structural.

Project Type:
One Unit Fossil Plant

Job Code	07/86	08/86	09/86	10/86	11/86	12/86	1st Qtr. 1987	2d Qtr. 1987	3d Qtr. 1987	4th Qtr. 1987	1st Qtr. 1988	2d Qtr. 1988	3d Qtr. 1988	4th Qtr. 1988	1989	1990	1991	1992
18DA	1	1	1	1	1	1	1	1	1	1	1	1	1	1	1	1	1	1
16JE	1	1	1	1	1	2	2	2	2	3	3	3	3	3	4	4	4	5
15AH	1	2	2	2	2	2	2	3	3	3	3	3	4	4	4	5	5	5
15BX	11	12	12	14	14	14	15	15	18	21	27	27	27	30	32	32	32	34
15CF	1	2	2	3	4	4	4	4	5	5	16	6	8	10	10	12	13	55
14AL	30	33	34	34	35	37	40	40	40	42	50	50	50	51	53	54	54	55
13AN	23	26	26	26	27	27	29	31	33	36	41	43	45	47	49	50	51	53
12AO	13	14	14	16	18	20	23	25	29	32	38	40	38	39	42	43	43	45
10EO	8	9	10	11	13	15	15	17	19	23	26	27	27	28	31	33	33	34
9AP	6	8	8	9	11	11	11	11	14	17	20	22	22	23	27	27	28	29
07UK	1	1	2	2	3	3	4	5	6	7	9	9	9	11	15	15	16	16
06SQ	1	1	2	2	2	3	4	5	7	7	9	9	9	9	11	12	13	14
05QD	2	2	2	2	2	3	3	4	7	7	9	9	9	9	12	12	12	13
05QF	1	1	1	2	2	2	3	3	4	5	7	8	8	9	12	12	12	12
05QG	1	1	1	2	3	3	3	3	4	5	7	7	7	7	9	9	10	10
05QI	1	1	1	2	3	3	3	3	4	5	6	6	6	6	8	8	8	9
04OL	1	1	1	2	3	3	3	3	4	5	5	5	5	6	7	7	7	7
03MB	1	1	1	2	3	3	3	3	4	5	5	5	5	5	6	6	6	7

of known components. More often, however, preliminary strategies involve at least some new products, technologies, or operating requirements not knowable with absolute certainty. Thus, managers must provide estimated staffing tables based on preliminary strategies—best estimates of what will be required in the way of human resources to accomplish each preliminary strategy. The question at this point, it should be reiterated, is not *whether* the organization has the human resources, but *what* human resources will be required by various strategies.

Staffing Demand for Each Strategy. When the preliminary strategies have been developed to the point where certain levels of production, the provision of certain services, or other organizational activities have been specified, human resources requirements are computed by adding the data provided by estimated and standard staffing criteria.

For example, project-oriented organizations can develop human resources models for each of the kinds of projects the firm handles. Typically, these models are aggregates of standard and estimated staffing tables for each component of the overall project. As shown in the Table 5-3 example, each of the projects proposed by preliminary strategies is determined to require a certain number of people—with specific, identifiable skills—to be employed over the period of time required to complete the project. Each project has a set of human resources requirements based on historical experience or the estimated staffing criteria of key managers. In this case, each project starts with a core team of key people, to which others will be added according to a specific staffing schedule.

The strategy for which staffing demands must be examined usually involves a mix of projects of different types, each with its own staffing criteria. In Table 5-3, projects that are part of the overall strategy are at different stages of development: some may already be under way, some may definitely be scheduled, and others may merely be in the planning stage. For instance, Project B, under ongoing projects, reflects the growth of staffing to a peak and a gradual tapering down. Eventually, when this project is finished, the staffing for Project B will be zero. In Project A, on the other hand, by 1986 the staffing level has already peaked; by 1990, the project is completed. Project I is still in the planning stage, and it is only in the later years on the chart that the build-up of staffing begins.

Human resources models may also reflect several levels of detail, as shown in the graphic depiction based on project staffing criteria, Figure 5-2. The top graph indicates that this project will take eight years and depicts the total human resources requirements over that time. At its peak, this project will involve about 400 people (whose specific skills are detailed in backup data), tapering off to completion.

The middle graph in Figure 5-2 shows one department's total human resources requirements for this project. Like the project-total graph, it shows a buildup and gradual reduction in departmental staffing needs. The final chart shows the project requirements over time for staff in a certain skills category—in this case, a type of systems analyst. As can be seen, this skill is not required

Table 5-3. Systems analysts load—by computer installation project.

	9/86	10/86	11/86	12/86	1st Qtr. 1987	2d Qtr. 1987	3d Qtr. 1987	4th Qtr. 1987	1st Qtr. 1988	2d Qtr. 1988	3d Qtr. 1988	4th Qtr. 1988	1989	1990	1991
Total	1,080	1,110	1,140	1,170	1,260	1,400	1,500	1,580	1,950	2,320	2,490	2,810	3,530	3,770	3,283
Ongoing projects	1,080	1,110	1,140	1,170	1,200	1,270	1,260	1,200	1,230	1,250	1,140	1,090	1,049	845	673
Project A	660	660	660	660	600	600	540	430	420	410	300	190	92	0	0
Project B	360	390	420	420	450	490	540	540	540	540	540	540	537	425	263
Project C	60	60	60	90	150	180	180	230	270	300	300	360	420	420	410
Scheduled projects	0	0	0	0	60	130	240	370	600	730	900	1,030	1,293	1,403	1,076
Project D	0	0	0	0	60	120	180	240	300	300	330	360	455	315	33
Project E	0	0	0	0	0	10	60	120	210	300	390	480	553	578	453
Project F	0	0	0	0	0	0	0	10	90	130	180	190	285	510	590
Planned projects	0	0	0	0	0	0	0	10	120	340	450	690	1,188	1,522	1,534
Project G	0	0	0	0	0	0	0	10	120	240	300	410	660	677	650
Project H	0	0	0	0	0	0	0	0	0	100	150	280	450	580	454
Project I	0	0	0	0	0	0	0	0	0	0	0	0	78	265	430

Figure 5-2. **Human resources models—by project, department, and skills.**

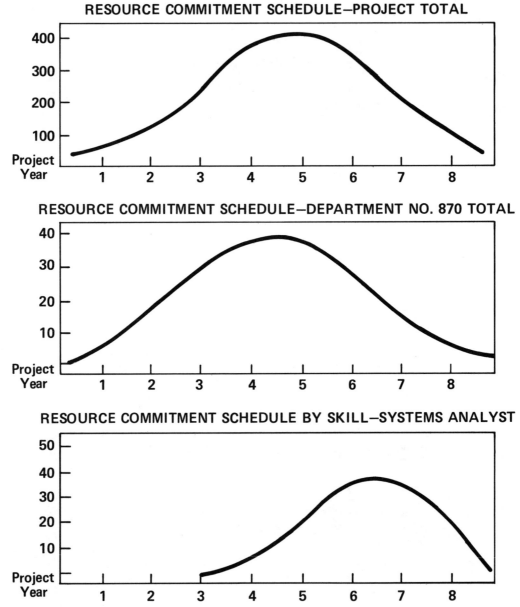

until the third year of the project, but a peak of some 30 such analysts will need to be available in the sixth and seventh years.

In order to evaluate strategies and their staffing demands as accurately as possible in this preliminary stage, as much information as can be obtained through experience-based staffing criteria should be used. Where new ventures or new technology dictate that a "best guess" is necessary, such estimates deserve special attention. As in other areas of the long-range strategic planning process, uncertainty requires more rather than less analysis and may include research and data gathering far afield from the immediate organization. But although the matching of strategies with their human resources demands should be as specific and accurate as possible—to avoid unpleasant surprises later on— the immediate objective at this stage of preliminary planning is to discard strategies that are patently unworkable because human resources will not be available. In some industries and organizations, this may leave a wide margin: If the strategy will require only unskilled workers in an abundant labor market, for example, hiring can bridge a wide gap. More often, however, especially in high-tech industries, strategies require skills that may or may not be readily available, and the first place to look for them is within the organization. This process, briefly described below, compares the operational demand forecast with the availability forecast generated by human resources planning.

Demand versus Availability and Strategy Selection

The next step, analysis of demand versus availability, is a conglomerate activity that includes both the preceding estimates of staffing needs for each strategy and—equally important—the human resources needed to accomplish existing and scheduled work. Total organizational demand is being sought, and unless the company is planning to discontinue present operations, the demand side of future strategies will include today's human resources demands and forecasts. This information is provided by the operational staffing demand forecast and is a product of the operational planning process described in Chapter 6. As discussed there, operational planning provides detailed forecasts of the short-term demand for personnel.

At the same time, the human resources planning system described in Part III provides forecasts of human resources availability, both for the short term and for the long-range planning horizon. This human resources availability forecast is initially based on a continuation of existing business needs; later on, as discussed in Part III, the availability forecasts will include overall planning strategies and the human resources strategies designed to achieve the levels and types of human resources needed to realize strategic goals.

For now, the purpose is to compare operational demand with human resources availability, to establish overall and specific categories of "variance"— the difference between human resources demand and availability. The determination of human resources variance is a key test for evaluating the viability of a strategy.

Are Strategies Adequate? For any given strategy, the preliminary determination of variance between demand and availability may be its death knell. If the difference between demand—what we need to continue operations plus what we'll need for this strategy—and availability is clearly insurmountable in the planning time frame, it may be necessary to discard this strategy as nonfeasible without further analysis. Eliminating the variance may require expensive training or hiring practices that are simply impossible given the current financial picture—a critical input from corporate planning at this juncture. Or the strategy may produce a nonviable "positive" variance, requiring layoffs or dismissals of large numbers of workers in whom the company has an investment—and with whom the company quite possibly has labor contracts.

In extreme cases, it is conceivable that a decision to discard a strategy may put the company out of business: If management must accept an irrefutable scenario that demands a strategy that cannot be implemented, the handwriting on the wall is clear. There is no point in following a strategy headed for frustration and loss.

Strategic planning requires a faith that there is a way for the organization to survive and prosper, however, and identification of a human resources variance often, simply means that planners must upgrade strategies, by making changes in either the demand side or the availability side. Also, the strategy may be revised or reformulated to change its human resources requirements, recycling staffing estimates as shown in the Figure 5-1 flowchart.

It should go without saying that upgrading a strategy in some organizations may be the ultimate objective of a human resources planning system. In other words, in actual practice, the process of revising a long-range strategy may be linked to changes in all human resources availability programs—including performance appraisal, evaluation of potential, career management, and succession planning systems—as discussed in Part III. At this stage in the discussion of the model, however, the focus is on preliminary strategies, meaning that the management interventions that proactively adapt the organization to a different future have not yet been initiated.

Also, it should be clear that the revision or upgrading of a strategy may involve more than the formulation of plans to increase human resources availability. Significant interventions of a financial or organizational nature may also be necessary. The purpose in preparing preliminary strategies is to be as comprehensive and detailed as possible, to show as specifically as possible the resources, actions, and timetables that accompany each strategy. Full detailing, including budgets, will take place later in the process for any strategy selected for implementation.

The strategic planning process should also consider the possible volatility of the environmental factors reflected in the scenarios on which the strategies were based. Constant attention to the key factors underlying each strategy, to take advantage of the system's flexibility in creating and adapting to new strategies, is essential.

A case in point is that of Grupo Industrial Alfa, S.A., a Mexican conglomerate involved in steel mills, tourism, food processing, capital goods, and other products and services. At the start of the 1980s, Alfa—Mexico's largest private company—was the darling of the international banks, which were more than willing to lend it any funds requested. At the time, Alfa was seen as the premier exemplar of the success of the new Mexican industrial development.

Then, in April 1982, the bubble burst. Alfa proposed a debt restructuring that would defer 70 percent of the parent company's interest payments on its $2.3 billion debt burden until at least the end of the year, after having suspended payments on most of the principal.[12]

What happened? A year earlier the company's problems would have been unthinkable, and its continuing success seemed assured. Some of Alfa's difficulties were caused by environmental factors beyond its control. The U.S. recession and the first devaluation of the peso severely affected the company's import business. High interest rates overburdened the debt-heavy firm, and since most of the debt was owed to foreign banks in foreign currency, the devaluation of the peso had further disastrous effects.

These financial difficulties might have been dealt with or at least weathered temporarily had the company not pursued a management policy that seemed logical at the time but turned out to have debilitating effects on the management of newer firms in the conglomerate. Past success had convinced Alfa that its managers could do no wrong: As Alfa acquired new companies, its own managers were sent in with calculators and preconceptions, interfering in businesses they did not always understand. Further, Alfa in this period seemed obsessed with managers having Ivy League MBA degrees and hired a disproportionate number of new managers having these credentials, regardless of their other talents or experience. Predictably, some of the most competent managers in the acquired companies began departing in frustration, leaving those firms in less experienced hands.

At the time, it has been reported, clearer heads at Alfa urged a slowing down of debt-financed acquisitions. But Alfa's top management, believing it was infallible, continued to pursue its empire building, which included the imposition of parent-company managers on all firms that came within its grasp. When the bubble burst, blame was widely distributed: Along with Alfa, foreign banks and the Mexican government took a share. But in retrospect, it is clear that a more flexible acquisitions approach—coupled with strategies assuring managerial competency through development, career planning, management succession, and other human resources planning techniques—would have minimized the impact of environmental change on the company.[13]

Much of the flexibility needed to be in a position to upgrade strategies on the basis of changing conditions is inherent in "what-if" analysis of hypothetical scenarios and the strategies they imply.

Strategic "What-If" Analysis. Even though the variance analysis at this stage is preliminary, it is very important that it be as accurately portrayed as possible. On its results may hang the future direction of the organization: Certain strategies will be discarded because the variance analysis shows they are unfeasible;

others will appear workable; and strategies based on hypothetical scenarios will have many different variances—some more easily closed than others. The analysis of what might be required for each scenario and strategy is a "what-if" process, a hypothetical exercise based on the realities of staffing requirements in each department, for each type of work.

To conduct this analysis, planners must be able to identify the variance for each strategy. Depending on the size of the variance, some strategies will have been judged unfeasible, but others will have one degree or another of feasibility. Human resources measures to close these gaps are not the only interventions, but for present purposes, they are the most important.

What will it cost to implement a strategy that calls for human resources interventions? As discussed in Part III, the factors that affect human resources availability have measurable costs, and these should be analyzed alongside each scenario-based strategy examined in the "what-if" analysis. Through many repetitions and in considerable detail—considerations that underscore the value of a computerized human resource information system—various strategies and the different environments represented by alternative scenarios can be largely quantified and "costed out."

In actual operation, this process will force the strategic planner to eliminate some favorite strategies from consideration. Strategies that the planner considered elegant, far-reaching, ambitious, and ideally suited to a changing world may fall by the wayside. In some cases, the human resources planner may be the villain of this piece, the bearer of the bad news that considerations of human resources availability preclude pursuit of a highly attractive strategy. More often, the human resources planner will be told that a given strategy is necessary, and this is when the real work needs to be done: The preliminary availability forecast was developed on the assumption that no interventions would take place to change that forecast, but it is also assumed that specific human resources planning interventions *can* change the availability of human resources, making the forecast compatible with the strategy of choice.

Up to a point, and at varying levels of cost, the gap, or variance, between the demands of a given strategy and human resources availability can be reduced or closed by the techniques and programs outlined in Part III. As will be discussed there, the ultimate responsibility of the human resources planner is to be able to provide decision makers with quantitative planning data about various combinations of human resources interventions, their impacts, and their costs.

Alternative and Most Likely Scenarios and Strategies

Whether or not an early analysis of human resources interventions affecting availability is required, preliminary planning should permit managers to select alternative scenarios and strategies at this point. These are the several models that will be incorporated into the organization's formal plan as alternative strategies to deal with different scenarios and provide needed flexibility in the long-range planning process.

Alternative scenarios and strategies are necessary for the same reason that strategic planning must be flexible: Uncertainties in the external environment and unforeseeable impacts on the organization require "reserve" strategies to prepare for events or developments that *could* occur.

The number and level of detail of alternative scenarios and strategies incorporated into the formal plan will be limited by resources. Time and effort are required to establish both scenarios and strategies, and managers will need to exercise judgment—based on the uncertainties that exist and their potential impact on the organization—in selecting the most likely, most significant, and most widely agreed upon scenarios on which to formulate strategies. In some cases, alternative strategies may be sweeping and fundamental, such as growth through acquisition versus retrenchment and divestiture. In other organizations, the "grand strategy" may be a constant, and alternative plans or substrategies may be built up to respond to different environmental conditions.

The net result of the foregoing process—from environmental scanning and scenario development through strategy development, testing, and selection—is the identification of the most likely scenario and strategy. At this point, using the data in the corporate data base, the process begins of specifically identifying the resource requirements of the primary strategy as well as making some assessment of the human resources that might be needed to implement alternative strategies. This identification is based, first, on an analysis of the operational demand for human resources: What quantities and qualities of human resources are involved in the actual and projected work of the organization? This subject, operational planning and control, is examined from a human resources planning perspective in Chapter 6.

6

Human Resources Planning and Scheduling at the Operational Level

Operational planning, the short-term analysis and determination of the quantity and types of people needed to perform the organization's current and upcoming work, is the very cornerstone of human resources planning. In order to arrive at meaningful demand forecasts for human resources requirements in the years ahead, planners must have an understanding of how existing human resources are used to produce the goods or services generated today and how changes in human resources usage specifically affect costs and outputs.

For human resources planners, the focus is always on "change." Too often, perhaps, we are beguiled by the future possibilities in new environments—the world on the horizon—and tend to give short shrift to the more prosaic details of actual operations in the here and now. Present operations are interesting only insofar as they are going to be changed—by new technology, different product lines or markets, change in the availability of human resources to do the work, or some other shift affecting human resources needs or supply.

To understand the impacts of change—or more important, to plan human resources to implement change—managers must first understand what it is that is being changed. Put in its simplest terms, a planner cannot know the impact of an additional ten workers unless he or she knows what those workers do, what they add to organizational output, and what they cost.

In most modern organizations of any size, operational analysis and planning are based on highly complicated management science techniques and statistical methods aimed at establishing quantified relationships between resources, time, and results. Further, while the operational planning process is virtually unique in every organization, its inherent frame of reference and ultimate objective are the assignment of costs: costs of tools and equipment, costs of materials and supplies, and costs of people. The operational planner, with no control over sales, can affect organizational profits only by reducing costs to the minimum allowable level needed to fulfill operational goals—which may involve anything from the completion of a hydroelectric power plant to the maintenance of a 24-hour newsstand.

Thus, the present chapter focuses on the costs of human resources in actual operations as well as operations research methods used in several industries to help determine and plan human resources costs. This material takes a necessarily different perspective on people than may be usual among human resources planners, but it is an essential perspective.

The Operational Planning Perspective: People as Costs

The overall strategic human resources planning system has three fairly distinct cycles: strategic planning, operational planning, and human resources planning. Each has its own perspective on human resources and its own analytical "mind-set," or frame of reference, for assessing organizational goals. Each of these ways of looking at and planning for human resources must be fully developed if the planning system is to be complete, and all three must be integrated in ways that reflect their mutual interdependence in proactive human resources planning.

At the strategic planning level, as discussed in Chapters 4 and 5, the numbers and characteristics of the present and future workforce are factors weighed with other factors in the development of optimal strategies to meet changing environmental conditions and organizational needs. Strategic planning requires the input and influence of operational and human resources planning, but its primary outlook is more general and theoretical than what would be needed for a close analysis of work and workers. Its perspective on human resources is necessarily abstract. In the strategic planner's eye, work and workers are numbers, the results of operational and human resources planning.

In operational planning, the focus is on the work of the organization today and in the immediate future and on the human resources needed to perform this work. The planner's perspective is to treat human resources as any other resource necessary to production—raw materials or equipment, for example. The reality of the work itself must be closely analyzed, and the human resources that perform the work are viewed primarily as units of cost or productivity associated with the completion of known tasks or processes.

At the human resources planning level, the focus is on the supply or availability of people to meet organizational goals, short- and long-term, and the programs and policies that will assure that availability. HR planners treat people as individuals, with the overall aim being to help make individual goals coincide with organizational goals and the primary focus being on "the people side" of this equation. Numbers are the results of human resources planning rather than its starting point or tools.

In one sense, then, integrated strategic human resources planning is a continuum of three different perspectives: the abstract, the concrete, and the human. Chapters 4 and 5, on strategic planning, have thus dealt with human resources as abstractions, and the perspective of the material in Part III, on human resources development and availability, will be essentially "human," or focused on people. The present chapter, on operational planning, brings the human resources planner's attention to bear on the concrete realities of work and the personnel costs of work.

Operational planning produces "bottom-up" forecasts of short-term demand. At any given time, the operational plan is a specification of the organization's level of activity, defined in terms of resources required to accomplish the specifics of operations.

At the same time, however, forecasts of operational human resources demand must be compatible with strategic plans. Thus, the operational planning system recommended by the model includes planning not only for active and scheduled projects or production levels but for "potential" work, which includes activities that the strategic plan indicates will be undertaken in the future.

The Narrow, Restricted Focus of Traditional Operational Analysis

Operations research and operational human resources planning are among the management science disciplines that have had "explosive histories" since World War II and have for years included "an impressive collection of systems analysis and design techniques," all focused primarily on minimizing costs and maximizing output of actual work in day-to-day operations.[1]

Since the earliest time-motion studies, managers have been seeking more scientific ways of analyzing what workers actually do on production lines and in offices and other work settings, and how these tasks might be made more productive. As the tools of analysis became more powerful in the postwar era, permitting examination and modeling of an increasing number of the many variables associated with tasks and processes, the management function of placing the optimal mix and number of human resources (as well as other resources) in the right place at the right time became increasingly detailed and scientific. The use of computers to create linear programming models that point out optimal assembly line balancing, for example, was already widespread in the mid-1950s.[2]

As valuable and informative as these computer-based modeling techniques have become, however—and they are indispensable in calculating the effects of changing hundreds of variables in the conversion of resources to output—the focus of most management science–based operational analysis is strictly limited to the realities of operations as they exist. From a human resources perspective, this means the identification of the people needed to do existing work and management efforts to minimize their costs by planning and scheduling people in ways that maximize their productivity.

It is our view that operational planning of human resources can also include relationships with overall strategic or long-range human resources planning, as shown in the model and the industry examples discussed in later sections of this chapter. Before that can be done, however, human resources planners need the clearest possible understanding of short-term operational requirements, a subject that can only be sketched in its broadest outlines here—because operations differ so much from one organization to another.

Typically, human resources planners in medium-size to large organizations with complex staffing needs are presented with personnel requirements "after the fact," based on determinations made by industrial engineers, operations research specialists, or managers who rely on the judgment of experts in the operational analysis of work. Depending on the level of sophistication of this kind of analysis, the human resources planner is more or less able to forecast immediate and short-term personnel requirements for the organization—the number and types of people needed at the present time and to handle various levels of changing output. Where management science techniques have been applied to fully analyze personnel requirements, optimize the scheduling of workers according to cost criteria, and produce specific plans and schedules for human resources loading to most efficiently achieve desired levels of output, the short-term objectives of operational human resources planning have been met.

In other organizations, human resources planners may have their work cut out for them: If existing methods for determining operational personnel requirements are inadequate, or provide no reliable short-term forecasts, human resources planners must find a way of estimating this critical information. As suggested earlier, no amount of long-range strategic analysis of human resources demand can be more than wishful thinking if not based on the realities of what people do to create today's and tomorrow's products or services—and what it costs while they do it.

Supervisor Estimates. In the absence of fully developed operational research information, one of the most commonly used sources of information for short-term forecasts is supervisor estimates. Such estimates are based on the reality that the person best informed about human resources requirements is the manager closest to the actual work, a reasonable assumption.[3]

The validity of supervisor estimates depends, of course, on supervisors' experience and intuition, but the insights of individuals are usually supported by rules of thumb, ratios and standard guidelines, and information observable from work accomplished in the present or in the recent past.

Rules of thumb, for example, are essentially decision heuristics used by supervisors as guidelines for short-term or output-specific staffing forecasts. The rule "Hire one additional salesperson for each $60,000 in increased sales" is an example. Because these rules are usually based on average performance, however, they insufficiently account for differences in employees. Also, it has been pointed out that rules of thumb tend to maintain the status quo by not incorporating change factors such as productivity improvement.[4]

Standard guidelines or staffing tables are also used by supervisors, drawing on the evidence of existing human resources levels as well as historical records, industrywide standards, and other sources. Such staffing tables can be quite sophisticated and detailed, as discussed in the construction industry example covered in a later section of this chapter.

Perhaps the least effective basis for supervisors' estimates, from an operational planning perspective, is the use of budget figures to determine staffing levels. A supervisor receives an allocation for staff and simply hires as many people as the budget permits. Budgets are of course a necessary constraint on operational human resources planning, but to use budgets as a starting point in determining staffing levels is to miss the whole point of operational demand forecasts: The organization's purpose is usually to produce output, not to employ as many people as possible.

In general, planners who must rely on supervisors' estimates for short-term forecasts can achieve the best results by following several guidelines:

1. Give supervisors enough information to make informed judgments, including what is known about past assumptions and expected workloads.
2. Ask the kind of questions supervisors can answer—that is, questions about the work and staff under the supervisors' control.
3. Don't insist on details not normally available to supervisors when round numbers or percentages will suffice for planning purposes.

The Model: A Pattern for Operational Human Resources Planning

Human resources planning at the operational level is in many ways a microcosm of the overall planning process. It can be a complete human resources planning system for short-term planning of the status quo, or changes that will affect only the quantity of resources and output in an otherwise constant environment.

Although the planning and scheduling of personnel at the operational level is necessarily different in virtually all industries, the general pattern of an operational planning system that is integrated with long-range straight human resources planning is depicted in Figure 6-1. This section of the overall model would be modified by organizations according to their specific operational characteristics and needs.

As can be seen, the model focuses on the realities of existing operational needs—from sales through staffing criteria—but also permits the introduction of long-range demand forecasts to prepare for "potential work," which form the basis for interventions and management resource allocations such as human resources loading schedules.

Sales. Sales, or output usage, are both the starting point and the ultimate objective of operational planning. For human resources operational planning, product or service objectives here characterized as "sales" are usually known levels or quantities of output, both as they exist today and as they are projected in terms of new sales goals by marketing planners. In the final analysis, sales may be heavily dependent on the efficiency of operational management techniques—including human resources planning—that serve to reduce costs or improve the quality of output.

Production Planning. This part of the process takes into account the differ-

Figure 6-1. **Detailed model of operational planning within the integrated human resources planning process.**

OPERATIONAL PLANNING

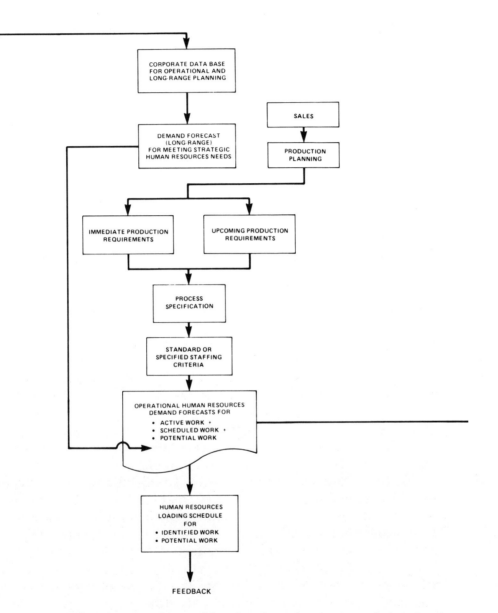

ences between sales forecasts and actual levels of production or other outputs. In manufacturing, for example, planners must develop a methodology that assures that products will be available in sufficient supply to support sales but below surplus levels that become excess inventory. The goal of most production planning is to set targets that provide optimal sales support at minimal costs, an objective that requires consideration of such factors as:

- Sales forecasts, as a starting point
- In-process inventory
- Inventory awaiting quality control release
- Inventory in distribution centers awaiting shipment to customers

Whether the output of the organization is products, projects, or services, production planners will have a fairly explicit idea of the quantities and types of output that are the short-term goals of operations. To determine the actual levels of operational production required, however, all aspects of the resource conversion "pipeline" must be considered, to determine exactly how much work actually remains to be done to achieve planned output levels.

Production Requirements. A knowledge of sales forecasts, actual production needs, and any process specifications used permits planners to develop production requirements, covering both immediate and short-term future needs. Production requirements at this stage are aimed at creating a schedule that will achieve desired output within a short-term time frame and are usually expressed in such terms as units per shift, transactions per day, or project milestones per working day.

In most cases, flexibility is added to the planning process by separating production requirements into the categories of immediate and upcoming requirements. Such a division may be a way of giving line managers and supervisors advance notice of near-term needs. Often, production managers can devise more efficient schedules if they are able to plan for production runs that will not only replenish stocks in distribution centers—or meet immediate needs—but add to inventory to meet expected demand.

Process Specifications. At some point in the operational planning process, planners usually turn to established process specifications, which quantitatively define the various components—from raw materials through labor—necessary to produce the smallest unit of production. Such specifications also prescribe acceptable criteria of quality or perfection and may be quite explicit in establishing skills levels for labor input, for example.

Standard or Specified Staffing Criteria. The definition of production requirements results, in turn, in the definition of at least two other requirements—for materials and for labor. Human resources planners at this stage are more or less aware of the nonhuman requirements of production—depending on the relationship between such factors as production technology and productivity, for example—but for present purposes, attention is focused on the number and kinds of people needed to do the job. What types of people, and how many, are needed to create a given level of output on the prescribed schedule?

Often, human resources requirements are the result of standard or specified staffing criteria established by an industrial engineering group. Such criteria usually provide tables showing each product type, machinery to be utilized, and number and skills of people needed to staff a production line or other operational format. In operations where individuals work alone, staffing criteria may be based on productivity rates per shift.

Operational Human Resources Demand Forecasts. The final computation of human resources required to meet the production schedule constitutes the operational demand forecast for human resources. For flexibility and to permit the introduction of strategic planning factors, three separate forecasts may be made, covering personnel required to perform:

- *Active work,* the actual operations in progress that will still be in progress tomorrow and may require the same or slightly different human resources (or an entirely different finishing cadre)
- *Scheduled work,* not yet started and using human resources but definitely scheduled at some point in the future and requiring certain fairly explicit levels of personnel and skills
- *Potential work,* or operational human resources demand forecasts based on strategic long-range planning

Data for the strategic, or "potential work," demand forecast come from the corporate data base for operational and long-range planning and its specific human resources requirements—demand forecast (long-range) for meeting strategic human resources needs. Normally, this forecast will not require any actual assignment of personnel. Rather, it advises operational management that certain minimal resources must be available for deployment if and when potential work becomes scheduled work.

In some cases, however, the long-range demand forecast may lead to the creation of project teams or added production staff "on paper," so that potential work may be quickly and efficiently staffed if it becomes a reality.

Human Resources Loading Schedule. The final item in the model depicting the pattern of operational human resources planning is the development of the human resources loading schedule. This can be a highly elaborate and scientific process—as discussed in the engineering firm example below—but its basic purpose is to assign people to jobs and shifts according to an overall plan.

As can be seen, the amount of data needed by the model and the requirements for analytical reports virtually dictate the use of automated personnel information systems in most medium-size to large organizations. Especially in the area of developing human resources forecasts for potential work, the use of computer-based "what-if" planning models to analyze the impacts of various alternative workloads is a practical necessity.

Operational HR Planning and Scheduling in Practice: Industry Examples

The ways in which operational human resources planning varies among industries and companies reflect a panoply of modern production methods, process requirements, and output variations as diverse as the kinds of work there are in the world.

Even the most consistently applicable generalities leave room for a vast range of realities. For example, operational planning is always considered to be "short-term" because it focuses on actual work being performed and the actual or scheduled outputs. Yet "short-term" in calendar time may be a matter of weeks for a ski resort operator, months for a clothing retailer, a year for a toy manufacturer, or 12 years for a builder of nuclear power plants.

More fundamentally, operational planning is definitionally intrinsic to the production of specific goods and services, the conversion of resources over time to output. The ways of accomplishing this conversion vary not only by products or services but according to different kinds of constraints and resource characteristics. For example, automobiles are not made the same way in the United States and Japan, for reasons that originate in cultural and societal attitudes shaped over the course of the history of these two very different countries.

Production technology affects operational planning, and so do an almost limitless number of environmental and specific factors that influence operational decisions. A factory with a ready supply of fresh water will do things differently than one without; sales volume dictates certain operational methods; and the availability of particular human resources skills may shape operations.

In the three subsections that follow—on operational planning and scheduling in manufacturing generally, on operational planning and scheduling in customer service industries, and on project-type planning as developed by an engineering consulting firm—several consistencies are evident:

- Operational planning is primarily concerned with implementing short-term work schedules.
- It includes both the determination of how the work is now being done— the numbers and skills needed—and ways of looking at future needs.
- It is usually done by line management, but for human resources planners to be effective, they must understand the organization-specific principles involved and how they affect future plans.

Operational Planning and Scheduling in Manufacturing

Methods of analyzing operational aspects of manufacturing and systems used to plan and schedule resources are invariably industry-specific and are usually company-specific, as well. The overall goal of the many different management science and operations research techniques in manufacturing, however, is essentially universal: to minimize costs without sacrificing quality.

Typically, organizations that manufacture products for sale develop highly sophisticated analytical tools based on a standard cost system. This system traces the movement of materials, labor, and overhead costs through stages, from raw materials procurement to distribution of the final product, localizing the value added to the product and operational costs at each stage of the manufacturing process. For most companies, the two main types of resources to be analyzed and planned for are materials and labor. (In the robot-intensive "factory of the future" the nomenclature may change, but the principles of cost analysis remain the same in operational planning.)

Material Standards. Materials in manufacturing are any tangible items necessary to the manufacturing process, and material standards establish specifications for raw materials prices, material flow, and material classifications. The material classifications to be considered range from indirect materials such as twine and cleaning agents, which are not part of the finished product, to raw materials, work-in-progress materials, and finished products, which may also include packaging.

An example of how material standards use standard cost data to analyze and track costs in manufacturing is shown in Figure 6-2, a process for specifying raw materials price standards. As can be seen, "standard prices" are used throughout: Set in advance by management, standard prices are the fixed charges for one unit of the material for one year and provide a yardstick of production value added to the material. In this example, the department is not allowed to pass on any gains or losses in material to the next department, although fluctuations in actual prices are accounted for as credits and lost or wasted material becomes "material usage variance."

Material flow control is normally a much more complex and detailed process than can be adequately covered here. An overview of the sequence of the process, however, usefully conveys its central theme: Every step of the manufacturing process is analyzed on the basis of costs related to usage, as measured against established standards developed from past performance and current productivity. As a result, strict accounting requires standard reporting forms and measurements from the time raw materials are purchased to the time finished goods are shipped to the customer.

Typical Material Flow Control Sequence. To measure efficient material usage against established standards, operational material flow sequencing in manufacturing proceeds in a manner such as this:

1. A purchase requisition orders the material from the supplier.
2. Upon receipt of this order, the supplier ships the raw material requested.
3. Warehouse personnel complete a formal record indicating quantity received and may have a sample checked for compliance with specifications. Today, most larger organizations are able to enter this transaction on computerized reports, which also include such data as balances on hand, time needed for reordering, minimum balance required, year-to-date material usage, and information from the last inventory.
4. Materials are entered in a raw material inventory system that produces a periodic—sometimes daily—report of materials on hand. This information is used by both warehouse people and the production planning function.

Figure 6-2. **Raw materials price standards.**

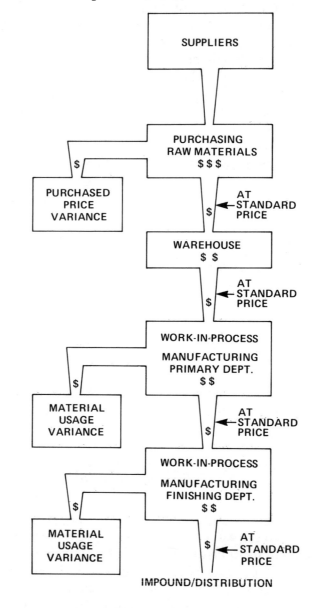

NOTE: MATERIAL CHARGED TO THE WAREHOUSE, TO MANUFACTURING,
AND TO IMPOUND/DISTRIBUTION IS ALWAYS CHARGED AT THE
PREVIOUSLY SET, FIXED PRICE, REGARDLESS OF WHAT IT
REALLY COSTS TO BUY. PURCHASING WILL ABSORB, OR GET
CREDIT FOR, PURCHASED PRICE VARIANCES.

5. On the basis of the production schedule, raw materials are delivered to manufacturing departments. The material becomes "owned" by manufacturing, and this is reflected in some kind of charge ticket (which is reversed if the material is returned as unusable).

6. Manufacturing adds to the value of the material by the imposition of standard costs—labor, overhead, or processes such as packaging. Also, each department has a materials waste allowance, a standard above which it must absorb the cost of waste. In this way, each department is held responsible for materials value variance.

7. Accompanied by forms transferring "ownership" of the material and its new standard price, manufactured goods are moved to the distribution center. Material costs here may be enhanced by storage or impoundment charges, warehouse overhead, shipping costs, or other standard costs.

Labor Standards. Operational planning and scheduling of workers—always viewed as standard labor costs—varies according to company-specific machinery, processes, products, collective bargaining agreements, incentive programs, and other particulars in manufacturing. Just as in the movement of material through the production process, however, labor costs at specified rates represent value added to products, based on established standards. Only the standard labor cost is passed on to the next department; the originating department remains responsible for any variances—positive or negative—generated by its productivity rates.

As with materials, labor is usually classified as being either direct or indirect.

Direct labor (again, always measured in costs) is that which is applied to convert resources to the items being produced. Any worker directly responsible for part of the production cycle is "on standard," whether or not paid by an incentive plan. Incentive rates are usually listed in a labor rate manual, which includes other information such as established base rates, standard minutes, and definitions of production units. Standard minutes represent the amount of time required by an employee of average skill and experience, working at a normal pace that allows for breaks and so on, to produce one unit of production. Standard labor costs are expressed as costs per unit of production, although a "unit" may be a gross of items. Other ways of viewing direct labor costs may integrate the costs of machines and workers—as in the costs of a team of workers needed to operate a given piece of production machinery.

Indirect labor costs are incurred by activities that are not directly responsible for conversion of resources to products that cannot readily be identified with units of production. These usually include the labor costs of cleaning work areas, for example.

Scheduling Workers by Standard Procedures. In actual operations, scheduling of workers is frequently guided by standard operating procedures (SOPs), which may be part of work rules negotiated in collective bargaining agreements or may be "side" agreements. In either case, they are documented explicitly for each product line or process.

Such publicly known SOPs establish specific guidelines for work procedures, including job bidding, incentives, seniority ranking, overtime scheduling, shift rotation, absenteeism, and staffing requirements. Supervisors schedule workers openly, to some extent based on workers' choices. For example, weekly staffing requirements might be set according to this kind of procedure:

1. A production coordinator distributes production schedules to supervisors showing output, the products scheduled for the week, or line processes to be completed.
2. Each supervisor lists the line number, product, number of shifts, and the number and types of workers necessary to run the line for a given output. A company labor code manual, based on past performance, gives the standard staffing requirements for each line and product.
3. On a scheduling board, the supervisor places employees on "home" jobs in order of job seniority. This selection is based on an office procedure manual.
4. If there are any unfilled jobs left when all home jobs have been assigned, these are posted within the department for 12 hours or some other agreed-upon period.
5. Employees sign up for unfilled jobs, often listing their top three choices in order.
6. In each department, a list is compiled of employees without jobs, ranked by seniority.
7. The supervisor assigns jobs by seniority and top choices, until all employees have been assigned to jobs.
8. The supervisor assigns employees to shifts and sets any rotation schedules. Normal shift rotation is first to third, third to second, and second to first.

Where the manufacturing environment is guided by SOPs based on collectively bargained labor agreements, decisions about which employees take different shifts—and sometimes are required to repeat shifts—are usually based on seniority rankings.

Other Staffing Procedures. In addition to union influences, human resources allocation in manufacturing may be determined by changing production requirements from day to day or week to week, by the skills needed to operate certain machinery, or by the output at some preceding stage of production. For example, certain processes are staffed according to the number of units delivered to the area: The handling of so many units per minute will require a certain level of labor.

When human resources loading is determined by tasks required to operate specific machinery, labor levels are usually the result of industrial engineering criteria aimed at optimal productivity, minimal downtime, and other factors that predetermine personnel loading.

Operational Planning and Scheduling in Customer Service Industries

Operational planning aspects of human resources staffing and scheduling in service industries—especially where the product consists of a continuing flow of services provided to a more-or-less constant stream of customers—are highly organization-specific and often require analysis using the most sophisticated mathematical optimization or stochastic (probabilistic) modeling techniques.

In service industries, production levels are frequently beyond the control of operational planning; one usually cannot decide to serve so many customers per day or hour, and set staffing levels accordingly. Other variables include: a wide distribution of services in many locations; different kinds of services as determined by provider or by customer needs; fluctuating rates of productivity associated with a wide range of different conditions; and sometimes unclear standards of service quality, such as the difference between fast and efficient restaurant service and a more relaxed, slower-paced dining environment.

Some examples of planning and scheduling issues include:

- Planning and scheduling of airline reservationists to ensure efficient response to telephone inquiries, optimal time spent on customer calls, and adequate staffing levels
- Establishing the number and routes of buses to maximize equipment use, fully utilize drivers, minimize employee overtime, and provide regular service to customers
- Scheduling the work hours and lunch breaks of bank tellers to match variable patterns of customer flow, reducing customers' waiting time in lines and optimizing existing personnel
- Planning staggered or flexible hours, such as the schedules worked by nurses in a nursing pool, to correspond with health-care service requirements, varying functions (emergency service versus operating room aid, for example), and the preferences or needs of the nurses
- Relating the need for part-time or temporary employees to levels of service activity, to reach an optimal balance between customer service needs and worker productivity

Clearly, the diversity and variability of the factors involved in service industry staffing situations such as these lend themselves to mathematical modeling and statistical analysis. Different techniques and combinations of techniques have been applied to help resolve these issues, and each organization will apply those methods that best suit its needs for accuracy, levels of service requirements, and access to data. The need to accurately establish staffing levels and scheduling of airline pilots, for example, is certainly more important than determining the number of car-hops needed at a drive-in restaurant—and the sophistication and cost of operational planning is likely to reflect this.

The example that follows illustrates one type of service industry function.

Airline Telephone Reservationists. Operational planning for the airline telephone sales force is a relatively simple process compared to planning for certain other types of service industry personnel; even so, the need for adequate and cost-effective staffing levels has led to the use of sophisticated techniques in the area of airline telephone sales. Some airlines use queuing theory models to assign staff, some use linear programming techniques, and some use both. Later in this section we will describe airlines that utilizes both these statistical methods to improve customer service significantly and, at the same time, to decrease telephone sales costs.

Telephone sales offices are not only labor-intensive, but must be staffed with experienced, well-mannered personnel many rungs above typical clerical workers in their ability and compensation levels. It would be too costly for such offices to be consistently overstaffed to meet occasionally heavy workloads. In fact, the idea of overstaffing reservation offices is such a widely recognized anathema in the industry that most airlines end up understaffing telephone sales offices. This understaffing is identified by a high lost-call rate, accompanied by lost business as customers receive prolonged busy signals or express annoyance when put on "hold."

The traditional approach airlines utilized to assess a growing workload was to work toward a ratio for each member of the telephone sales force and to compare the ratios to each other. In this ratio the numerator represents the number of calls received and the denominator represents the number of calls the reservationist is expected to handle. The number of calls received is determined by taking a count of calls after the latest staff increase. The number of calls to be handled is the actual number of calls the airline believes a reservationist should be able to answer per hour or per shift. The problem with this ratio of past calls received to calls expected is that it does not take into account future growth and gives little attention to the particular characteristics of calls that affect productivity—for example, the fact that some calls may be more complex and may need to last longer than others.

To create a human resources forecasting model of future needs, one airline first collected historical data on workloads. This was done month-by-month going back two years and day-by-day for the most recent three months. Days of the week were analyzed, showing no significant variations in weekdays but considerable variations in the characteristics of Saturday and Sunday calls.

Next, a queuing model and a linear programming model were developed on the basis of a series of assumptions and constraints, including:

- Average service time of $3\frac{1}{2}$ minutes for weekday calls and $2\frac{1}{2}$ minutes for weekend calls
- A company standard of service stating that not more than 10 percent of telephone callers should wait more than 20 seconds before service commences

- An exponential distribution of incoming calls for each given half-hour time unit
- An assumption of equal efficiency among sales reservationists
- Shift lengths of $8\frac{1}{2}$ hours
- Staggered shifts that start on either the hour or the half-hour

These constraints were quantified and applied to the computerized queuing and linear programming models. The computer printouts that were generated consisted of the following information for each day of the week:

- Number of staff required for each shift
- Start and finish time per shift
- Lunch schedule per shift
- Total staff required for the day

Thus, by incorporating certain assumptions about staffing procedures, the airline came up with mathematical models that more accurately predict staffing needs by simulating actual conditions. For example, through model simulation the airline discovered that a very small cutback in staff resulted in considerable increases in customer waiting time.

The critical finding, however, was that a reduction in the average service time per call was the most effective way to increase productivity and permit cuts in staff size. Shaving off as little as 30 seconds from the average time per call was found to produce considerable savings.

The costs of such sophisticated statistical modeling techniques, which include expenses for research, computer time or facilities, and model testing, can be fairly steep. Because of the high potential savings involved, however, such techniques can repay their costs in less than one year. In the difficult business environment of the airline industry, workforce planning techniques such as these are expected to be used more and more and to attain even higher levels of sophistication.

Project-Basis Operational Planning: Engineering Firm Example

The varieties and permutations of techniques used for operational planning are as diverse as the universe of kinds of operations planned for, multiplied by the range of possible operations research approaches that might be used to study and quantify such concepts as value added, unit costs, and the costs of human resources. As noted in Chapter 3, all but the simplest operations require an automated system to cope with the demands of analyzing operations and projecting specific resources needed to create value added or products.

But while management science today offers a broad array of such automated techniques for operational planning, the particular method selected should not necessarily be "the latest thing" in statistical analysis or computerized infor-

Figure 6-3. **Operational planning and control in an engineering firm.**

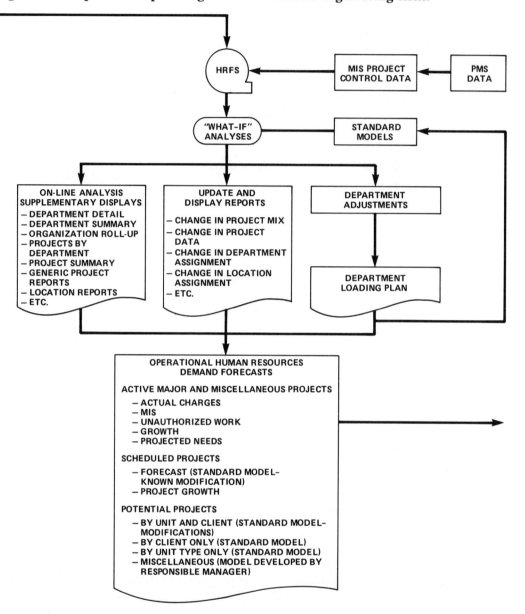

mation system technology. It is more important that the method used to examine operations and anticipated demand be imitative of actual operations, appropriate to the realities of operational objectives, or intrinsically "native" to the kind of work being analyzed.

Thus, this section, which presents a system designed for an engineering firm in the heavy construction industry, illustrates a somewhat different procedure and set of methods than that depicted in Figure 6-1. As shown in Figure 6-3, this system moves from data provided by critical path method (CPM) scheduling techniques through a series of segmented "what-if" analyses to reach human resources demand forecasts for active, scheduled, and potential projects.

The underlying reasons for this approach are based on several distinctive characteristics of engineering operations. Among them:

- Engineering firms handle projects rather than creating manufactured products, performing processes, or providing ongoing services.
- Productivity criteria in engineering are based on the actual expenditure of workdays, instead of budgets or workday outputs.
- Clients are billed on the basis of workdays expended, not necessarily a percentage of the project completed, in part because the engineering consultant's product (such as drawings and specifications) does not always represent constant inputs of resources. Two apparently similar drawings, for example, may require significantly different amounts of time—for reasons that are critical.
- Many projects are bid on a lump-sum basis, setting the price in advance, but work must be controlled through the monitoring of workdays expended to meet specified milestones, as illustrated in Figure 6-3.

The three basic sources of data in the system shown in Figure 6-3 are *PMS data*, or project measurement system data, which are part of a project's CPM (critical path method) schedule, specifying milestones during the project and main elements of work that remain to be accomplished; MIS *project control data*, which use PMS data to develop performance references in the management information system (MIS), producing a series of reports showing various levels of detail for actual and projected work; and *HRFS*, the human resources forecasting system, a software package that uses MIS data on projects to produce reports and roll-ups showing actual forecast staffing by project and other categories. The other elements in the figure are each explained below.

Standard models are mathematical models of projects that are used as references for determining the status of a project, its staffing needs, and its scheduling.

"What-if" analysis permits planners to examine the effects of various conditions and changes in such factors as product mix, department assignments, location assignments, and other elements. The computerized system permits displays of such data as department detail, organization roll-up, projects by department, generic projects reports, and location reports.

On-line analysis supplementary displays provide an instant analysis of the status of any project at any time.

Update and display reports, a product of "what-if" analysis, present various computer-generated outputs defined by the variables used to calculate the result.

Department adjustments are made within departments, which have the capability of working "what-if" analyses for their own internal planning and examination of staffing alternatives. Departments can also include potential projects, using standard staffing models or new models for unique projects.

Department loading plan is a tool growing out of the use of CPM scheduling, discussed in greater detail below.

Operational human resources demand forecasts represent the net result of the foregoing analysis of data originating in the MIS and modified through the testing of alternatives. These forecasts, which must be compatible with the strategic corporate plans discussed in Chapter 4, are in this case based on projects classified as:

- *Active projects*—ongoing work with known levels of activity and staffing requirements, updated regularly as conditions change or work is completed
- *Scheduled projects*—those with a high probability of being performed, for which load projections normally start with standard staffing packages and become more detailed as specific needs are identified
- *Potential projects*—the stuff of long-range strategic planning, whose requirements are based on standard project staffing package criteria

Capabilities and Highlights of an Engineering Planning System. The engineering firm system shown in Figure 6-3 is designed to provide management with these computer-generated results:

- A clear picture of organizational human resources requirements and concurrent supply, with both summary and detailed reports available for analysis
- Forecasts by project, by groups of projects, and by combinations of current and future projects
- Forecasts by department, groups of departments, or job families
- Summary reports for any year or combination of years, by project or organizationwide
- Data for examination of human resources trends in any other combination or relationship

In the system depicted, two of the most important management devices employed to obtain these results are critical path method (CPM) scheduling, which establishes workdays in detail and permits analysis of resource loading, and the use of standard project staffing package estimates for long-range planning.

Critical Path Method Scheduling and Resource Loading. Operational planning for work done on a project basis is often accomplished through the use of the critical path method, a planning and scheduling technique first employed by Remington Rand on a plant built for Du Pont in 1957. By showing which operations in a project are critical to the completion date—and which have "slack," or can be performed with fewer resources without affecting final completion—CPM also permits planners to optimize the application of human and other resources to each part of the project. This resource loading capability permits

Figure 6-4. **Critical path network.**

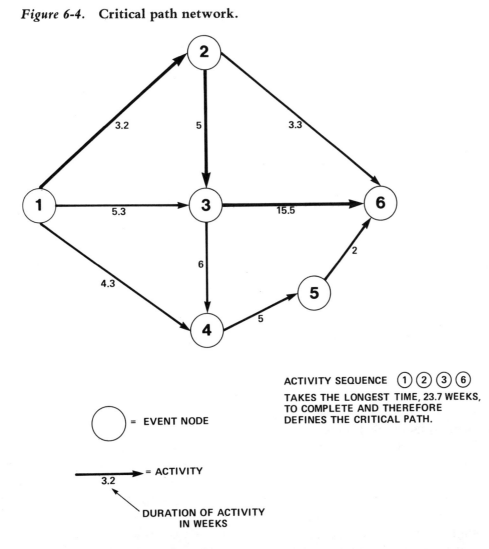

ACTIVITY SEQUENCE ① ② ③ ⑥
TAKES THE LONGEST TIME, 23.7 WEEKS,
TO COMPLETE AND THEREFORE
DEFINES THE CRITICAL PATH.

◯ = EVENT NODE

─────▶ = ACTIVITY
  3.2

= DURATION OF ACTIVITY
  IN WEEKS

management to test and determine optimal staffing levels at each stage of the project for each activity.

In any major project made up of many activities, only a certain number of tasks control the overall schedule and completion date.[5] These tasks are sequential; they must be completed before some other task can be done. In building a house, for example, a heating system must be in place prior to plastering.

The first step in CPM is to list each activity in the project and its duration with anticipated or typical resources, and then construct a diagram showing the relationships between these activities.[6] Activities are represented as arrows, leading from activities that must be done ahead of them and to tasks that cannot start until these activities have been completed. Nodes between the arrows stand for "events"—dates of completion, in the final diagram. Thus, in Figure 6-4, activity 3–6 cannot be started until activities 1–3 and 2–3 have been completed.

Figure 6-5. **Dummy arrow.**

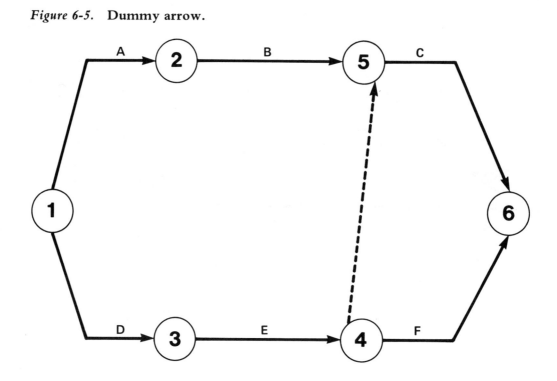

Other activities, not dependent on or determinant of these activities, might be represented as parallel lines.[7]

When all activities that are part of the project are shown in their necessary sequence, and each is assigned an expected duration, one path through the diagram will take the greatest amount of time. This is the critical path, critical because any change in the time required for any of its arrows or tasks will affect the final completion date. Dummy arrows represent dependencies that restrain the start of an activity—but that are not in themselves an "activity" to which time and resources can be assigned. The dotted line in Figure 6-5 is such a dummy arrow. A dummy arrow might signify a supplier's delivery of materials, for example.

In a typical major project, only about 10 percent of all activities are on the critical path.[8] Clearly, the use of CPM to identify those activities, which are the only ones worth monitoring to stay on the overall schedule, is an immediate advantage. In practice, however, the payoff in CPM comes from alterations in the critical path. For example, managers may use additional labor to complete a critical job in three days instead of eight, apparently bringing final completion five days closer. But because the critical path is the one that takes the longest time through the project, the speeding of one activity may shift the critical path entirely: The original CP may have been just three days longer than some other path.

New critical paths may also occur inadvertently, without the planner's intervention: If an activity that should have taken six days takes eight, in fact, this may be enough to shift the longest path through the project to include this delayed task.

Thus, each activity in the project has the potential for being critical, if it takes enough time. How much time? That is the key question answered by CPM "slack" times. Each task that is not on the critical path has a certain amount of slack time between its expected duration and the duration that would affect the overall schedule, or make it critical. Slack time is usually expressed as the difference between late finish and early finish: Some jobs might have a day or two of slack; others, months. Tasks on the critical path have zero slack, of course.

Obviously, activities with greater slack time can often be postponed and people moved to more critical tasks in the resource loading process.

Resource Loading Examples. Resource loading techniques lead to a diversity of scheduling tools in addition to the simple assignment of more or less resources to a particular activity. These include the formation of partial networks, the determination of schedule limits, the creation of resource feasibility envelopes, and resource loading in a constrained environment.

Partial networks can be developed to analyze and manage complex tasks. For example, a highly specialized pump is needed to replace an existing pump. Its specifications and acquisition will require two engineering resources, electrical and mechanical engineers. As shown in Figure 6-6, partial networks can be constructed showing what must occur in what sequence.

Because so much interface occurs in the two networks—the locations of the interfaces are the events with common numbers—a combined network must be built to show a timing framework and the interdependencies involved. This network is shown in Figure 6-7. The durations of all activities and the resources required are determined as nearly as possible by historical data, staffing packages, and other estimating resources. These data are input to the computerized network, which prints out the critical path, shown in Figure 6-7 as a dotted line.

Determination of schedule limits is based on the determination of slack time, which permits the establishment of early- and late-start schedule limits for each activity. These limits, depicted within boxes in Tables 6-1 and 6-2, show the maximum time each activity may take without affecting the critical path.

For the early-start schedule, resources are loaded, or scheduled to begin, at the leftmost, or earliest, bars. On the late-finish schedule, resource loading occurs as late as possible.

Accumulations of these activity schedules produce staffing load resource distributions in the form of S-shaped curves, as shown in Figure 6-8.

In construction and other industries, S-curves are used to show changing labor requirements over the life of a project. Normally, a project such as the building of a dam requires relatively few people at first, builds to a peak, and then tapers off. The S-curve shows cumulative worker days on the project, so curves for the total labor requirement or for any given skill are S-shaped, starting from zero, rising inexorably as worker days are added over time, and almost leveling off as the project nears completion.

Figure 6-6.   **Partial CPM networks.**

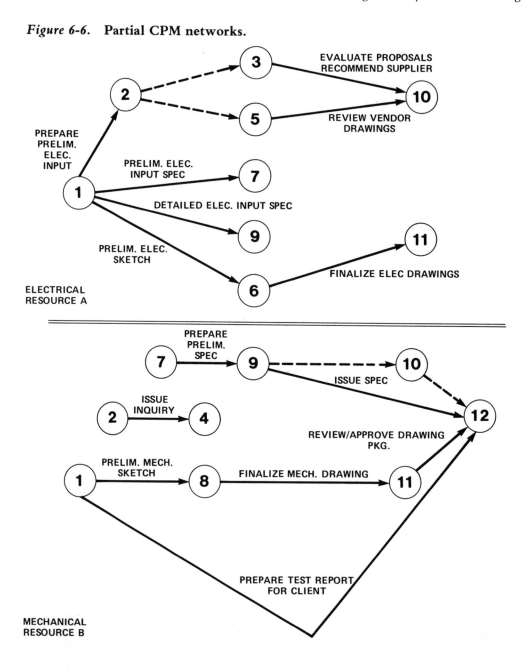

The plotting of two S-curves on a single graph, as shown in Figure 6-9, creates a "resource envelope" that provides project managers with highly useful decision data. For any skill or for the project as a whole, planners can plot two curves: One depicts worker days needed at various times on an early-start schedule; the other shows when people will be working if the schedule is based on late-start times, the maximum allowable interval before the critical path is affected. The former curve shows human resources being used earlier, but both

Figure 6-7. **Partial networks combined.**

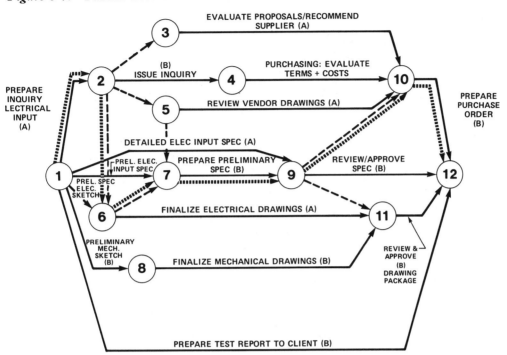

lines end at the same point, because the curves show cumulative worker days needed.

The envelope defines the upper and lower limits of staff loading, a feasibility range for human resources planning. If planning calls for a level of worker days that extends out of the envelope at any point, as shown in Figure 6-9, this indicates nonfeasible human resources planning. The straight line in the graph shows that too many people will be available early in the project, with some likely to be idle and unproductive, and that not enough people will be available at the end of the job to complete work on time.

The envelope also provides a quick indication of how critical a skill is to the project at a given moment. The horizontal distance between the two curves at any point in time indicates the time slack of the skill being plotted: If long, the supply of the skill can be delayed without jeopardizing project completion; if short, the demand must be met promptly, and the skill is critical.

The vertical "time slack" line between the two curves is the staffing slack, indicating the range of human resources usage possible at that time. If short, it indicates that the craft is critical, and availability must meet demand. When the slack is greater, it indicates that shortages of the skill can be absorbed without affecting the overall duration of the project.

CPM can also be used to test HR availability in a constrained environment. In actual operations, the hundreds of different skills needed on a construction project or other complex projects are not available in unlimited supply or at a

(Text continues on page 146.)

Table 6-1. Early-start envelope resource loading worksheet.

ACTIVITY	DUR	RES	1	2	3	4	5	6	7	8	9	10	11	12	13	14	15	16	17	18	19	20	21	22	23	24
1, 2 – PREPARE INQUIRY ELEC. INPUT	6	A4	4	4	4	4	4	4																		
1, 6 – PRELIMINARY ELEC. SKETCH	4	A2	2	2	2	2																				
1, 7 – PRELIMINARY ELEC. INPUT SPEC	2	A3	3	3																						
1, 8 – PRELIMINARY MECH. SKETCH	6	B3	3	3	3	3	3	3																		
1, 9 – DETAILED ELEC. INPUT SPEC	5	A3	3	3	3	3	3																			
1,12 – PREPARE TEST REPORT	5	B4	4	4	4	4	4																			
2, 4 – ISSUE INQUIRY	3	B3							3	3	3															
3,10 – EVALUATE PROPOSALS/RECOMMEND SUPPLIER	4	A3							3	3	3	3														
5,10 – REVIEW VENDOR DRAWINGS	6	A2							2	2	2	2	2	2												
6,11 – FINALIZE ELEC. DRAWINGS	5	A3							3	3	3	3	3													
7, 9 – PREPARE PRELIMINARY SPEC	10	B5							5	5	5	5	5	5	5	5	5	5								
8,11 – FINALIZE MECH. DRAWINGS	4	B4							4	4	4	4														
9,12 – ISSUE SPEC	5	B2																	2	2	2	2	2			
10,12 – PREPARE PURCHASE ORDER	8	B5																	5	5	5	5	5	5	5	5
11,12 – REVIEW/APPROVE DRAWING PACKAGE	4	B3																	3	3	3	3				

RESOURCE A		1	2	3	4	5	6	7	8	9	10	11	12												
STAFFING LOAD		12	12	9	9	7	4	8	8	8	8	5	2												
CUMULATIVE		12	24	33	42	49	53	61	69	77	85	90	92												

RESOURCE B		1	2	3	4	5	6	7	8	9	10	11	12	13	14	15	16	17	18	19	20	21	22	23	24
STAFFING LOAD		7	7	7	7	7	3	12	12	12	9	5	5	5	5	5	5	10	10	10	10	7	5	5	5
CUMULATIVE		7	14	21	28	35	38	50	62	74	83	88	93	98	103	108	113	123	133	143	153	160	165	170	175

DUR = DURATION IN MONTHS OF ACTIVITY
RES = TYPE (A OR B) AND QUANTITY OF RESOURCE REQUIRED

Table 6-2. Late-finish envelope resource loading worksheet.

ACTIVITY	DUR	RES	1	2	3	4	5	6	7	8	9	10	11	12	13	14	15	16	17	18	19	20	21	22	23	24
																		TIME IN MONTHS							
1, 2 – PREPARE INQUIRY ELEC. INPUT	6	A4	4	4	4	4	4	4																		
1, 6 – PRELIMINARY ELEC. SKETCH	4	A2			2	2	2	2																		
1, 7 – PRELIMINARY ELEC. INPUT SPEC	2	A3					3	3																		
1, 8 – PRELIMINARY MECH. SKETCH	6	B3											3	3	3	3	3	3								
1, 9 – DETAILED ELEC. INPUT SPEC	5	A3												3	3	3	3	3								
1,12 – PREPARE TEST REPORT	5	B4																				4	4	4	4	4
2, 4 – ISSUE INQUIRY	3	B3										3	3	3												
3,10 – EVALUATE PROPOSALS/RECOMMEND SUPPLIER	4	A3													3	3	3	3								
5,10 – REVIEW VENDOR DRAWINGS	6	A2											2	2	2	2	2	2								
6,11 – FINALIZE ELEC. DRAWINGS	5	A3																3	3	3	3	3				
7, 9 – PREPARE PRELIMINARY SPEC	10	B5							5	5	5	5	5	5	5	5	5	5								
8,11 – FINALIZE MECH. DRAWINGS	4	B4																	4	4	4	4				
9,12 – ISSUE SPEC	5	B2																				2	2	2	2	2
10,12 – PREPARE PURCHASE ORDER	8	B5																	5	5	5	5	5	5	5	5
11,12 – REVIEW/APPROVE DRAWING PACKAGE	4	B3																				3	3	3	3	3

RESOURCE A		1	2	3	4	5	6	7	8	9	10	11	12	13	14	15	16	17	18	19	20	21	22	23	24
STAFFING LOAD		4	4	6	6	9	9	0	0	0	0	2	5	8	8	8	11	3	3	3	3				
CUMULATIVE		4	8	14	20	29	38	38	38	38	38	40	45	53	61	69	80	83	86	89	92				

RESOURCE B		1	2	3	4	5	6	7	8	9	10	11	12	13	14	15	16	17	18	19	20	21	22	23	24
STAFFING LOAD								5	5	5	8	11	11	8	8	8	8	9	9	9	15	14	14	14	14
CUMULATIVE								5	10	15	23	34	45	53	61	69	77	86	95	104	119	133	147	161	175

DUR = DURATION IN MONTHS OF ACTIVITY
RES = TYPE (A OR B) AND QUANTITY OF RESOURCE REQUIRED

Figure 6-8.   **S-curves—cumulative human resources requirements.**

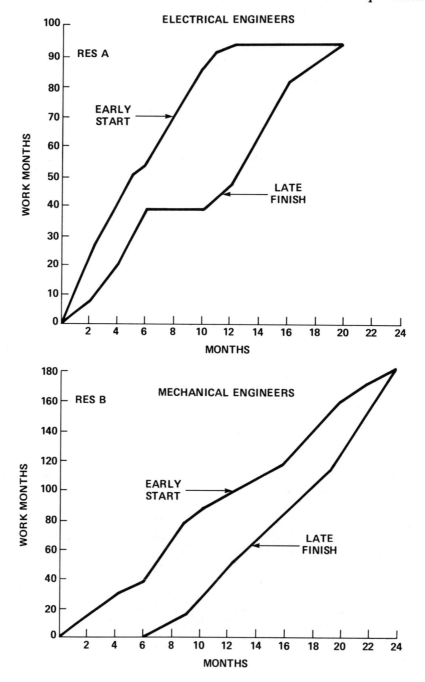

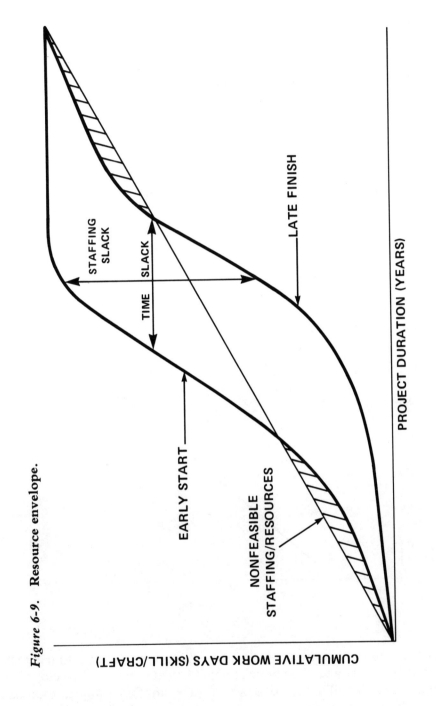

Figure 6-9. Resource envelope.

Figure 6-10. **Test availabilities of resources.**

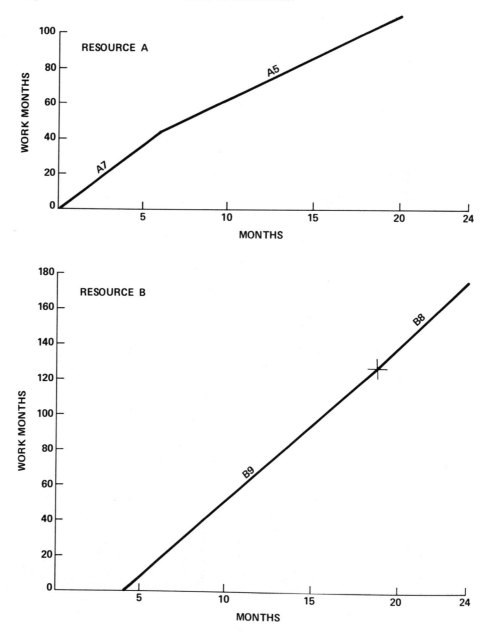

constant cost to the organization. It is one thing for a planner to use techniques such as early and late worker hour curves to create resource envelopes showing how many people will be needed when—and another thing to establish a balanced staffing load of resources that will optimize the match between this demand and constraints on human resources availability. The skills may not be available in sufficient numbers at any given time, may be too expensive to acquire

Table 6-3. Staff loading by resources availability.

ACTIVITY	DUR	RES	1	2	3	4	5	6	7	8	9	10	11	12	13	14	15	16	17	18	19	20	21	22	23	24
1, 2 – PREPARE INQUIRY ELEC. INPUT	6	A4	4	4	4	4	4	4																		
1, 6 – PRELIMINARY ELEC. SKETCH	4	A2	2	2	2	2																				
1, 7 – PRELIMINARY ELEC. INPUT SPEC	2	A3					3	3																		
7, 9 – PREPARE PRELIMINARY SPEC	10	B5							5	5	5	5	5	5	5	5	5	5								
2, 4 – ISSUE INQUIRY	3	B3							3	3	3															
1, 8 – PRELIMINARY MECH. SKETCH	6	B3										3	3	3	3	3	3									
5,10 – REVIEW VENDOR DRAWINGS	6	A2							2	2	2	2	2	2												
1, 9 – DETAILED ELEC. INPUT SPEC	5	A3							3	3	3	3	3													
3,10 – EVALUATE PROPOSALS/RECOMMEND SUPPLIER	4	A3												3	3	3	3									
6,11 – FINALIZE ELEC. DRAWINGS	5	A3																3	3	3	3	3				
8,11 – FINALIZE MECH. DRAWINGS	4	B4																4	4	4	4					
10,12 – PREPARE PURCHASE ORDER	8	B5																	5	5	5	5	5	5	5	5
1,12 – PREPARE TEST REPORT	5	B4	4	4	4	4	4																			
9,12 – ISSUE SPEC	5	B2																				2	2	2	2	2
11,12 – REVIEW/APPROVE DRAWING PACKAGE	4	B3																					3	3	3	3

RESOURCE A

	1	2	3	4	5	6	7	8	9	10	11	12	13	14	15	16	17	18	19	20	21	22	23	24
AVAILABLE	7	7	7	7	7	7	5	5	5	5	5	5	5	5	5	5	5	5	5	5				
STAFFING LOAD	6	6	6	6	7	7	5	5	5	5	5	5	3	3	3	3	3	3	3	3				
REMAINING	1	1	1	1	0	0	0	0	0	0	0	0	2	2	2	2	2	2	2	2				
CUMULATIVE USAGE	6	12	18	24	31	38	43	48	53	58	63	68	71	74	77	80	83	86	89	92				

RESOURCE B

	1	2	3	4	5	6	7	8	9	10	11	12	13	14	15	16	17	18	19	20	21	22	23	24
AVAILABLE	–	–	–	–	9	9	9	9	9	9	9	9	9	9	9	9	9	9	9	8	8	8	8	8
STAFFING LOAD	4	4	4	4	4	0	8	8	8	8	8	8	8	8	8	9	9	9	9	7	10	10	10	10
REMAINING	-4	-4	-4	-4	5	9	1	1	1	1	1	1	1	1	1	0	0	0	0	1	-2	-2	-2	-2
CUMULATIVE USAGE	4	8	12	16	20	20	28	36	44	52	60	68	76	84	92	101	110	119	128	135	145	155	165	175

DUR = DURATION IN MONTHS
RES = TYPE (A OR B) AND QUANTITY OF RESOURCE REQUIRED

Figure 6-11. Usage plot.

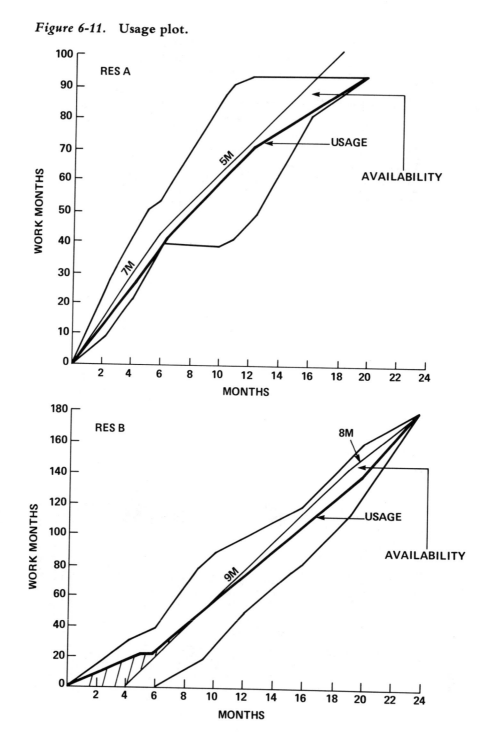

temporarily, or may be needed on other company projects at the same time. The CPM-developed slack times become highly useful in balancing staffing demand under constraints, permitting resources to be loaded in a virtually linear fashion over time to stabilize staffing. A rule of thumb might be to plan a human resources curve that remains within 20 to 30 percent of early- and late-start curves.

Availability, as shown in Figure 6-10, indicates that any given skill will usually be available on a linear basis: Resource A, or electrical engineers, will be available in a head count of seven for the first 6 months in the example, with five being available for the next 14 months. These data are entered into the computer—for perhaps as many as 100 different skills—along with planned staffing load data, derived from the planning curve constructed on the basis of resource envelopes. The computer loads the resources as evenly as possible, calculating the differences between availability and planned demand, detailed for the two skills in Table 6-3.

This permits the workload simulation or test shown in Figure 6-11, which indicates the difference between resource availability and usage, or demand, at any point in the project. The critical number is resources remaining, the margin after the planned staffing load has been subtracted from availability.

This kind of availability testing tells whether or not the project will be completed with available resources, permits loading that will prevent impacts on the completion date, and allows planners to load human resources more evenly throughout the project—within the limits of availability constraints.

The CPM and test availability procedures reduce the risk of a delayed project by simulating expected conditions of resource availability and timing. The system cannot take into account unforeseeable events such as bad weather or late deliveries, and it is not recommended that these unknowns be incorporated in the model. In the event that they occur, a new critical path and additional test availabilities should be prepared. In any case, the CPM system should be regularly updated to improve the accuracy of scheduling and human resources planning.

PART III

The Supply Side: Availability Analysis and Planning

A central premise of this book and the planning system it describes is that the future availability of human resources in the organization depends, first and foremost, on existing human resources and planning and development systems that operate in the present to forecast and shape tomorrow's skills, talents, and managerial competencies. Part III, consisting of Chapters 7 through 9, explores the major aspects of this availability, focusing special attention on managers and professionals, whose costs and value to the organization usually put them at the forefront of strategic planning concerns.

Chapter 7, on personnel information, identifies the kinds of information planners need about people and their jobs as a basis for planning in the modern organization. Thanks to the capabilities of today's information system technology, more data than ever before about employee skills, experience, capabilities, their costs, and the contribution they make to organizational objectives can be currently and accurately maintained and used as the basis for a broad range of management reports relating this information for planning purposes. Examples in this chapter illustrate some of the ways cumulative data can be presented to top management—showing trends, cost-benefit relationships, and other personnel data formats that underscore the critical importance of planning.

Chapter 8 covers the main kinds of human resources planning and development systems needed by most modern organizations to proactively shape human resources availability to meet the short- and long-term demands of operational and strategic planning. While the primary focus is on managers and professionals—with emphasis on appraisals of performance and potential, career management, and succession planning—the guidelines and procedures discussed have wide applicability across occupational categories. To the extent possible, planning for production workers, clerical people, sales personnel, and other kinds of human resources should likewise be systematically integrated with overall organizational goals and objectives. For example, the criteria for performance appraisal may differ for different classes of employees, but they can always be designed to reflect organization-specific needs and implemented and evaluated in ways that support other human resources programs similarly designed as part of an integrated management and planning system.

Chapter 9 deals with human resources forecasting, focusing on the availability side of the supply-demand equation. In an integrated system, of course, strategic and operational factors account for the demand factor in human resources forecasting—the business needs and constraints that call for different quantities and qualities of personnel in the years ahead.

On the availability side, this chapter explores a highly effective network flow method of forecasting based on career planning. Adjusted for attrition, this approach is uniquely realistic, provides managers and planners with the ability to intervene in the factors that shape availability, accounts for individual aspirations and career goals, and—most important—can be designed in ways that proactively create the kinds and numbers of people needed by the organization to meet its business goals.

7

Personnel Information: The Basis for Planning

Information about people, their jobs, and the effects of change on the workforce is the basis for human resources planning and development in the modern organization. In order to analyze the costs and capabilities of the existing workforce, to design career management and other human resources programs that have impacts on these costs and capabilities, and to forecast the future availability of human resources to meet organizational objectives, managers require information that is up-to-date, accurate, consistently defined, historical, and available in a range of formats showing key relationships.

In most complex organizations with more than a few hundred employees, these requirements virtually necessitate the mechanization of data. The use of a human resource information system, as discussed in Chapter 3, makes possible the cost-effective collection, updating, and reporting of information on the many factors involved in human resources planning and development—from skills inventory data to historical flows of human resources movement in the firm.

Further, in the flexible, integrated planning system we propose, information about people and their jobs must be available to meet the demands of quantitative analysis and comparison with strategic and operational data. To assess the ability of existing human resources to meet organizational needs, at knowable costs, human resources must be understood in an organizational context.

Finally, the human resources activities considered critical in planning proactively for the future—to shape the human resources needed because of the demands of strategic and operational plans—require constant tracking, analysis, and adaptation in a flexible planning system. Intuition or management judgment may tell the planner that a change in career pathing structure, for example, will produce a greater number of managers at a certain level in the organization. But how many, what will be the effects of attrition, and what will these managers cost? And what would be the effects of not making the change?

The sections that follow in this chapter depict some of the general categories of personnel data, usually presented as summaries of statistics, that can provide the decision-support information needed to answer such questions. The summaries and trends shown in the figures here exemplify presentation formats that effectively communicate such data to top management, although other formats—including the use of color graphics—may be more suitable to specific needs. Also, these are not the only areas of personnel information that may be important to the organization: Chapter 3 covers the kinds of detailed data, under functional modules of an HRIS, that may be needed by specific functions of personnel. Here, however, the emphasis is on overall human resources and data needed for planning and development.

Employee Population by Job

Perhaps the surest and most readily grasped indicator of what an organization really does—its purpose and actual business—is a view of the major job titles, professional disciplines, and occupational specialties of the employee population. The U.S. Congress, for example, has in recent years been made up largely of people who are lawyers (48 percent in the Ninety-eighth Congress)—a fact decried by some commentators as suggesting a failure of "representative" government but obviously a clear indicator of the chief business of Congress: to make laws.

Figure 7-1. **Ad agency company population—by job classification.**

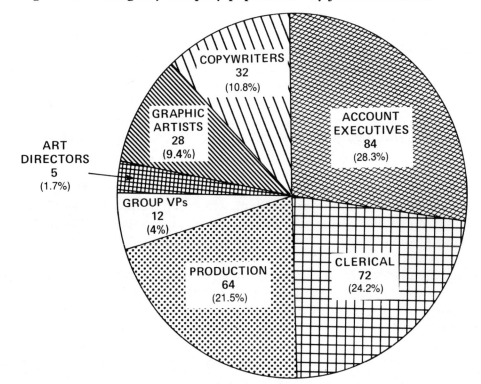

Figure 7-2. **Distribution of engineers.**

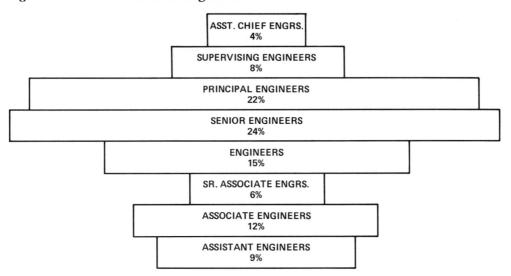

Figure 7-1 shows an overall snapshot of a company's population by general job and skill classification—what people do in the organization. In other kinds of organizations, such a breakdown might include sales personnel, maintenance staff, production workers, physicians, or any other occupational categories utilized. In any case, the overall population depicted in this way provides an immediate picture of what the organization does.

More important for planning purposes, population data by function can be periodically analyzed for change and examined in greater levels of detail—department, location, or according to any other classification (age, race, and sex, for example) resident in the employee data base.

The percentage distribution of the job levels of engineering discipline positions in a company at one point in time is shown in Figure 7-2, for instance. Figure 7-3 shows where these different titles or levels of engineers work in the organization, and Figure 7-4 shows the same engineers—plus others added by an expanding and reorganized firm—two years later.

Displays such as this show planners at a glance the trends in job populations, which should be attributable to actual operational trends. In the electrical design engineering department, for example, there should be a business reason for the relative shrinkage of the senior engineer population. If not—if senior engineers are leaving for better jobs or retiring at a disproportionate rate, for example—then management will want to undertake developmental program changes that will address the issue. Revisions to career paths or modified succession system criteria may be in order.

Job classification data may be general (such as simple breakdowns of management versus nonmanagement employees) or highly specific (such as tables showing hundreds of job function codes, broken down by division, department, location, or other segment of the organization).

Figure 7-3. **Population distribution of engineering departments (August 31, 1984).**

x - ref:
p.273

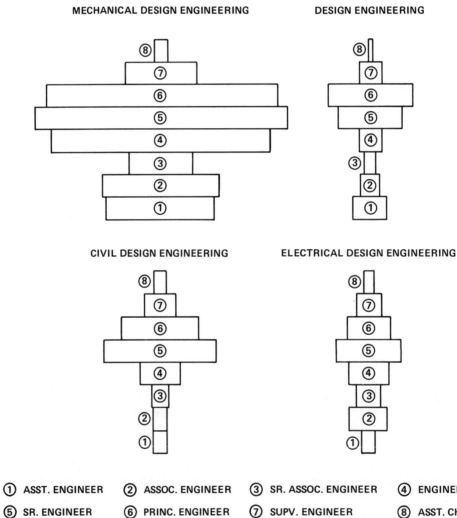

MECHANICAL DESIGN ENGINEERING

DESIGN ENGINEERING

CIVIL DESIGN ENGINEERING

ELECTRICAL DESIGN ENGINEERING

① ASST. ENGINEER   ② ASSOC. ENGINEER   ③ SR. ASSOC. ENGINEER   ④ ENGINEER

⑤ SR. ENGINEER   ⑥ PRINC. ENGINEER   ⑦ SUPV. ENGINEER   ⑧ ASST. CHIEF ENGINEER

Figure 7-4. **Population distribution of engineering departments (August 31, 1986).**

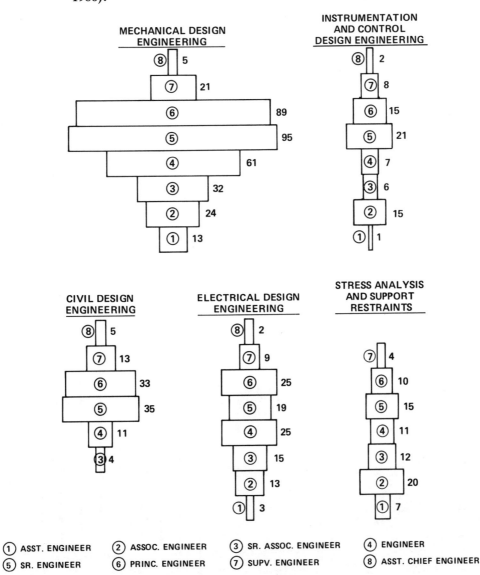

Pay Characteristics: The Case of Salaries

Wage and salary compensation continues to represent the major cost factor of human resources, reason enough for overall analysis of pay characteristics and trends. An organization's present and future pay structure is clearly a "strategic" issue because such a large share of operating expenses goes to wages and salaries. The accumulations of pay data shown here as examples focus on salaries, of primary interest in management development planning.

(Text continues on page 161.)

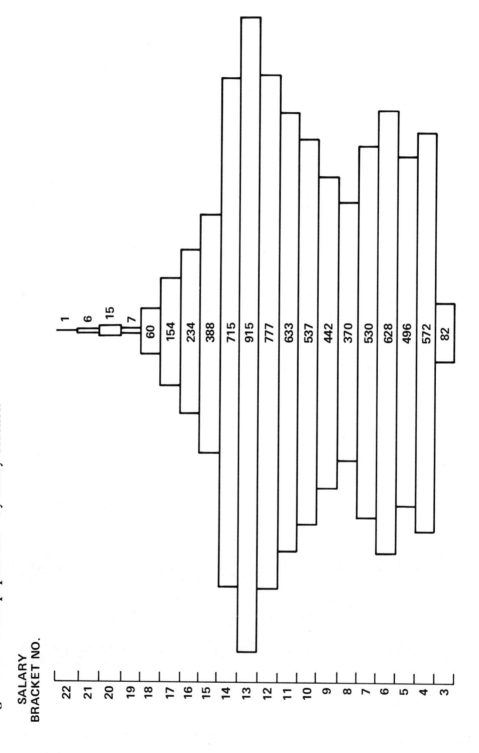

Figure 7-5. Total population—by salary bracket.

SALARY
BRACKET NO.

Figure 7-6. Comparison of actual salaries with midpoint of salary curve.

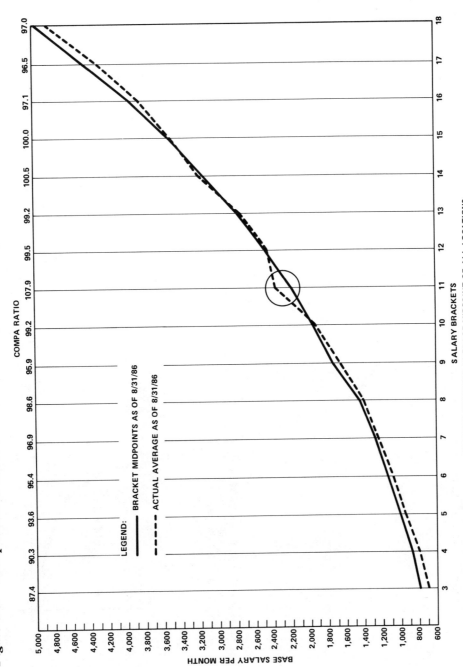

NOTE: BRACKETS 3-8 MIDPOINTS REPRESENT THE WEIGHTED AVERAGE MIDPOINT OF ALL LOCATIONS.

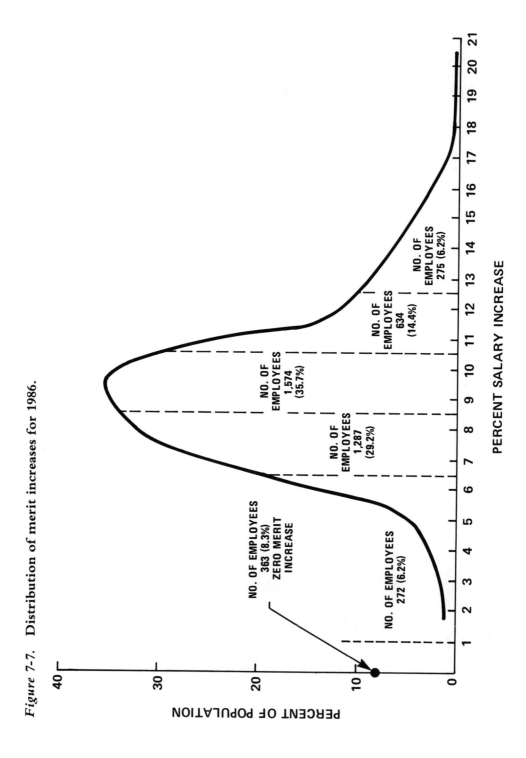

Figure 7-7. Distribution of merit increases for 1986.

Figure 7-5 presents an overall view of the salaried population by bracket, from the CEO to 82 support workers. In many companies, this kind of display would assume the shape of a pyramid—the greatest number of employees are paid the least, and there are fewer supervisors at each level of pay to the top. The organization depicted in Figure 7-5, however, is in a high-technology industry, with a preponderance of technical and professional personnel earning relatively high salaries. Specific analysis of such data will depend on what the salary brackets mean, of course. In some cases, a graph in this shape might mean that the organization is "fat" with midlevel supervisors and that not enough lower-level managers are available in the firm to meet future needs.

More detailed salary analyses are shown in Figures 7-6 and 7-7. Figure 7-6 highlights the fact that managers in salary bracket 11, on average, are being paid well above that bracket's midpoint, calling management attention to a situation that will bear further study. Figure 7-7 provides a quick picture of the effects of merit pay increases in a single year, showing that most employees received salary increases in the 6.5 to 10.5 percent range.

Another type of salary analysis is illustrated in Figure 7-8. In this figure

Figure 7-8. **Average length of service—by bracket (October 1986).**

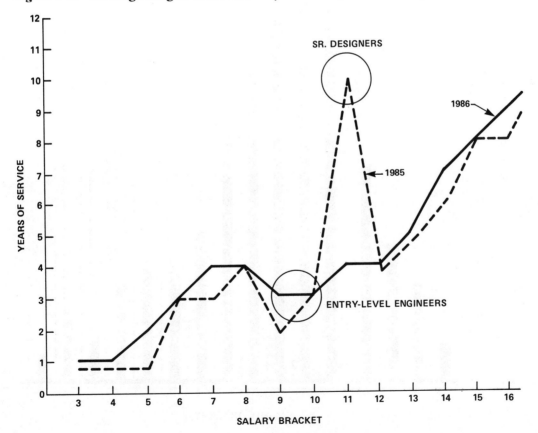

average length of service is correlated with salary brackets for the job classifications of senior designer and entry-level engineer over two years. The dotted line, for the former year, shows that the organization had a conspicuously large number of senior designers with seniority at that level. The "smoothed out" solid line, for the following year, was the result of management action that created an intermediate level in the organization in order to accommodate this group.

Figure 7-9. Employee sex—by bracket (October 1986).

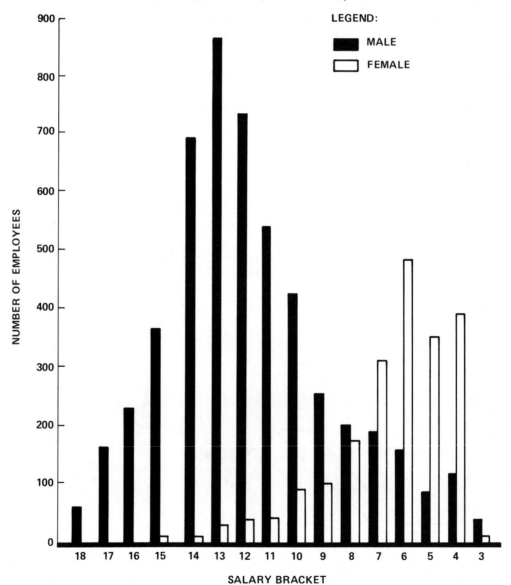

Demographic Data: Beyond EEO Requirements

The need for age, sex, and race information to meet regulatory requirements may have been a prime reason for the development and use of the human resource information systems that provide the wealth of personnel data available in many organizations today. Certainly, HRIS technology "paid for itself" in the early days by mechanizing EEO data collection and reporting procedures. Today, however, most companies can usefully analyze employee populations by age, sex, EEO "protected class," and other demographic information, including educational attainments and skills experience.

Beyond EEO requirements—which for companies with comprehensive affirmative action plans in effect, may involve voluminous, frequent reports on progress toward goals and timetable dates for numerous jobs across the organization—demographic data provide important management insights for human resources development programs. For example, a company seeking to attract and develop a growing share of female managers—because the business needs them, as much as to be an equal opportunity employer—would do well to examine present career paths, succession plans, compensation policy, and other programs for any significant differences in the way men and women are treated.

Figure 7-9, for example, showing the different numbers of men and women

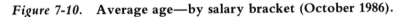

Figure 7-10. **Average age—by salary bracket (October 1986).**

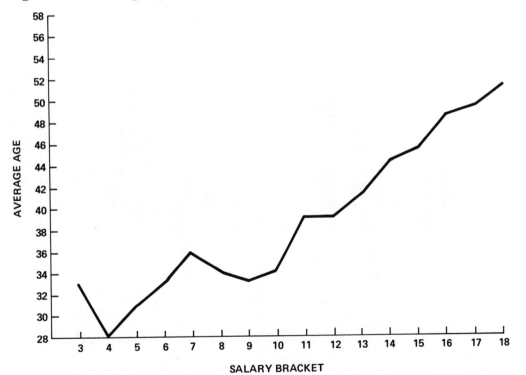

Figure 7-11. Engineering degrees (October 1986).

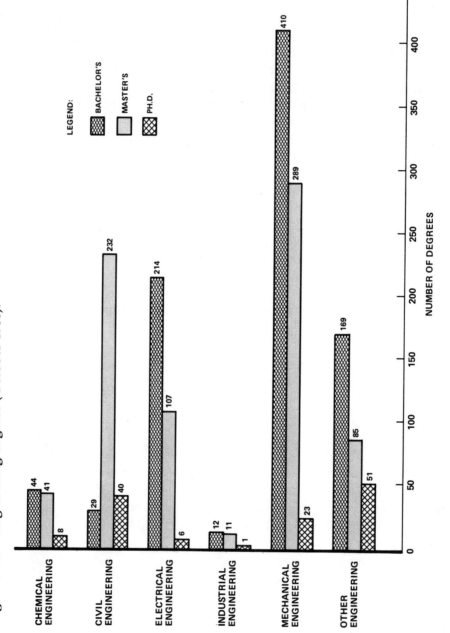

NOTE: EACH EMPLOYEE IS COUNTED ONCE AT THE HIGHEST DEGREE ATTAINED. THOSE WITH THE SAME LEVEL DEGREE IN DIFFERENT DISCIPLINES ARE COUNTED IN THE CURRENT FIELD OF EMPLOYMENT.

in each salary bracket of a company, is typical of organizations managed largely by men or where few women seek careers as professionals. In the organization depicted, most female employees are in clerical and lower-level management positions.

Figure 7-10 shows an aggregate picture of average employee ages in salary brackets across a company. More detailed analysis of the age of various levels of managers, skills areas, and departments is a critical need in developing career programs of all kinds and projecting future availability of human resources. In the graph shown, most of the salary brackets below nine are clerical and experience high turnover rates that produce a variable age-salary correlation. In the higher brackets, average age corresponds with salary.

Virtually every human resources development program worthy of the name is based on general and specific data about the skills, talents, experience, and education of the existing workforce. Skills inventories, which typically provide this kind of data on individuals for accumulation in overall reports, are discussed in Chapter 3. An example of such a report is shown in Figure 7-11, a chart that counts each employee with an engineering degree once—at his or her highest level of attainment. Other reports might show types of degree by department—a key factor in developing career management programs—and attrition data by type of degree.

Benefits Costs and Trends

Increasingly, the cost of staffing levels and projections of future costs of personnel cannot be accurately forecast without improved techniques for identifying noncash compensation costs and future trends in these costs. Figure 7-12 shows one company's benefits costs compared to salary costs for different job levels. Many U.S. firms report spending over 30 percent of employee costs on benefits.

With benefits costs accounting for such a large share of compensation, and some benefits costs—notably, health insurance—escalating at rates far in excess of inflation, planners must work more closely than ever with benefits administrators, pension actuarials, and other compensation professionals to devise means of controlling these costs in the present and more accurately projecting benefits expenses in the years ahead. The introduction of new forms of noncash compensation—such as dental insurance, 401K plans, prepaid legal insurance, and deferred compensation—and the introduction of flexible or "cafeteria-style" programs of benefits administration have only served to complicate the task of benefits planning.

In many organizations, the cost of employee pensions is a critical factor in shaping management development programs or policies on retirement. Figure 7-13 shows the escalating costs of pension payments in one organization over an eight-year period, for example. Other data that should be understood by planners include the number of vested and active employees, market value of the trust fund, and actuarial data projecting pension costs in the years ahead.

(Text continues on page 171.)

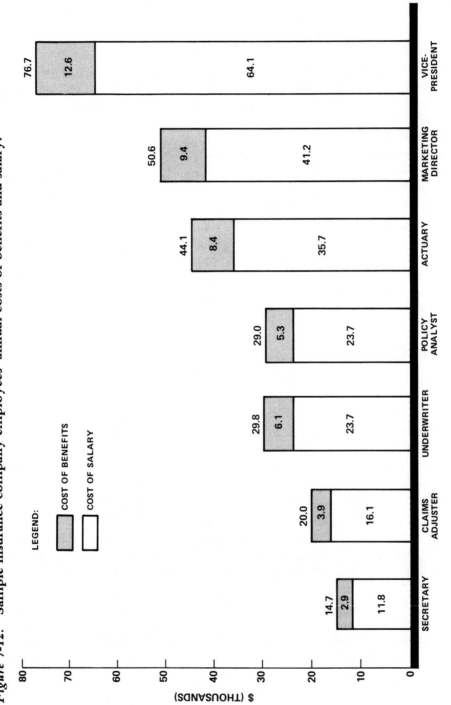

Figure 7-12. Sample insurance company employees' annual costs of benefits and salary.

Figure 7-13. **Pension payments over eight years.**

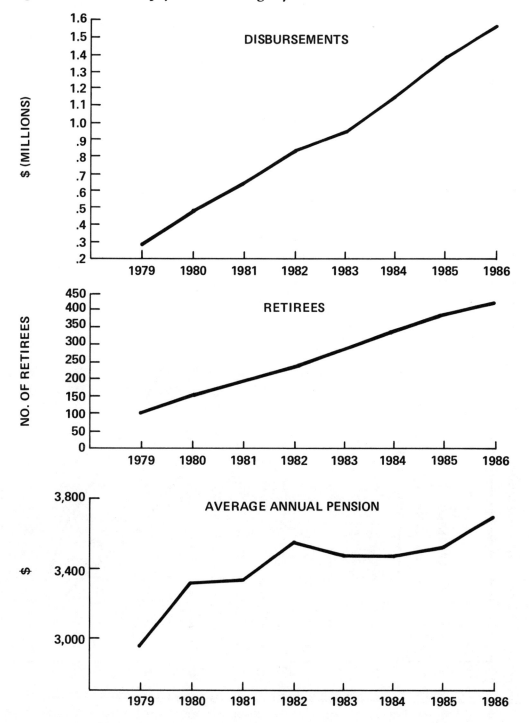

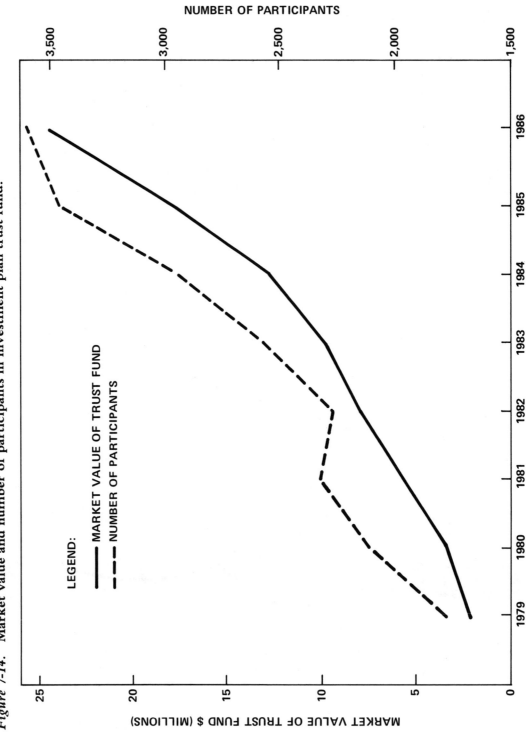

Figure 7-14. Market value and number of participants in investment plan trust fund.

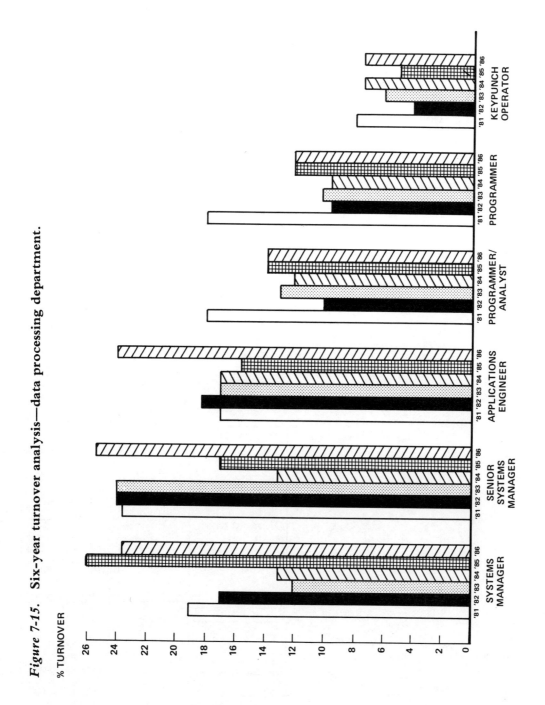

Figure 7-15. Six-year turnover analysis—data processing department.

Figure 7-16. **Reasons by bracket for retiring or remaining employed.**

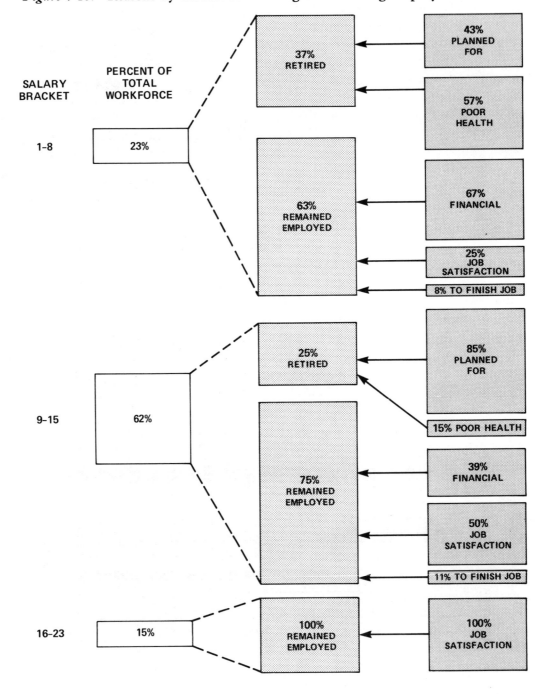

Similarly, the cost of employee investment plans, an example of which is charted in Figure 7-14, should include relevant details such as the number of participants, market value of the fund, and eligibility projections.

Attrition Statistics: Key Availability Factor

As discussed in greater detail in Chapter 9, attrition analysis is a cornerstone of human resources availability forecasting. Attrition data are important to the design of career development programs, succession planning, and the appraisal systems, as well—especially where unwanted turnover resulting from voluntary separations is an issue.

Analysis over time, such as the six-year chart shown in Figure 7-15—broken down by job classes, departments, or locations—can pinpoint turnover problems and perhaps suggest remedial interventions. The higher turnover rates for several classes of engineers shown in Figure 7-15 in the last year covered by the chart, for example, may indicate the need for an improved career path in these classes.

Figure 7-16 isolates attrition through retirement by groups of salary brackets,

(Text continues on page 176.)

Figure 7-17. **Hires for growth and turnover.**

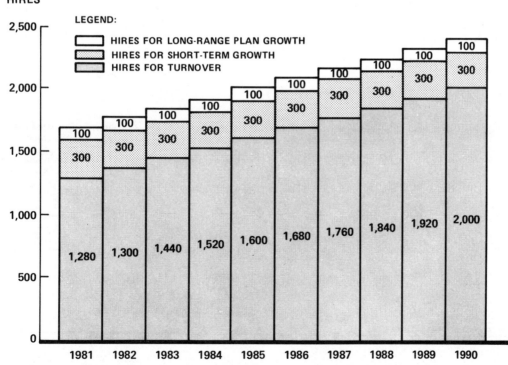

Figure 7-18.   **Percentage distribution of degrees—by field of study (to 1988–89).**

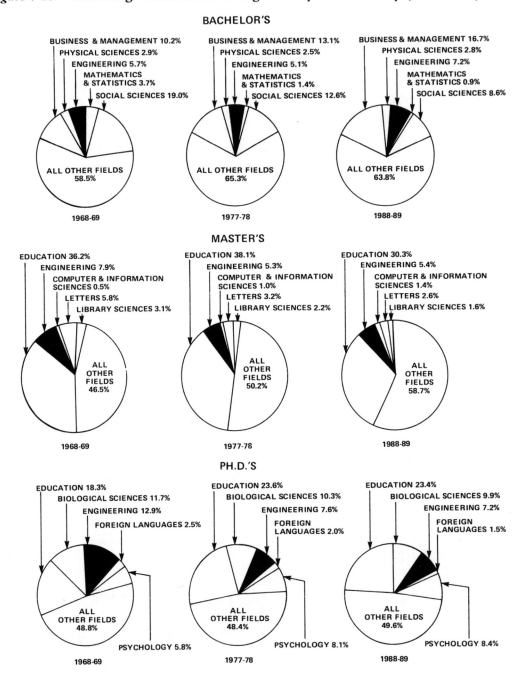

SOURCE: NATIONAL CENTER FOR EDUCATION STATISTICS (1980), TABLES 15, 16, AND 17.

Figure 7-19. **National engineering and construction salary survey.**

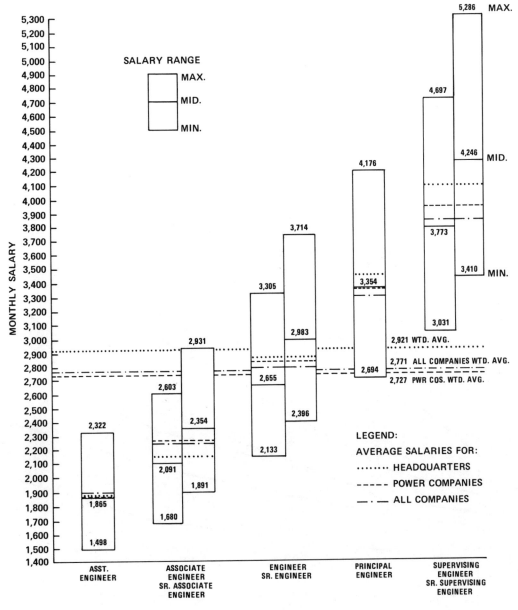

Figure 7-20. **Salary trends compounded 7.0 percent annually (1980–90).**

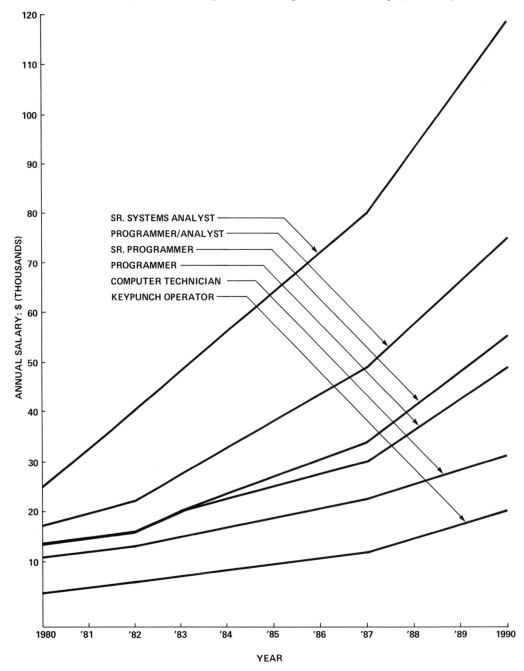

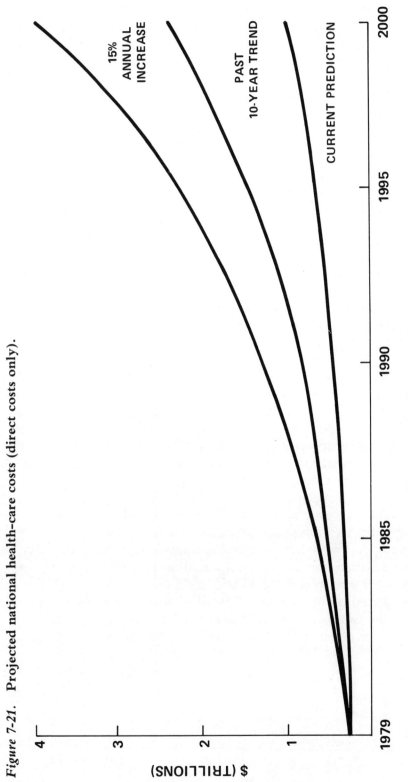

Figure 7-21. Projected national health-care costs (direct costs only).

providing aggregate data on percentages of those eligible for retirement who actually retired, those who remained with the company, and the reasons given for either decision. One insight immediately evident in this display is that employees in the lower salary brackets are more likely to remain employed for financial reasons.

Another kind of display, illustrated in Figure 7-17, shows a forecast of organizational hires needed to replace turnover in the next ten years. In most firms, data such as these will underscore the importance of further study of the reasons for turnover and subsequent actions—such as career development programs—to reduce its incidence.

External Data Affecting Human Resources Development

Organizational needs will dictate the kinds of external, or environmental, factors that should be watched and planned for in the design and operation of human resources development programs. As discussed in Chapter 4, the external human resources environment that has an impact on the organization can include population demographics, labor market conditions, skills shortages in specific areas, formal education, and the actions of competitors affecting labor markets.

For example, planners will normally want some data on general educational trends, such as the trends in college degrees shown in Figure 7-18. Projections of the supply of specific types of degrees in the years ahead—when compared with other data—can provide an overall view of recruitment needs.

Salary survey information, such as that depicted in Figure 7-19, is usually available from research organizations, trade associations, or consulting firms specializing in these data. Although salary surveys are notoriously unreliable as guides to setting specific pay rates—the problem of job comparability in the organizations surveyed has not been adequately addressed, for the most part—trends in industrywide salary practices bear tracking.

Among economic trends affecting human resources, few have had the impact that inflation has had on compensation policies in recent years. Figure 7-20 shows, for example, the effects of a 7 percent average inflation rate over a ten-year period on certain jobs. Trends in specific kinds of employment costs, such as medical insurance, indicate even greater inflation ahead. Figure 7-21 shows several projections of U.S. health-care costs to the year 2000.

8

Management Development Programs: Key Concepts and Strategic Implications

Inevitably, management development is a complex process with strategic implications at every step of the way. Whether done well or poorly, the programs and policies that characterize appraisals, succession planning, and career management will shape the kinds and numbers of management skills available to the organization in the years ahead. It is a process in well-managed companies that:

- Defines critical incumbencies at various levels of management and sets criteria for succession planning
- Identifies managers with potential for growth who may be suitable candidates for leadership in the future
- Establishes individual career development plans that include training, developmental experiences, rotation, and other forms of development
- Provides feedback on progress, permitting correction and improvement of the development process

The techniques and specific mechanisms of management development will vary greatly among organizations. Our purpose in this chapter is not to prescribe techniques, nor even to suggest which part of the employee population should be considered "managers" and included in management development programs. Rather, the focus in the sections that follow is on the strategic implications of *any* management development program and on key design concepts that will help assure that these programs are capable of being systematically integrated with strategic plans.

The Role of Evaluation in Shaping Availability

The role of evaluation in a systematically integrated organization is, or can be, fundamentally strategic: Both performance appraisal systems and methods for appraising potential have the effect of rewarding and developing certain kinds of characteristics and capabilities among managers and professionals, in a sense "creating" the kinds of human resources available to the organization in the years ahead.

Conceptually, an ideal performance appraisal system looks at individual "pasts" in order to create an organizational future. The framework and criteria for looking at past performance, the techniques used to rate or rank employees, and the specific relationships of appraisals to compensation, career development, training, and other human resources programs should be conditioned by specific organizational requirements, as determined by the systematic analysis of the variance between human resources demand and availability.

Appraisal of potential is a quintessential planning process. Unlike performance appraisal, which looks to the past, appraisal of potential attempts to assess the capabilities of individuals to become effective managers in the future. This assessment presupposes a planning view of the kinds of capabilities needed by organizational managers—especially upper-level managers who will lead the firm—in the years ahead, adding another dimension to the future-orientation of the appraisal of potential. Without this strategic view of the future needs of the organization, of course, no "solution" to the very difficult job of evaluating individual potential will help select tomorrow's effective leaders.

Performance Appraisals and Strategic Goals

As one of the oldest human resources functions—and one that has assumed increasing importance as organizations seek to improve productivity, nurture and reward outstanding performance, and better analyze and motivate managers' and other employees' actual contributions to organizational work—performance appraisal has reached a high level of sophistication and technical elegance in many firms. Not uncommonly, behavioral scientists, job analysts, compensation specialists, training and development people, systems experts, and professionals in company-specific disciplines all have a hand in the development of appraisal criteria, techniques, and applications.

Any of these methodologies has the potential for success, if effective in meeting strategic objectives. In general, however, we have found that the most effective techniques are those that are characterized by two features: widespread support and understanding by employees; and effective appraisal instruments, carefully designed around job-related criteria and developed as part of a systematic approach that links appraisals to individual and organizational goals and also permits regular evaluation of the appraisal system itself.

If performance evaluation is to be part of the strategic planning process, as we recommend, it must be more than just a method of allocating merit pay, motivating employees, and providing criteria for succession planning. All of these are important subobjectives of an effective program, but the main purpose of a strategic performance appraisal system is or should be human resources availability: what the program does to help assure the continuing and future availability of the human resources needed by the organization to achieve strategic goals.

This means that the specifics of any performance appraisal system will depend on organizational needs. If the overall human resources planning function is truly proactive, it means that performance appraisals, along with all other personnel functions, must serve to create the quality and number of people needed in the near and long-range future. Different timetables may apply, but the overall program should be designed with the long-range view in focus.

For example, such details as the weighting of specific criteria (and the criteria themselves) should not remain mired in the past. A company that has always valued "customer service" above all else, for instance, may be moving into an intensely competitive environment where sales volume or cost cutting is more critical to survival. The performance appraisal criteria should reflect that. If managers are being promoted and rewarded for reasons that applied to yesterday's organization, the system is not strategically based.

In large, complex organizations, the strategic plan may call for the development of a number of highly specialized, job-related skills and aptitudes to meet human resources demand in the years ahead. This may require the use of numerous evaluation forms—each with a somewhat different set of criteria or rating scales—to accurately assess performance in specific areas. The organization needs this kind of specific detail to establish and improve training and development programs, as well as to promote and compensate according to the strategic plan. The individuals being rated need this kind of job-related specificity in order to believe that their jobs, and what they actually do in their jobs, are the basis for their value to the organization.

Such a plethora of different evaluation forms may seem a cure worse than the disease of overly generalized criteria. The use of human resource information systems (HRISs), as discussed in Chapter 3, can minimize manual data collection and reporting—once in operation—and can be economically feasible for large firms. Further, depending on organizational human resources needs, evaluation instruments can usually be broken down by general classes of employees.

Appraising Different Groups with Different Instruments

At a minimum, employers using performance appraisal systems have always distinguished between at least two classes of employees, exempt and non-exempt. Today, most complex organizations—and especially those in high-tech industries employing growing numbers of professionals and technicians—should consider a different "minimum" classification system: Different instruments and evaluation procedures normally apply to at least three categories of workers—managers, professionals, and the nonexempt; a somewhat different approach is needed by organizations in matrix management modes. Whatever classification system is used, of course, it should be based on needs dictated by strategic plans.

Figure 8-1. **A simple checklist for performance appraisal.**

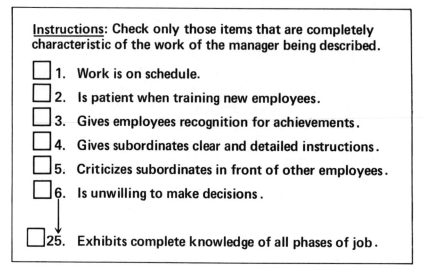

Instructions: Check only those items that are completely characteristic of the work of the manager being described.

☐ 1. Work is on schedule.

☐ 2. Is patient when training new employees.

☐ 3. Gives employees recognition for achievements.

☐ 4. Gives subordinates clear and detailed instructions.

☐ 5. Criticizes subordinates in front of other employees.

☐ 6. Is unwilling to make decisions.

☐ 25. Exhibits complete knowledge of all phases of job.

Managers. The effectiveness of a management appraisal system depends on such factors as the objectivity of ratings, the job relatedness of criteria, comparability of appraisal results, and the relevance of the appraisal process to strategic goals. In some organizations or departments, all of these factors may be accounted for by a simple measurement system—such as one based on sales volume per quarter. More often, management appraisal will be based on company-specific checklists, rating scales, and evaluation procedures carefully designed to further specific management development needs.

An example of a simple checklist is shown in Figure 8-1. Such a list is designed to be comprehensive, leaving no characteristic important to the organization out of the evaluation. In actual application, of course, raters for different kinds of functions in the organization would each be asked to assess managerial characteristics particular to his or her given function. One form of more specific checklist is shown in Figure 8-2, a "forced-choice" instrument that requires raters to assign specific values to specific characteristics.

Ranking methods used in performance appraisals recognize the reality that not all managers perform equally and have the added advantage of providing comparative evaluations from the same rater. In ranking, one supervisor normally ranks all managers within a function or span of control, using the same criteria.

Rating scales based on management-by-objectives (MBO) criteria are theoretically superior to virtually all other methods of performance appraisal. The distinguishing characteristic of an MBO approach is that it uses performance standards that have already been determined.[1] Each position is analyzed for its critical job requirements, its "yardsticks" of successful incumbency, and a goal or set of goals is defined. The appraisal process is simplified because raters need

Figure 8-2. **A forced-choice checklist for performance appraisal.**

Instructions: Statements descriptive of managerial performance are grouped below in blocks of four. For each block of statements, indicate which statement is most like and least like the manager being described. Place an ☒ in the appropriate column.

Most | Least |
--- | --- | ---
☐ | ☐ | Does not get the facts necessary for making decisions
☐ | ☐ | Receives constructive criticism well
☐ | ☐ | Can be promoted when the opportunity arises
☐ | ☐ | Gives credit to others for work well done
☐ | ☐ | Accepts the opinions of subordinates
☐ | ☐ | Quickly analyzes a situation
☐ | ☐ | Coordinates the activities of his or her department to facilitate work flow
☐ | ☐ | Has minimal knowledge of other departments' work
☐ | ☐ | Follows through even when the going gets tough
☐ | ☐ | Expresses himself or herself clearly and convincingly
☐ | ☐ | Is willing to make decisions
☐ | ☐ | Knows how to present a report with all the facts
☐ | ☐ | Always follows company policies and procedures
☐ | ☐ | Has a well-organized approach to any problem
☐ | ☐ | Can put ideas across to others effectively
☐ | ☐ | Can take constructive criticism without getting angry or upset

only determine the degree of success realized in achieving these goals or objectives. Performance appraisal interviews, furthermore, can focus on specific progress or lack of progress toward defined goals—which in most cases have already been communicated to the employee being appraised.

An effective MBO approach usually includes provision for the following:

- *Objectives* that are spelled out in advance and understood by all concerned, possibly separated as quantitative and qualitative goals, but including both "maintenance" goals reflecting basic duties and incentive goals
- *Criteria,* or specific methods of showing observable and measurable progress

- *Target dates*, which may include overall completion dates as well as phase or percentage completion dates for each objective
- *Performance measurement* at appraisal time or on target dates, by specific criteria, at which time supervisors can compare actual and targeted performance and make evaluations

On paper, the MBO method appears to answer all the needs of performance appraisal. In practice, organizational life is not always so readily quantified and measured. For one thing, MBO puts a great deal of pressure on employees to achieve specific goals. Pressure in itself is not necessarily a bad thing, if the goals are valid and important to the organization. The problems with MBO as an appraisal method emerge from the difficulty inherent in defining, clearly and quantitatively, the goals or objectives of each position.

Especially at the upper levels of management, job descriptions for managers deal in intangibles not easily translated into goals, criteria, and target dates. Moreover, job descriptions cannot account for the interdependence of much managerial activity. And if a manager fails to achieve his or her objectives because of others, the performance appraisal system should not force the manager (or supervisors) into a position of needing to blame those others to get (or give) a good performance rating.

In addition, the setting of objectives and targets for many kinds of work—especially in service industries and among professionals—may require a subtlety and sophistication beyond the reach of simple quantification. To the extent that objectives become "qualified" by intangible characteristics and generalized impressions, the MBO system loses its objectivity and usefulness as a means of assessing one manager's performance using another's form. While it is expected that the rater is the person who is in the best position to know what the employee has been doing, this may not always be the case. The employee may be too new to evaluate properly, or the form may simply be in the wrong hands. And by having a "no assignments in this area" code, the form can be designed to apply to a greater population of managers, some of whom will have new business responsibilities and others of whom will not.

Finally, management evaluation should include provision for narrative comments. These comments permit raters to be more specific, explain ratings, or point out particular strengths or weaknesses not adequately identified—in the rater's view—by the items on the form. In addition, the comments—which may be mandatory or optional—help with the evaluation of the ratings and raters, as discussed below.

Professional and Technical Employees. Evaluation of the performance of professional employees has long posed problems for results-oriented business concerns. Accurate measurement of performance requires clear job descriptions, for one thing, and many professionals—research chemists, systems analysts, legal advisers, designers, and so on—contribute to the organization in ways that cannot be readily described in advance.

For example, a structural engineer working on a wind-shear problem created

Figure 8-3. **Professional employee evaluation: petroleum engineering consultant.**

EMPLOYEE NAME	DATE

The following rating scale should be used for level of performance:
1. Performance is exceptional.
2. Performance is outstanding.
3. Performance is effective.
4. Performance is acceptable.
5. Performance is unsatisfactory.
UD Insufficient knowledge of employee's performance at this time.
NA This employee has had no assignments in this area.

1. REVIEW OF PERFORMANCE OF ASSIGNED WORK

LEVEL OF
PERFORMANCE
(Circle One)

A. KNOWLEDGE AND APPLICATION

1. Maintains and upgrades the necessary knowledge of technology related to current and desirable assignments.   1 2 3 4 5 UD NA

2. Keeps current with technology related to work of personnel reporting to him or her.   1 2 3 4 5 UD NA

3. Demonstrates an understanding of
   a. job duties and responsibilities.   1 2 3 4 5 UD NA
   b. departmental standards and procedures.   1 2 3 4 5 UD NA
   c. applicability of relevant industry standards, codes, and guides and causes for departure from them.   1 2 3 4 5 UD NA
   d. applicability and limitations of engineering analytical methodology.   1 2 3 4 5 UD NA

4. Anticipates information required to complete work assignments and solve technical problems with the least amount of delay.   1 2 3 4 5 UD NA

5. Completes assignments in a timely fashion when all required information is available.   1 2 3 4 5 UD NA

6. Produces definitive engineering solutions in the form of analytical reports, specifications, etc.   1 2 3 4 5 UD NA

7. Discusses technical problems on an appropriate level with colleagues and experts in the field.   1 2 3 4 5 UD NA

8. Assimilates ideas and follows them through to a logical conclusion.   1 2 3 4 5 UD NA

OVERALL RATING – KNOWLEDGE AND APPLICATION	1 2 3 4 5 UD

by a plan revision might spend hours or even weeks working out a solution. Another engineer might come up with a different solution—a variation that appears adequate—instantaneously. But if the variation ends up costing much more, in materials or reduced safety margins, the former engineer is surely more "efficient."

Obviously, the first requirement of the process of evaluating professional and technical specialists is that the methods used should incorporate professional standards and technical criteria specific to the activity. Forms may be developed for each specialty, as shown in Figure 8-3, or for general applicability

Figure 8-4. **Professional employee performance appraisal: generic.**

EMPLOYEE NAME	DATE

The following rating scale should be used for level of performance:
1.   Performance is exceptional.
2.   Performance is outstanding.
3.   Performance is effective.
4.   Performance is acceptable.
5.   Performance is unsatisfactory.
UD   Insufficient knowledge of employee's performance at this time.
NA   This employee has had no assignments in this area.

1. REVIEW OF JOB PERFORMANCE

	LEVEL OF PERFORMANCE (Circle One)
A. QUALITY AND QUANTITY OF WORK	
1. Makes plans, establishes priorities, and carries out multiple assignments in a systematic and organized fashion.	1 2 3 4 5 UD NA
2. Submits work that is thorough and accurate.	1 2 3 4 5 UD NA
3. Produces the required volume of work on schedule.	1 2 3 4 5 UD NA

OVERALL RATING – QUALITY AND QUANTITY OF WORK	1 2 3 4 5 UD

Comments: _____

_____

_____

to professionals, as shown in Figure 8-4. Either way, raters must usually be from the same discipline or have the same qualifications as the technical or professional employee, to assure that performance criteria and actual job performance are sufficiently understood. A strict MBO approach, focusing on objectives that are difficult to define and measure, may be the worst way to appraise professionals.

Because professionals often work in teams or departments where they interface with the management hierarchy at many levels, the matrix approach to their performance appraisal—discussed below—may be especially effective.

Clerical and Nonexempt Employees. All employees must be accorded the same opportunities for advancement, if for no other reason than that equitable treatment is mandated by the equal opportunity laws. The main mechanism for ensuring equality of opportunity is a consistent, universally applicable performance appraisal system covering all employees, whether they have the basic qualifications to advance into management ranks or not.

In many organizations with a heavy commitment to job security, promotion from within, and career development programs such as training and tuition reimbursement, evaluation of the performance of clericals, production workers, and other support personnel is taken as seriously as management appraisal.

As a rule, the form used in these appraisals applies to all employees in a class—such as office workers, technical support personnel, or production line employees.

Matrix Organizations. Particularly among the growing ranks of professionals and technical specialists in modern organizations, many employees are responsible both to a technical department—such as the legal department—and to an immediate supervisor on the current job or project. Thus, an additional form from the project supervisor will complement the professional evaluation instrument discussed above.

There are many other reasons for establishing a matrix form of management—to assure continuous development of all managers at a certain level, to maximize skills needed in more than one department, or to distribute decision-making power across the levels where decisions must be made quickly—but from an appraisal perspective, each matrix organization is characterized by multiple assessments. That is, usually, a single supervisor using one form cannot adequately evaluate an employee. All interfaces in the organization must be considered, a requirement that may add complexity to the design of performance appraisal methods but is essential to the fair and comprehensive evaluation of the employee's performance.

Analysis of Appraisals: Rating the Raters

No matter how effectively forms are designed and data are systematically entered into the performance appraisal system, this information is susceptible to error or inadequacy unless carefully analyzed before it becomes part of the employee's permanent record. The major area deserving analysis, the part of the process most susceptible to error or misjudgment, involves raters.

Being human, raters bring their own values, perceptions, and preconceived criteria to the job of performance appraisal. No matter how well prepared by the human resources department or how specifically instructed by clear definitions, criteria, and ranking systems, supervisors can be "unequal" in several ways.

Some will be excessively generous at all times, some too strict; others will be lenient as a rule but intolerant of one kind of deficiency, such as lateness, which colors all other characteristics being evaluated for that employee. Still others may highly prize a quality such as accuracy, and a high mark on this trait will produce a "halo effect" that influences all other ratings.

For any of a number of reasons, from old-fashioned "cronyism" to fear that the subordinate is out for the rater's job, performance evaluations can be biased because of different raters' attitudes and values. In addition, raters may not see performance the same way in May as they did in January.

These kinds of inconsistencies can be systematically addressed through mechanisms that collect data on raters and their ratings, for analysis by human resources specialists and department heads. The reports produced by such systems provide the means of identifying "problem" appraisers as well as pinpointing inconsistencies by raters or by department.

For example, the average value of all appraisals by a given rater can be compared to companywide data. Past appraisals by any one rater, or within a department, can be compared with current ratings. In organizations where matrix management applies, or dual appraisals for professional disciplines, different ratings for the same employee can be compared.

The purpose of such summaries of appraisals is to enable department managers or other officers to meet with supervisor-appraisers to determine the reasons for anomalies. It is important to emphasize that such differences are not always "rater problems" but may be department problems or may mean that the anomalous rater is to be congratulated. It could even be that the "different" rater is the only one in the organization who understands the appraisal process.

Feedback: Developmental Application of Appraisals

The most "strategic" component of a successful performance appraisal system—apart from an original design that focuses on the real human resources needs of the organization—concerns the actual use of appraisals: What actions, by individuals or by the organization, occur as a result of appraisals?

Inevitably, performance appraisals affect compensation. Whether the relationship is direct and explicit (as in a salary review based on ratings or merit increases tied to ratings) or indirect (as when appraisals are but one factor in a promotion decision), there is almost always a relationship between performance and pay.

We regard this as a fact of life and neither harmful nor necessarily beneficial to an effective appraisal process. Some human resources managers feel otherwise: The main purpose of performance appraisals should be developmental, they say, to help employees achieve individual and company goals through behavior modification, training, or other change that improves performance.

But despite all the attitudinal studies showing changes in the value systems of workers, and despite the fact that managers and professionals are often more motivated by "the work itself" than by other considerations, compensation remains the main reason why people work. At the very least, it is seen as the yardstick of success. More important, from the company's perspective, compensation resources are not limitless. If pay-for-performance is a good idea in principle (and few would say it is not), there must be a consistent, fair, and timely method of measuring the performance of individuals.

Motivation is the key goal of performance appraisal applications. In meetings with supervisors and upper management, employees must be provided with rating data in ways that are clearly associated with personal and organizational goals: what needs to be done to improve, or take advantage of, an appraisal or series of appraisals. Thus, as shown in Chapter 1 in the flow diagram of the integrated planning model (Figure 1-1), performance appraisals—along with evaluation of potential, discussed in the following section—are directly linked to the career development process.

In smaller organizations, this linkage may be accomplished merely by providing space on the evaluation form for a supervisor's "development recommendations." If the number and kinds of human resources development options applicable to a rater's subordinates can be readily understood by the rater, this may be a decision the rater can make effectively.

More often—and particularly in larger firms with a range of training, educational, and other development programs (including job rotation, sabbaticals, leadership experiences, and so on)—professionals in the human resources development department should be involved in any recommendations based on appraisals.

In addition, appraisals related to compensation require the regular analysis of changing variables by the salary administration department. If performance appraisals are producing merit pay increases for 95 percent of all managers, or for most managers in engineering but for only a few in marketing, either the appraisal system or the merit pay system may require a new approach. At a minimum, in organizations where appraisals have pay consequences, supervisors who make appraisals should understand the effects of different ratings.

In an integrated human resources planning system, the appraisal process is linked to these other human resources functions—including appraisal of potential and overall planning—through information. Using data and information flows appropriate to organizational needs for analysis and decision making, the most widely scattered departments and disparate functions in the firm can understand, support, and work synergistically toward overall strategic human resources objectives. For large organizations, the technology of the HRIS makes possible the consistent, timely collection of relevant information. It also offers reporting capabilities that provide those data to managers promptly, cost-effectively, and in formats designed to permit analysis.

Appraisals of Potential: Leadership and the Strategic Perspective

Past accomplishments alone are not always the best indicators of future capabilities in managers. Achievements at one level of the organization or an ability to "get things done" when objectives are clear, limited to the short term, and readily recognizable as bottom-line results do not necessarily predict future success—or even competence—at higher levels. Thus, organizations seeking ways to evaluate the capabilities of managers for future positions, to offer guidance for management development and succession planning systems that will help provide management capabilities in the years ahead, and to help managers develop career plans that will merge individual and corporate goals have undertaken the assessment of potential among managers, through techniques that have had varying levels of success.

Evaluation of potential is inherently difficult to the extent that it must focus on people rather than jobs. For upper-management positions—where job descriptions are less precise and such intangible qualities as leadership, innovation, team building, and integrity are required—appraisal of potential is most difficult. For the most part, no valid predictors of upper-management success exist to guide the assessment process, although several innovative perspectives are suggested later in this section.

For professional and technical positions—which make up a growing share of jobs in the modern organization—tests of knowledge within a particular field present no major difficulties. Bar exams, civil service examinations, and professional licensing are all types of appraisal of potential tests involving knowledge, and organizations can devise job-specific test instruments to assure that candidates for jobs requiring specific knowledge and technical skills possess those attributes. Professional and technical management positions, however, require more than knowledge: To effectively manage a group or function with a role to play in overall organizational activity, managers must have such qualities as the ability to plan, coordinate, motivate, negotiate, improvise, budget, and communicate—or some ineffable blend of these and other qualities that adds up to "leadership ability."

In virtually every field of endeavor, the human qualities needed to lead organizations defy easy measurement. Historians debate whether "the times make the man" or vice versa. In professional sports, it is axiomatic that "great players make lousy managers" (in part, because they haven't the patience to help and lead less talented athletes). In science, discoveries may be made by solitary geniuses, but organizational efforts, such as the U.S. space program, are led by talented bureaucrats, such as Wernher Von Braun (who insisted that he was the only top scientist in the space program who was *not* a genius).

In organizations with a clear mission and purpose, the task of assessing the potential of future leaders is simplified by the definition of job requisites that match organizational goals. One company may need managers who can cut costs; another will need marketing people; others will require greater technical expertise of one kind or another. The overall strategic goals of the company may indicate different kinds of needs for different department heads—an innovator in research and an accountant in purchasing, for example.

Thus, the factors that make up an ideal leader, or the top level of managers who will shape the organization's future, are anything but generic. Appraisal of potential for these positions must be based on organizational conditions and needs as outlined by the strategic planning process: What kind of leadership do we need to meet our strategic objectives?

Still, the conviction persists that there must be some general guidelines or techniques available to help identify the managers of today with potential to become tomorrow's leaders. Leadership is far too important to leave to chance, individual ambition, or the vagaries of personnel shifts and changing priorities in the executive suite. What kinds of distinctions are worth making among potential leaders, beyond the skills and experience levels dictated by strategic plans?

Research on the predictive ability of various means of identifying leadership potential indicates that no specific approach has been consistently valid—at least for upper-echelon managers. Korman and others have found, for example, that:

- Intelligence is a fair predictor of first-line supervisory performance, but no conclusive evidence relates intelligence test scores to success in higher-level positions.
- Objective personality inventories, including tests of leadership qualities, have shown little predictive validity.
- Personal data analyses, from biographical reviews to work references, are adequate for midlevel managers, less so for upper-management jobs.
- Prediction methods based on aggregate techniques that include judgmental approaches, such as peer rankings and assessment centers, are generally superior to single psychometric or performance measurements, but no evidence supports a widespread correlation applicable to all leadership positions.[2]

While it is possible that any of these or other techniques *might* be effective in predicting future leaders, it is far more likely that the system for appraising potential that "works" in a given organization will be based on organization-specific strategic plans. In addition, however, there are two highly useful "perspectives" that should be considered in developing leadership potential criteria and a system for appraising candidates for upper-management positions: The first is "process" evaluation, the analysis of *how* the manager has achieved past performance; the second is, appropriately, the strategic planning perspective, a way of looking at management potential as a function of the individual's ability to understand, appreciate, and implement the requirements of the overall strategic plan.

Appraising Managerial Process as Well as Performance

The process by which a manager achieves performance levels can be a far stronger indicator of top management potential than the performance levels themselves. In certain situations—and especially for a certain style of manager—the "how" of results is more predictive of future leadership ability than the results themselves.

The observation of managerial process is often disdained as a "soft" approach to appraisal—in assessments of both performance and potential—by results-oriented managers who insist on a measurable, bottom-line approach. Others may turn to results as the only valid criterion out of frustration and despair, having found no infallible psychometric test of future leadership ability and management success.

An appraisal system that focuses only or primarily on results can cause more problems than it solves, especially in the upper ranks of management, where behavior "at the top" sets a style emulated by subordinates. A managerial process that "gets things done" but is in actuality harmful to the organization—if rewarded by favorable appraisals and consequent increases in status and salary—becomes the model of executive behavior in the firm, multiplying its harmful effects.

It is quite possible, for example, for a manager to achieve results in the manner of Attila the Hun, terrorizing others and perhaps destroying careers in order to achieve short-term results—a bottom line that looks good to pragmatic managers interested only in measurable accomplishments. Often, such a manager may be deliberately brought in as a "troubleshooter," to get a lackluster department moving or correct a situation that needs "straightening out."

When the organization rewards these results with another position, the same thing is likely to recur. But typically, our Attila's successor fails to achieve the same results. The successor inherits an organization that is probably demoralized, possibly missing some of its best people (those with the most promising job opportunities elsewhere), and certainly behind on any long-range or developmental projects that do not contribute to short-term results. The results-oriented manager continues to move up, each time producing results that are both quick and measurable, and each time the successor fails.

Ironically, the failure of the successors only serves to strengthen the reputation of these tough, no-nonsense managers. When the same results are not forthcoming under the newcomer, another "Attila" may be sought; but in many cases, the damage has been done, and no amount of whip cracking will restore the balanced working conditions and concern for planning essential to productive work. In such cases, it is the organization that suffers, at least until managers are found who can rehabilitate morale, set appropriate goals, and manage the job in a way that puts organizational goals ahead of career ambition.

Results are critically important in the appraisal process, especially if they reflect the objectives of strategic plans. The reasons for results—or lack of results—may be even more critical, however. These reasons can be discerned only through empirical observation, a review of behavior from a perspective of understanding that "results aren't everything" and that overall organizational objectives condition the validity of results per se.

Leadership and the Strategic Perspective: A Pragmatic Approach

Because the critical needs or characteristics of leaders required in the company of the future are organization-specific, discernible only through analysis of strategic plans based on the realities of existing conditions and a view of the future, it is only pragmatic to say that leadership requires a capacity for strategic planning. If the leaders sought are to be conscious of their role—not unwitting pawns manipulated by offstage strategists—they must know why they are leaders. To be effective, they must be able to accomplish strategic aims and devote whatever talents and energies they possess to the leadership of the organization toward those aims.

If strategic planning were a simple process, or its goals fixed and readily understood, this requirement would be widely shared by most managers. The essence of the plan could be summarized on a page or two, and each prospective leader could memorize it.

To be effective, however, strategic planning must be a constantly changing process, flexible enough to meet changing needs, visionary in some ways and immediately practical in others, and inevitably, extremely complex. The requirements of strategic planning offer some highly suggestive "clues" to the development of a framework and methodology for appraising the potential of leaders needed to implement long-range organizational plans.

If there is such a thing as "the mind of the strategic planner," an ideal intellectual proclivity or mental outlook for planning ahead, it surely includes an ability to think about many different things at once and grasp the idea that many of these things are related somehow, in connections that can be understood and anticipated. Strategies to deal with the future must take into account a vast range of specific, variously related organizational, operational, environmental, and human resources factors. And the "effects" of strategies—specific human resources programs and activities—are themselves causes of change.

The complexity that human resources planning must deal with exists on several levels. First, there is the range of dissimilar factors to take into account, from corporate financial considerations to the market supply of specific skills. Next is "level of detail" complexity, which may include the need to understand production line variables, the time-cost curves of each operation using labor, or the determinants of turnover in a given department or age group. Finally, there is the inherent complexity of cause-effect planning, which requires an understanding of relationships and their degree of interdependence: If we change x, what happens to y (and therefore z, which is influenced by y), and how large are these changes and when will they occur?

Strategic planning also requires an ability to assimilate and at least generally understand a broad range of different kinds of information—from production specifications to the probable impact of age distribution on markets. Whether the planner is primarily an accountant, a computer scientist, a marketing expert, an architect, or a generalist with no specific disciplinary qualifications, the ability to grasp the basics of all areas that relate to organizational activity and plans is essential. With few exceptions—notably, those rare individuals who seem to manage by inspiration—effective leaders have this same capacity.

Analogical Reasoning. One kind of measurable intelligence characteristic that might suggest leadership potential—given the complexity and multidisciplinary nature of the organization or a major department—is analogical reasoning. This consists of "the extraction of a relationship in one realm," such as economics, and the mental creation of a "closely equivalent" relationship in another realm as well as the ability to see differences.[3]

Most effective managers of complex organizations have neither the time nor the capacity to understand all aspects of operations. But a usable understanding of any area is possible through analogy: Laws of physics are frequently invoked to understand economics, for example. The strategic planner—as well as the manager of a complex company—needs such analogies to grasp relationships that may be obscured by technical jargon, specialized terminology, and the realities behind the language of each discipline or function.

Time-Span Capacity. Another characteristic shared by both effective strategic planners and most leaders is the ability to work and think in abstractions over time. The greater the period of time that can be clearly envisioned as "the present," the longer a person will be able to execute planning-directed work and make necessary revisions in the overall plan—based on both present conditions and a changing view of the future.

This is of course a clearly valuable trait in a strategic planner and was also put forth decades ago by an English psychologist concerned with measuring managers' actual responsibilities and their potential for positions of greater responsibility. Elliott Jaques, who developed his views during 25 years of study at a top manufacturing firm, provides some provocative insights in his work *A General Theory of Bureaucracy*.[4]

In most hierarchical organizations, according to Jaques, "levels of bureaucratic organization" require time-span levels ranging from several months to ten years. By time span, Jaques means the planning horizon of the immediate job as well as the individual manager's ability to conceive tasks that take that long and execute them successfully over the period. At the lower levels of management, these times are relatively short, lengthening all the way to the CEO's office.

Further, Jaques postulated that individuals *inherently* possess different capacities to work effectively within these time spans. The further ahead a person is able to formulate goals, plan to reach them, execute the plan, and make necessary changes in plans—the greater the person's ability to manage at higher levels, depicted graphically in Figure 8-5.

One highly provocative, but potentially useful, finding of Jaques's time-span analysis is that this particular kind of ability to work and deal in abstractions is usually related to age and experience: Work capacity, he found, has a regular and predictable pattern of growth among individuals, which correlates directly with chronological maturation. Even though the critical capacity is "inherent," time and experience expand a person's time-span ability, as illustrated in Figure 8-6.

Jaques identified seven strata (see Figure 8-5) to differentiate between the levels of abstraction coincident with ability to work and plan in different time

Figure 8-5. **The relationship between time-span levels and leadership potential.**

	Stratum	Time-span	Level of Abstraction	Equitable Payment (1975)	Maximum No. of Employees (labour intensive)	Types of Unit			Normal Location of Work Facilities	Nature of Group
						Industry & Commerce	Military	Civil Service		
ABSTRACT Indirect or General Command	VII		?			Corporation	Army	Perm. Sec.	World-wide	?
		20 yrs		£70 000	150 000					
	VI		Institution creating			Group	Corps	Deputy Sec.	In several nations	?
		10 yrs		£35 000	20 000					
	V		Intuitive Theory			Full D.-M.	Division	Under Sec.	Spread over one nation	?
		5 yrs		£18 000	2500					
	IV		Conceptual Modeling			Medium-sized Business	Brigade	Asst. Sec.	Regional	?
		2 yrs		£8000	350					
CONCRETE Direct Command	III		Imaginal Scanning			One-man Business or Unit	Battalion	Princ'l	50 000 sq. ft.	Mutual recognition
		1 yr		£4800	50					
	II		Imaginal Concrete			Section	Company Platoon	Asst. Princ'l	5000 sq. ft.	Mutual knowledge
		3 mths		£3000	1					
	I		Perceptual-Motor Concrete			Supervisors & Shop & Office-floor	NCOs & ORs	Clerical & Office Supervisors	Supervising up to 500 sq. ft.: Shop & Office Floor up to 150 sq. ft.	Face-to-face

Source: Elliott Jaques. <u>A General Theory of Bureaucracy</u>
(London: Heinemann, 1976), p. 153.

spans, from 3 months to over 20 years. At the lowest level, 3 months—a level of abstraction he names "perceptual-motor concrete"—the individual is suited for shop-floor supervisory positions. At the top, "institution creating" individuals can run a multinational corporation employing thousands.

Obviously, the two "key perspectives" in designing a technique or system for appraising potential are closely related, or can be. Analysis of the "process" by which managers achieve results is perhaps the only valid way of determining whether their behavior, policies, and priorities are "strategic," guided by the long-range requirements of the organization.

Managers who set production goals, allocate resources, and make decisions on a range of issues from time off to raw materials acquisition do not perform all of these tasks in isolation from one another. A common thread, or several, conditions each act or each decision not to act. An appraisal system that effectively evaluates management potential for greater responsibilities should be able to (1) determine what these "guiding principles" in the manager's work are—whether they are results alone, the (possibly multifaceted) needs of the strategic

Figure 8-6. **Maturation of work capacity over time.**

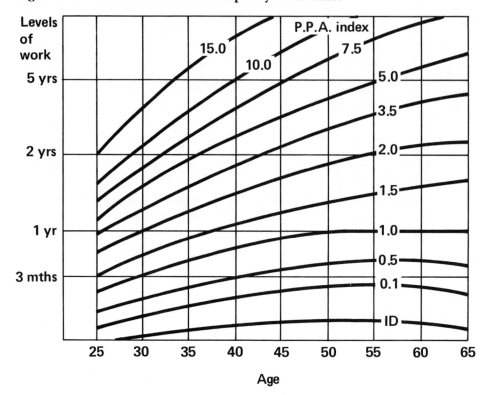

Source: Elliott Jaques, A General Theory of Bureaucracy (London: Heinemann, 1976), p.164.

Note: The growth of a person's work capacity will follow the capacity growth curve that intersects his or her work capacity represented in time span at any particular age.

or long-range plan, or simply personal ambition; and (2) observe and evaluate the process of accomplishing goals and results.

If a manager is unable to think and work strategically, considering many aspects and their relationships over a relatively long planning cycle, the system for appraising potential should be able to identify this weakness—which may or may not be "inherent" but is almost certainly a hindrance to strategic leadership.

The Role of Appraising Potential in Career Development

One way to look at the management development process is to view it as a continuum of four kinds of activity, focusing separately on positions, people, programs, and progress:

- *Positions.* Management development must first identify the key management positions in the organization that require succession planning, development, and a process for assuring continuity. Each of these jobs, whether they number two or three at the top or hundreds across many departments and locations, must be clearly defined as to its requirements—now and to accomplish the goals of strategic plans.
- *People.* Managers and people who might become managers must be evaluated, through appraisals of performance and potential, using criteria relevant to the requirements of management positions.
- *Programs.* Career development programs—training, education, leadership experience, and other management development background programs—must be created on the basis of organizational needs, so that individual career plans can be devised to prepare people for positions at higher management levels.
- *Progress.* Feedback mechanisms to assess progress, both of individuals along career paths and of the overall management development system in providing the quality and quantity of managers needed in key posts, furnish the data needed to adjust or correct the development process—by offering new programs, changing criteria for appraising performance or potential, revising succession plans, or reclassifying key positions.

Central to this process, and traditionally more controversial than any other aspect of management development, is the evaluation of people. Evaluation's purpose is selection, and selection requires comparisons. To compare people in terms of their past accomplishments is hard enough; to compare people for positions they may hold in the future—where job requirements may be quite different from what they have experienced in the past or present—requires a philosophic approach. There are no perfect predictors of future performance, no infallible guidelines for appraising potential, and no known yardsticks that guarantee success in picking one manager over another for a higher position.

Instead, there are many different indicators of management potential: The most effective method or set of methods used by the organization will usually reflect needs identified by strategic and operational planning.

The candidate's performance in career development programs is one valid measure of potential, in most cases, and the outcome of the appraisal will often indicate a need for a particular program to improve a manager's readiness for a higher job.

Appraisals of potential in the aggregate, from an organizational point of view, may suggest the need for new career development courses or programs—such as job rotation or leadership seminars. At times, if the needs of the organization for future managers are greatly different from the "available" cadre of potential managers, the appraisal process may trigger major changes in recruitment policies, career planning practices, performance appraisal methods, or succession planning. As a general rule, more people have potential than ever realize their potential. But if a valid, strategically sound, organization-specific, job-related appraisal system turns up fewer high-potential candidates than there are critical positions of leadership, a serious personnel problem exists in the firm. If nothing else, an effective system for appraising potential will show the existence of this problem, the first step in its correction.

Succession Planning for Operational Needs

The primary task of succession planning is to plan the sequence of personnel moves so that candidates for key positions are known in advance of actual need. This prior identification permits development to improve a manager's "readiness" to succeed to specific positions and provides concrete decision-making information needed to minimize the chance of poor choices or the adverse impacts of unplanned vacancies that can disrupt the continuity of management.

An effective succession planning system is both an extension of career planning and a system based on a somewhat different perspective than career planning. The perspective here is "what's best for the organization," in such terms as management continuity, ability to survive lost leadership, capabilities of managers in new markets or new environments, and other priorities that arise from organizational needs and goals.

The goals of succession planning can be simply stated:

- To identify the critical positions in management
- To identify coming vacancies in those positions or when and to what job their incumbents will move
- To identify the managers who would fit into these vacancies

In most large organizations, the accomplishment of these goals requires a systematic or mechanistic approach. Even if there are only a dozen or so jobs identified as "critical," a change in one of those jobs could have repercussions far down the organizational hierarchy or in a distant department. More important, a systematic approach to gathering and maintaining needed data on succession charts assures uniformity of basic criteria for the development of candidate lists. Where these data are extensive, succession planning systems benefit from the efficiency of computerized systems.

A mechanistic approach that assures initial objectivity and consistency with overall strategic policies lays the groundwork for the exercise of management intuition and other "nonmechanistic" selection methods by the managers who will actually be making the choices of successors at the highest executive levels. We recognize the reality that top jobs are rarely filled "automatically," no matter how effective the succession planning system. In these cases, however, it is the systematic succession planning program that permits decision makers to say "all other things are equal" regarding two or more candidates—so that some unmeasurable quality or currently required talent determines the final choice.

Whether done formally and elaborately or informally and subjectively, however, the results of an initial succession evaluation of this sort should not be "carved in stone." Basic managerial competencies change with experience, maturity, and external events—including the taking on of new responsibilities—and a succession planning system should stay abreast of these changes.

Basic Requirements and Typical Shortcomings of Succession Planning

In general, the extent to which an organization has developed a successful and ultimately useful succession planning system can be determined by asking questions such as these:

- Does the system incorporate the policies and goals of other human resources programs—such as career planning—as well as overall strategic planning goals?
- Does it show qualified replacements to fill key management positions across the organization?
- Are gaps in management succession identified immediately?
- Is the system connected to management development in some way?
- Does it permit analysis and implementation of corporate policies such as the promotion of women and minorities?
- Does it show whether or not talent is being fully utilized—which jobs are "dead ends" and where there may be logjams or overqualified managers?
- Does the system identify managers by sufficient criteria, from appraisals of performance and potential through specific skills experience?

In most organizations, the answers to the majority of these questions are only partially positive. For example, lines of succession may be clearly drawn in profit centers, but not in other essential departments. Or top management may "know" who is in line for positions of increased responsibility, but no one has prepared succession charts to formalize planning and anticipate the possible impacts of unexpected change. In other companies, the answers to these questions are largely positive, but only for the short term: The system will be fine if business needs do not change and as long as present managers largely remain in place.

For a succession planning system to achieve all or most of its true goals, certain key elements must usually be incorporated in its design. Some of these key elements will be more important to some organizations than others—depending on company size, technological requirements, turnover rates, new business needs such as diversification, and other company-specific requirements—but each should be considered in the design of the system.

The key elements of a system that will effectively identify and track future management requirements and ensure the availability of managers for vital positions include these imperatives:

1. Future staffing needs must be completely delineated on the basis of operational plans—by units, projects or division, and so on—and projected changes.
2. Operational management criteria must be developed for positions determined to be critical. This is usually achieved through job analysis and may result in the creation of detailed specifications for each job.
3. Management profiles of present managers must exist in some accessible form. These profiles include all relevant data, uniformly measured, in such areas as appraisals of performance and potential, experience and skills, education, salary history, and personal career goals.
4. A formal methodology for identifying, nominating, and selecting successors to key positions needs to be in place. Often, executive committees make final decisions, after the human resources planning function has developed a system that produces succession charts, candidate lists, and other decision-support data.
5. The system must be able to communicate succession plans to managers from the CEO to potential successors at the lowest-level critical job. New data and changes need to be promptly incorporated, continuing attention must be paid to the development/training needs of prospective successors, and all managers should know "where they stand" with respect to possible promotion.

The complexity of the system designed to currently identify candidates for each position depends on the needs of the organization and the succession policies developed to meet those needs. In some strictly hierarchical companies, for example, a move at the top may have a simple, easily tracked "domino effect" down the chain of command. In other firms, career paths may be both horizontal and vertical. Specialized, highly technical departments may need specifically qualified managers, while consumer marketing managers can have more generalized talents. Where the candidates come from in the organization to form the "bench" for specific positions is largely determined by the structure of career paths, described in the section on "Career Management" below.

In most large organizations, the ramifications of change in a key position are potentially enormous and difficult to assess in advance. Managers have specific skills needed for a given job, but they are not necessarily all in the same department or location; transfers and relocations occur in several directions; and degrees of "multidisciplinary" abilities exist and must be evaluated: Do we need a person who is a product manager first and a sales rep second, or vice versa? The complexities of large organizations with diversified operations usually require the development of a mechanized or automated succession planning system, as discussed below.

An Automated Succession Planning System

The use of a mechanized information system as the tool to implement a succession planning system—specifically, a succession planning module in the human resource information system (see Chapter 3)—has these critical advantages:

- *Comprehensiveness.* The data base can be quickly and completely reviewed for possible candidates for succession to each key position, omitting no one, based on specific criteria or qualifications.
- *Currency.* Because changes are made automatically, and related changes are made at the same time, automated systems do not become stale or out-of-date. This automatic updating is especially important in large organizations where the promotion of one manager will have extensive "ripple" effects on successor lists at various levels and in numerous departments.
- *Completeness.* Because so much data can be stored in the data base, related tables, and reference files, automated systems permit a level of detail and range of qualifying information not feasible with manual systems. These data can include ratings and appraisals, experience in skills, training data, educational background, and other employee profile information, as well as employee preferences generated by the career planning system.
- *Responsiveness.* When decision makers need information on which to base a selection, candidate lists and the characteristics of candidates can be promptly provided. In addition, changes can be "tested" for their impacts on other positions in the organization, without waiting for extensive analysis of replacement charts or other manually maintained planning tools.
- *Integration with strategic planning.* By making it possible to economically analyze, manipulate, and correlate different kinds of data about individuals and positions, an automated succession planning system makes feasible the integration of succession planning with strategic planning—a critical feature of succession planning. Without the ability to project future needs in key positions, based on changes wrought by the strategic plan, succession planning methods are little more than record-keeping systems for perpetuating the status quo.

Figure 8-7 shows one configuration of a mechanized succession planning module. A candidate list is compiled matching position requirements with candidates gleaned from the human resources data base. Future organizational needs are also specified and the HRIS data base searched for these candidates.

In this system, succession reports are produced automatically, on an annual basis or more frequently, for use by managers in analyzing succession and making decisions. In an automated system, these reports can take the form of "turnaround" documents, such as that shown in Figure 8-8.

If, for example, the decision is made to promote J. K. Small to another position, the supervisor or management review committee simply marks the turnaround document appropriately—a penciled arrow moving Colby across the form shown in Figure 8-8 will do. The turnaround document is then sent to the information center, where the change is made and a new chart is pro-

Figure 8-7. **HRIS succession planning data flow.**

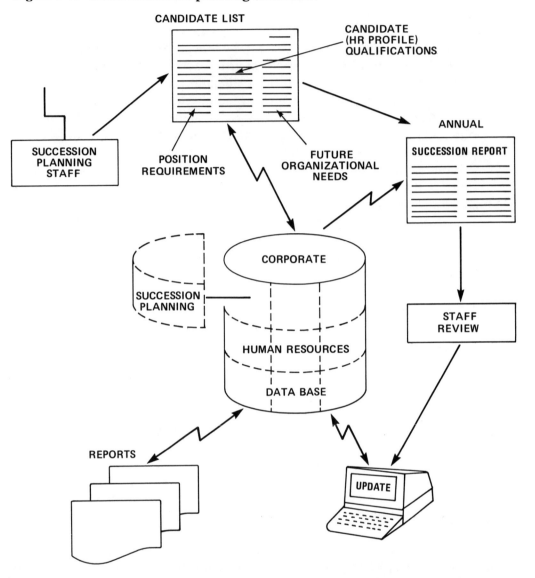

duced. This updated version can be reviewed by managers, approved, and returned to the information center for entry into the succession planning system.

The change entered in the automated system can affect a broad range of other reports, such as open position control, vacancy listings, new assignment postings, or others covering a wide array of possible management information needs.

In addition to the benefits of automatic updating of related reports, the mechanized system often carries with it several "built-in" aids to accuracy and compliance with standard procedures. For example, the system can be designed

Figure 8-8. Management succession chart.

INCUMBENT				REPLACEMENT CANDIDATES				
NAME POSITION DEPARTMENT EMPLOYEE NO. POS. CODE, SSN	P E R	P O T	NOTES	REPL RANK	NAME PRESENT POSITION DEPARTMENT EMPLOYEE NO. POS.CODE, SSN	P E R	P O T	APPROX. WHEN READY
SMALL, J. K. SUPERVISING ENGINEER QUALITY ASSURANCE ENGINEERING 761-002 15BX 095363000	B	A H		1	COLBY, S. T. PRINCIPAL ENGINEER QUALITY ASSURANCE ENGINEERING 441-276 14AL 085244058	B	B	4/87
				2	COHEN, V. A. PRINCIPAL ENGINEER QUALITY ASSURANCE ENGINEERING 441-292 14AL 467704107	B	B	10/87
				3	YOUNG, R. B. ASSISTANT CHIEF-VENDOR QA REP VENDOR QUALITY ASSURANCE 850-405 14IP 154508353	B	B	6/89

so that a "warning message" appears on the report if some predetermined protocol or rule is being violated by the change. It may be, for example, that a person is in line for promotion into a job that carries a lesser salary (not uncommon in organizations plagued by wage-compression problems), a situation managers will want to know about, if not avoid.

At a minimum, the automated succession planning system should provide timely and accurate answers to questions such as these:

- Does the succession require external recruitment efforts, or is there sufficient "bench depth" for this position?
- Are potential successors available in sufficient numbers and qualifications for critical positions?
- Who are the people qualified to move up? Are they the same people for many different positions?
- What gaps are likely to occur in succession charts—because of retirement patterns, for instance—and how soon?
- What kinds of training and development programs may be needed because of a weak succession chart for a specific position?

Used to its full potential as a strategic planning tool, however, an automated succession planning system also makes feasible the analysis of "what-if" situations, such as the staffing of new departments, restructuring along new lines of responsibility, or ventures into new products or services.

Response to Unscheduled Vacancies. Whether the succession planning system is automated or not, no amount of careful planning can take into account all of the possible events and developments—from plane crashes to new business bonanzas—that can create unexpected vacancies for which no successors have been planned.

Automated systems, however, are particularly well suited to *responding* to such crises through some form of contingency replacement cycle procedure. Such procedures require the expeditious search of management ranks for specific qualifications, states of readiness, and possibly a lengthy list of criteria—including individual preferences and goals—and only the power of a computerized system working on a comprehensively detailed data base is likely to provide the information about potential successors as quickly as managers need it.

Integrating Succession Planning with Strategic Planning

The goal of the management readiness and succession program is ultimately strategic: Where will the top executives of the future come from in the company, and who will be their replacements in critical positions? Such an evaluation requires a view of long-range needs for top managers, executives who may differ markedly in qualifications and characteristics from today's managers. The company may be in an industry being deregulated, for example, or entering new markets. Workplace technology may be changing the needs of entire departments, administrative functions, or production processes.

Typically, however, the succession planning process focuses on the status quo: What are the critical management positions in the company, and who in the firm is available to step into those positions? This is a necessary focus as a starting point for the integration of succession planning with strategic planning, but it should be borne in mind that the systematic succession planning procedures required to identify successors must ultimately be geared to strategic plans. The procedures may well provide a list of "the cream of the crop" according to track records and all other measurable criteria, but if these managers are unsuited to the task of leading a different organization in a different environment, time and effort have been wasted.

As an extension of career planning and management, succession planning must also be closely integrated—following the same guidelines, priorities, and strategic goals—with the human resources management function. And because it relies heavily on criteria established by appraisals of performance and potential, it is also logically related to these personnel functions. In the system we propose, human resources programs affecting the availability of people and skills are inextricably related to one another, gaining synergistic impacts on common goals and objectives—rather than working at cross-purposes or without regard to priorities and programs being pursued by other functions in the human resources department.

The "tie that binds" in this case is the strategic human resources plan, the long-range view of what the quantity and quality of human resources should be to meet organizational needs and how much "variance" exists between present personnel availability and the demands of the future. The means of bridging this variance, or strategies, are the product of integrated management effort. No other approach is possible, given the systematically inclusive nature of the integrated model.

Thus, the succession planning function does not usually act independently in setting strategic policies or goals. But it does play a vital role in supplementing or "filling out" strategic plans and in elaborating on the specific strategies used by the organization to have the managers needed for the new markets, new technologies, changed environment, and different management characteristics that will make the firm successful in the years ahead.

For example, it may be that the company is in an industry undergoing fundamental business change, such as the banking industry, where deregulation and technology are having swift and far-reaching impacts. The qualities that made "good managers" in banking ten years ago are far less important in the newly emerging competitive environment. Banks are offering different kinds of financial services, and both markets and the technology for serving markets are in the midst of a revolution. In banks with fully developed succession planning systems, these changes and the new strategies they have prompted are being planned for: New criteria are being added to employee profiles, new skills and experience codes are being used, and traditional lines of succession are being reevaluated for their relevance to the changing business organization.

As is discussed in greater detail in Part IV, the integration of succession planning and other human resources activities with "the demand side" of the business—demand created by both strategic planning and operational requirements—is, or shoud be, the guiding principle of human resources planning.

Career Management: Basic Concepts and Integration

Career management's purpose is to merge the career plans and goals of individuals with the objectives of the organization, through procedures and policies that help individuals identify and act upon the congruence of individual aspirations and corporate needs. Its overall aims—most important, the development of managers to meet the needs of the organization in the years ahead—are dictated by selfishly organization-specific requirements. To realize its aims, however, career management requires the active, committed involvement of the individuals whose careers are being "managed."

A first requirement of an effective career management and planning system, in our view, is complete honesty. Too often, the fact that the organization has its own reasons for career planning suggests to human resources people that these reasons should be kept secret from career-minded employees. The implication is that "if they knew where we're headed, they wouldn't want to come."

In fact, few things could be more harmful to an organization's future managerial excellence than a career planning approach that grooms the wrong people for the wrong jobs, or the right people for jobs that may not exist, or not enough people for critical positions in the years ahead. In the most fundamental sense, all excellent managers "select themselves" for career progression, through more diligent effort, the acquisition of needed skills and education, and whatever other activities are perceived as requisite to organizational approval and promotion.

A career planning and development program based on known organizational objectives, openly communicated to all employees, with systematic procedures designed to maintain and enhance employee involvement in the process, is not only "fair" to all employees; it is also eminently practical. Employee commitment and involvement in the planning system is essential—as well as inevitable, among the career-minded—but the question remains: Commitment to what?

In the integrated career management system shown in Figure 8-9, techniques and procedures are used to provide employees with the clearest possible view of the organization's future and their possible careers in that future. Such a system has the following main objectives, goals that should guide the design of any career planning system:

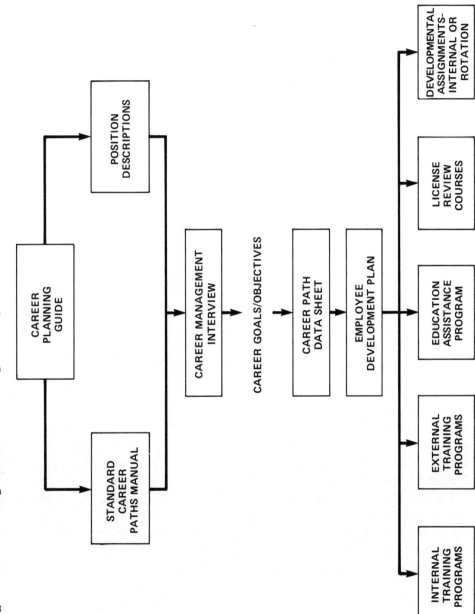

Figure 8-9. An integrated career management system.

- *Concurrence of employee-organization goals and needs,* based on the realities of organizational requirements and the employees' self-assessment in light of those requirements
- *Identification and tracking of development needs,* so that individuals are clearly informed, appropriately guided, and prepared for future positions, and the organization can shape and monitor the effectiveness of development
- *Enhanced employee involvement,* as fully informed employees select career paths based on position requirements and the overall strategic human resources plan, consult regularly about possible changes, and are periodically and systematically reminded of progress
- *Uniform procedures,* openly explained and applicable to all participants in career planning, providing data needed by the organization to monitor and improve the effectiveness of career management
- *Availability forecasting,* based on the individual and aggregate plans of managers, the capabilities of the developmental activities, and the requirements of positions in the years ahead

Basic Design Concepts of Effective Career Planning Systems

Before proceeding to a discussion of the recommended mechanisms and outputs of an integrated career planning system (see Chapter 9), a review of the basic concepts that apply to the design and effective use of any career planning approach is in order. These basic concepts are career pathing, self-assessment, and career counseling; the definition of these concepts fundamentally shapes the nature and effectiveness of the career management process.

Not only should the developers and managers of the career management and planning system have a clear understanding of these underlying concepts. All employees in the organization who are or will be participants in career planning should have the same understanding, requiring an internal employee communications effort characterized by openness, honesty, and repetition. There are many ways to misunderstand the goals and purposes of a career management system—as many as there are different employees with subjective perspectives, individual hopes and fears, and private agendas for the years ahead.

For example, many organizations do not include lower-level managers in career management, and others include only some midlevel managers. Companies have been known to omit entire departments from career planning, such as the data systems organization, where it may be felt that the work performed is "too specialized" to help prepare managers for positions of responsibility managing "what we really do in this company—make and sell widgets." Other organizations do not permit managers to participate in career planning until they have been with the company for five or more years.

These "left-out" members of the organization may make up a substantial share of managers and may even include most of the people for whom the organization will be doing career planning several years later (or when someone realizes that the costly turnover in the data systems organization is the result of dead-end jobs). What kinds of myths, misunderstandings, and discouraging impressions of the career planning system do these employees carry around with them?

Most damaging to the organization, many "future" participants in the career planning system will develop the view that they are simply not considered important to the organization: They have no future here, unless they "get lucky" or happen to be in the right place at the right time. Unfortunately, some of the most talented and capable people in the firm are also the most career-minded—especially among the new wave of female managers seeking long-term vocations—and these are precisely the managers who will be most affronted by their omission from career planning and most likely to become turnover statistics. The importance of clearly defined and communicated concepts of career management becomes even more evident in situations where nonparticipants turn to supervisors for information about the program and receive inaccurate, unclear, or divergent perspectives on the aims of the system. If the participants in career management do not understand its objectives—what it will do as well as what it will not do—career planning is unlikely to succeed.

For example, the concept of the career path should be understood as a highly flexible, dynamic idea, not an immutable career straitjacket. In some organizations, to shift metaphors, managers may see themselves on a tightrope as they proceed along their career path: All is lost if they do not advance along the prescribed course, and a slip is fatal.

A more flexible approach to the design of career paths is shown in Figure 8-10. This is one of many possible "sets" of paths in a major organization. Others are still more elaborate, full of an even greater number of possibilities.

Most of the myths and misunderstandings about career management—such as that it "guarantees" jobs, perpetuates past promotional practices, or is designed with only the managerial elite in mind—can be dispelled by open, widely disseminated information about the basic concepts involved in the process and the reasons for having a system.

Not all organizations, at all times in their history, will have the same reasons for career management, of course. Some will be guided by the need to develop more technically oriented managers, for example, while others may be seeking ways to thin the ranks of midlevel managers seeking promotions in the years ahead. Strategic plans must guide the specific purposes of the system, which would change as plans change.

In all cases, however, the basic concepts that should be widely understood and subscribed to by employees remain important: What is meant by career pathing, self-assessment, and counseling, and what role will these activities play in creating my future with the organization?

Career Pathing. Career management implies that positions of greater responsibility in the organization require certain kinds of experience and acquire skills or education and that these requisites can be identified and "made to happen" through the joint effort of individuals and the organization. Conceptually, these experiences and qualifications form a "path" to the higher position,

Figure 8-10. **Career path options.**

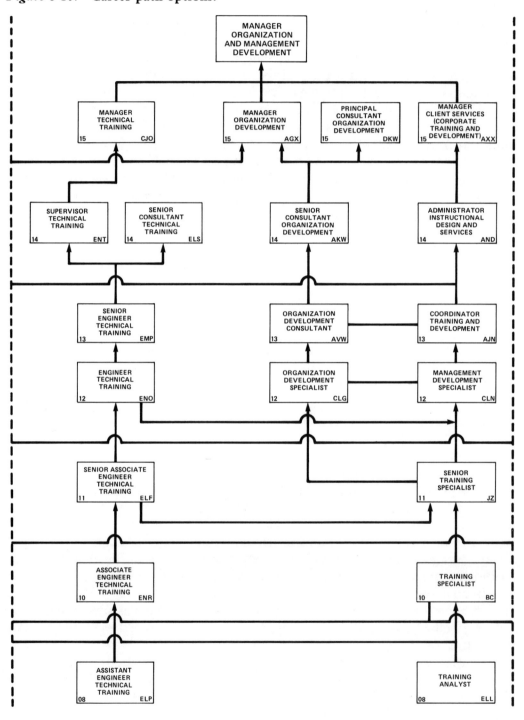

marked out by specific job incumbencies and developmental activities such as training and education.

There may be many paths to the top, or to any ultimate position the individual aspires to. The purpose of defining a single path, and second choices or alternative paths, is not to enforce a rigid structure of career progression on each employee. Instead, the reason for career pathing is identical to the reason for career management: to help bring individual goals into congruence with organizational goals. Employees are shown where the jobs are in the present and future organization and what they must do to get there. The individual employee makes the "choice" of which path to follow, but it is always a choice informed by organizational opportunities and constrained by organizational needs for each position.

A second reason for career pathing—closely related to the goal of marrying individual and organizational goals—is strictly organizational: Career path data can be used to forecast the future availability of managers in the organization and show which developmental efforts are needed to assure required availability in the future. The management of a career pathing program may necessitate efforts to redirect individual ambitions, add or subtract development activities, change the career path requirements of jobs, or intervene with any of the other tools available to human resources managers—from recruitment to early retirement programs. The career path data—showing where people expect to go, how soon, and how they plan to get there—provide a view of future availability that can be matched with the strategic plan, and appropriate action can follow. The forecasting implications of career paths are explored further in Chapter 9.

The development of realistic career paths requires, in the first place, valid job content analysis. Frequently, this analysis leads to the development of job families, groups of jobs with similar work requirements. Thus, a career path may lead through any one of several (or several dozen) specific jobs at a certain level, each capable of providing the individual with the requisite abilities to handle the next job up the path.

Not all steps in a career path need be upward, of course. Any number of lateral moves may be necessary to prepare a manager for a move to a position of greater responsibility.

Once the career paths have been realistically developed—based on actual job content and the requirements of incumbency—the focus of attention shifts to the employee, who must select a path that meets his or her professional needs and aspirations. It should go without saying, however, that career paths must be regularly reviewed and updated, as job requirements change, organizational priorities shift, and surpluses or shortages are forecast as the result of strategic plans.

Self-Assessment. If career paths are realistic and based on organizational needs, accurate self-assessment will permit individuals to select a career path that merges their interests with those of the organization. "I fit here," the employee says in effect, and if this turns out to be true, the career management system will be successful.

The self-knowledge required to accurately predict one's satisfaction or effectiveness in the future is not easily come by, but this knowledge need not be absolute. General tendencies and interests—such as career anchors—can shape the major outlines of a career path.

Often, self-assessment for purposes of career planning is seen as including the totality of life. It has been suggested, for example, that it should take the form of statements about individual egos, affiliations, family, and beliefs, as well as views regarding the role of work in life.[5] Others feel that self-awareness can come only in the context of the job, through trial and error in the organization.[6]

In practice, we have found that the most effective self-assessment techniques are those that take into account all individual interests, tendencies, and capacities that relate to organizational requirements. In some companies, this may mean behavioral analysis; in others, an emphasis on technical knowledge; and in some, creativity.

One important part of the self-assessment process is that it should explicitly say to the individual that the organization wants him or her to be satisfied, interested, and "happy," as well as good in the work. If this much is accomplished, the employee grasps the most important truth about career planning: Self-interest is, or can be, the same as organizational interest.

Finally, no self-assessment should be carved in stone. No matter how honest or accurate an individual may be at the age of 26, interests and goals may shift markedly in a few years. More often, actual experience in jobs can alter or sharpen perceptions of the kind of work that satisfies individual needs, and the career planning system should incorporate regular review mechanisms that permit managers to revise their career paths for personal reasons—as well as to take advantage of changing corporate priorities.

Career Counseling. Inevitably, there emerge "gaps" between individual choices for career paths and organizational needs. The organization may find that too many people want to progress along the same career paths—causing traffic congestion, if allowed. Entire departments may project as understaffed. Certain "plum" locations—in San Francisco or Paris—may be oversubscribed. Or an individual may simply be wrong about the results of self-assessment or have misunderstood its purpose.

The initial career counseling activity is the supervisor-employee interview. This occurs well after employees have had sufficient time to examine and select from career paths and is primarily concerned with negotiation, adjustments, or redirections that may be needed to close any gaps between organizational and individual needs and aspirations. Later on, career counseling becomes more concerned with developmental activities—what the individual needs to do to continue on his or her career path.

The negotiation phase of career counseling is a form of "reality testing" of individual career path choices. This is usually necessary to assure that:

- Job descriptions, and the requirements of specific positions on the path selected, are clearly understood by the employee

- The career path currently meets organizational needs
- Self-assessment has been generally accurate
- The organization, through the supervisor, has an opportunity to influence career path choices in ways that satisfy the demands of strategically determined human resources objectives

The supervisors or other management representatives who conduct these negotiations with individuals should be well prepared in advance and should be skillful in leading interviewees—where necessary—to new career path choices. Knowledge of the requirements of positions, at least insofar as the path is within one department, is essential. Also, the interviewer must be familiar with the qualifications, work characteristics, and capabilities of each interviewee—through either documentation or empirical evidence.

For example, if an employee expresses an interest in a sales career, ending as a marketing vice-president, and the supervisor knows the person to be completely unsuited to work involving personal relationships, the supervisor might find a way to make a technical or other type of career path more attractive. More often, the needs of the organization require a shift in a career path (if any shift is necessary), but this is as much an opportunity as it is a problem.

The opportunity is this: At the very point that an employee is made to realize that he or she can select a career path that is valued by the organization—leading through experience and development to a place where the employee is "needed"—the marriage of individual-organizational goals has taken place. In some cases, of course, the differences between what an employee wants and what the organization needs may be irreconcilable. This interview is as good a time as any to find that out, and the employee and organization should be able to part company amicably, respecting each other's honesty.

Beyond the negotiation interview, career counseling is critical to permit changes in either the employee's or the employer's priorities. Often, as noted earlier, especially in the early part of a career, jobs turn out to be something other than expected, or performance indicates the need for a change in course. Regular supervisor-employee interviews should continually provide a means of updating career paths.

A final, and in some ways most important, purpose of career counseling is its link with career development activities. Supervisors or other interviewers can work with the employee in ascertaining the career development programs needed at the present stage of the career path, help set schedules for training and other courses, make suggestions where appropriate, and encourage the employee when necessary. The counselor can assure that the individual is completing development work on schedule and at the required levels of performance.

Obviously, the skills and knowledge required of interviewers in an effective career counseling system are considerable. A knowledge of organizational needs, the requirements of jobs, and the characteristics of development activities are just the foundation. In addition, the interviewer at the "negotiation" phase must know employees—perhaps better than employees know themselves, at times.

To the extent possible, an interviewer's role should be passive, allowing the employee to fully express personal needs and professional goals. If these match the organization's needs, the session can be short and easy. The negotiating skills of the interviewer come into play when employees must be made to revise their career plans to achieve a closer congruence with organizational goals. As suggested earlier, however, this can be a golden opportunity to explain the real purpose of career planning, the matching of career goals with long-range strategic business goals.

9

Forecasting Human Resources Availability and Attrition

A key premise of this book is that human resources planning can "close the gap" between the human resources in today's organization and future demands dictated by strategic and operational planning. Earlier sections in Part III—on career planning, appraisal of performance and potential, and succession planning—focus on human resources programs that close that gap. First, however, the gap needs to be identified and then defined in ways that point up the most effective means of reaching objectives.

In predicting future personnel needs—shortages, surpluses, and the specific skills and talents required, when, where, and in what number—the HR forecaster must consider all of the following kinds of factors:

- Today's human resources—the skills, abilities, costs, development needs, future plans, and other known characteristics of the people on hand
- Human resources flows—the movement of people in and out of the organization, transfers, and promotions
- Organizational HR objectives, as determined by strategic and operational planning, which may include different skills mixes, changing budgetary constraints, the impacts of technology, or merely the continuation of existing levels of productivity and growth in a constantly changing world

Because most of these factors change over time, and human resources change especially, traditional methods of "manpower planning" have never been universally satisfactory.

In the years since the early 1960s, the state of the art of human resources forecasting models has made rapid strides. The advent of human resource information system (HRIS) technology provided access to detailed planning data about the characteristics of employees ("stocks") and their movement into, within, and out of the organization ("flows"). Yet as pointed out by the results of a 1984 survey of 300 major companies, "While state-of-the-art techniques (e.g., flow models) are easily available . . . there is very little indication that businesses are availing themselves of these tools."[1]

Typically, the textbook methods for forecasting human resources availability, including highly sophisticated statistics-based techniques developed by academics and consultants in recent years, are not adopted by organizations for one or more of the following reasons:

- They are *incomprehensible* to most managers and human resources planners responsible for the design and operation of forecasting methods.
- Most models are *incompatible* with forecasting tools used to project future demand for human resources created by strategic and operational plans and are often irrelevant to specific human resources needs, organizational characteristics, and time frames required for integrated planning.
- They are *inflexible* as personnel planning tools in many cases, providing inadequate or nonexistent opportunities for human resources planners to adjust the variables that influence forecasts, to change human resources availability (in reality or on paper, in "what-if" planning) through personnel program interventions.

Mathematical models arrived in the world of human resources planning—with a vengeance, some would say—in the 1960s in the United States, coincident with the arrival of computerized information systems capable of collecting the enormous amounts of data these models use and permitting fast calculation of their internal equations.

A model is a simulation of reality, a scaled-down version of the overall situation or problem. It contains "working parts" corresponding to all of the factors that influence outcomes in the real world, connected by mathematical equations that represent the relationships between these parts in the real world. Thus, if a factor is changed or constrained in a certain way in the model, the other parts of the model will move or be affected in ways that correspond to what would happen if such a change were made in the real world. How well the model's actions correspond with actuality, of course, depends on how well the model is constructed: whether relationships have been accurately represented by equations, for example.

One benefit of a model in forecasting is that it permits "what-if" analysis "on paper," a sort of trial-and-error method that avoids the real-world consequences of error. And the use of analytical models, which simulate the actions of the organization and its human resources, can clarify causes and effects. Modeling permits managers to examine aspects of personnel movement that cannot be observed directly. Models may be strictly descriptive, showing actual historical and current data, relationships, and movement; or they may be "normative," incorporating goals and objectives—the numbers and qualities of human resources needed at future times in various places in the firm.

Walker has classified four basic types of models that have been used in human resources planning, from simple to integrated, each with successively greater scope, level of technical complexity, and applications versatility.[2] Others use classifications such as the above descriptive-normative distinction, or identify some models as "strict-flow" (Markov or renewal models, which show the flow of personnel from one period to the next) and some as aggregate programming models, organizational design models, or input-output models.

Apparently, the science and art of human resources forecasting has reached unprecedented levels of sophistication in the 1980s, with every other issue of many planning journals reporting a new way to account for change in forecasting models using longer and more subtle equations, employing multiple regressions, and encompassing a greater array of possible variables.

Most forecasting models available today (see section on "Other Human Resources Forecasting Techniques") require that the planner either understand advanced statistical techniques or employ the services of a statistical expert. More important, the human resources planner may not fully understand the factors that can change future availability or be in a position to effect change through program intervention.

In the balance of this chapter, we will examine the network flow method, the most effective model, in our view, for forecasting human resources needs in an integrated HR strategic planning system. We will then turn our attention to other forecasting techniques—both simple and statistical—and assess their potential utility from the human resources planner's perspective. And finally, since the organization's human resources are not fixed in place, the process of estimating attrition, or the continuing loss of personnel over time, will be considered as a key element in forecasting the future availability of human resources.

The Network Flow Method of Forecasting Based on Career Planning

In human resources forecasting, the goal is not merely to take two snapshots—one of today's organizational situation and another of the future—and compare them for surpluses and shortages. Such a comparison tells us nothing about the best way to "get from here to there," so that the skills and talents needed in the future have been acquired at the least cost.

In the recommended system, shown partially in Figure 9-1, human resources forecasting concerns itself first and foremost with the internal availability of people—an availability shaped by HR development programs.

In the overall model of the integrated HR planning system, as depicted in Chapter 1 (Figure 1-1), career management is the third critical step—after appraisals of performance and potential—in the human resources planning and development process. A fundamental change in the process occurs with this step: Planning moves from the "evaluation mode" of appraisals, which seek to assess the capabilities of individuals now and in the future, to a "developmental mode," the goals of which are to shape the human resources needed by the

Figure 9-1. **The human resources availability forecasting function within the integrated human resources planning system.**

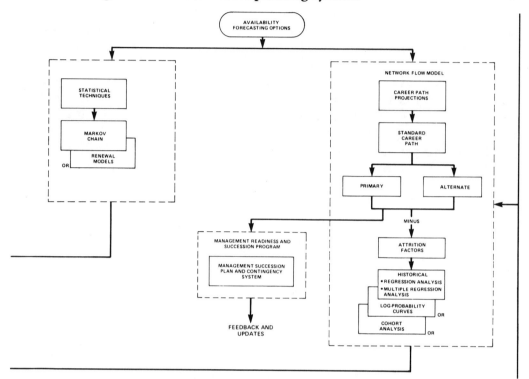

organization in the years ahead. The thrust of career management is to provide a systematic, active set of procedures and devices that will enable the organization to merge individual and organizational goals and objectives and, further, provide the means of reaching these objectives.

The HRIS Advantage: More Information and Involvement

The advent of human resource information system technology has paved the way for the development of career planning information systems that permit an economically viable solution to some traditional problems of career planning. Two examples follow.

Insufficient personnel data hamper the organization's career planning managers, who may have a better inventory of their furniture than they do of their people. A critical need of career planning—as well as of succession planning and virtually all management selection programs—is sufficient information about individual qualifications, accomplishments, experiences, compensation history, personal interests, professional credentials, and both vocational and avocational interests and pursuits.

Inadequate organizational information about the future and continuing needs of the firm is fatal to career planners—who can only guess at career paths, timetables, and organizational priorities in the future—and is fundamentally discouraging to individuals seeking to project themselves into the organization's future. Without specific information on opportunities ahead, the requirements of particular positions, and detailed progress reports and revisions based on actual career events, employees will soon lose confidence in career planning's credibility or in the company's good faith in even creating a program.

Data systems, and specifically the development of the skills inventory or human resources inventory (HRI), furnish the tools needed to solve these problems at an economically justifiable cost. Moreover, the procedure used in most organizations with an HRI to put this information in the data base requires employee involvement, a key characteristic of effective career planning.

The HRI and Career Management

The foundation of the HRI data base is a collection of individually prepared forms or profiles, each completed by the employee. Supervisors may check and verify certain information, and in some cases, a panel may confirm specialized data, but the basic data in the HRI profile originate with the best source of information about the individual—the individual himself or herself.

Typically, the HRI information entered by the employee consists of work experience or skills codes, product or market experience, educational and training courses completed or underway, language skills, licenses and certifications, and some indicators of career preferences, relocation limitations, and outside interests. In addition, supervisors or managers may include ratings of performance and potential, or codes that can extract data from interfaced appraisal systems. In the integrated system, the employee profile carries career path information as well and the development requirements—the courses and other developmental activities needed for future positions on the career paths— projected for the individual.

The HRI document listing all of this information is usually—and most effectively—a turnaround document; that is, a form filled out by the employee, submitted to the human resources information center for processing, and "turned around" as a printed report to the employee for verification and periodic updating.

The sections of the HRI that most directly bear on career management, career paths, and developmental activities are discussed in greater detail in the sections that follow. The overall procedures for creating HRI data, however, have a bearing on the efficiency of a systematic career planning approach. These procedures incorporate the key characteristics of self-description, self-nomination, and openness, while using the power of today's computer technology to permit the inclusion of voluminous amounts of personal and professional data that could not readily be collected, stored, and retrieved without a mechanized system.

The use of a turnaround document to gather information for the HRI and make periodic changes is a procedure ideally suited to the employee-involvement and personal decision-making needs of an effective career planning approach. The process by which the employee fills out the HRI, at least initially, is not easy, but if managers are presented with adequate instructional material—and know that their careers will be affected by what is in their HRI—the problems can be manageable.

The first time an employee completes an HRI form, its requirements may seem daunting. He or she is asked to enter codes for different kinds of work experience or "skills," for example, which may require reference to a list of codes many pages in length. In addition, there is a code list for schools, as well as for internal training courses, languages, certificates, and other categories of information. Later on, in another iteration of the turnaround process, the employee will be asked to enter codes for career paths and the development plan.

The effort required on the part of the employee is not necessarily a hindrance to the process. Rather, it can help involve the employee in assuring that his or her profile information is accurate, up-to-date, and useful to the organization. More important, the employee knows that this document will be used by the organization to create his or her future, and if the system is well designed, the employee will be motivated by the conviction that the HRI "works."

Career Paths as Forecasts

An effective career planning system can also provide the basis for a uniquely "proactive" availability forecasting approach, one that solves some of the practical problems associated with implementation of statistical models and also provides human resources planners with the ability to make interventions that will change forecasts.

To illustrate, persons in a certain salary bracket, in certain jobs, and in a given age group (cohort) are likely to retire at a particular rate, move laterally at another rate, be promoted at another rate, and so on. In a descriptive model, the forecast shows what will happen to groups of people (human resources stocks) over time because of past movement expressed as probabilities. (Optimization models, discussed later in the chapter, start with the desired outcome and work backward but are based on the same mathematical representations).

What can the human resources planner do to change the outcome of a statistically modeled forecast if the most important variables turn out to be beyond his or her control? For example, it may be that the statistical model shows age to be the most important determinant of promotion: People don't get moved into certain levels before they turn 40. There may be good reason for this, but it is not immediately apparent to the planner. Moreover, there is little the planner can do, in a realistic time frame, about people's ages.

Using a network flow approach based on career paths, however, the planner works with career path variables that are largely within the control of the organization. In a typical "what-if" exercise, for example, the planner can quickly see what would happen to human resources availability for a given job if a required training course were speeded up or even eliminated.

A network flow model is simply a collection of "elements" connected by "links" representing relationships. In a career path–based network flow model, the elements are typically job positions, although they might be salary levels, skill codes, management levels, job families, or other employee classifications. The elements are linked, as they are in career paths, by the requirements of progress along career paths over time. Thus, the links represent training courses, development experiences, time in certain jobs that must be completed before progression to the next job, and so on.

For any individual—and for aggregates based on any number of classifications such as a job function code—the computerized career path information can produce actual head-count availability at any time in the planning cycle. Employee John B. Smith will be "available" as a code 123 manager on a given date in the future, and so will X number of others, minus expected attrition. For this simplified forecasting system to work, however, career planning must be fully integrated with overall business and strategic planning.

How the Network Flow Model Works

In actual operation, the network flow model of forecasting human resources availability is based on individual career path projections developed in a highly sophisticated career management system. The use of regularly updated, comprehensive information about position requirements, organizational needs, and "variances," or the gaps projected between supply and demand for people with different capabilities or job titles, helps participants select career paths on the basis of actual company needs in the years ahead.

Ideally, the selection of career paths begins with an intensive self-assessment program that helps identify individual goals and capabilities and proceeds through the provision of information about the requirements of different kinds of jobs, the roles of different kinds of work in organizational strategic plans, and counseling with supervisors who are expected to be knowledgeable and up-to-date about career path realities in the organization.

Actual career paths are selected from among the possibilities. As can be seen from the example that was shown in Figure 8-10, standard paths typically include a range of possible moves from any position—laterally across departments, in some cases—but each possible path represents actual positions, experience needed for a successive position, and the relationships between positions in the organization.

Here, the network flow model "elements" are the job positions in career paths, identified by position codes and salary brackets. In other variations, these elements might be skill groups, management levels, or any other category that suits the planning needs of the company.

In the network flow model, these job position elements are interconnected by links representing movement between positions and indicating the amount of time (minimum to maximum) required to move from one position to another. For example, a link might represent a training course needed to qualify for a certain job, a course with a known duration. At any given time, an employee with this link on his or her career path will have the duration of this course included in estimates of when he or she will be available for positions that occur beyond the training course on the career path.

Thus, the network flow model based on career paths is a reflection of what has happened and will happen in the company, assuming career paths have been accurately designed on the basis of actual organizational needs and individual capabilities and goals. Forecasts show the numbers of actual people who will be available at each "element," or job position, in the future, at any time in the planning cycle. In a computerized system, hundreds or even thousands of different elements and linkage characteristics can be accounted for.

Moreover, as indicated in the depiction of the network flow model on the right-hand side of Figure 9-1, this approach permits planners to produce the results of "what-if" analysis based on any number of "alternative" career paths created by changing the variables in the paths. For example, present policies and procedures may indicate that a particular employee must spend at least one year in a given position, attend a certain management development course for six months, and work in a certain discipline for a total of three years before moving into a higher job on the career path. If the integrated human resources planning system outlined in Figure 1-1 (Chapter 1) indicates that organizational demand for this employee in this higher position supersedes the importance of all or some of this preparation, an accelerated career path can be devised as an alternative, tested as a "what-if" scenario, and implemented or not according to its impacts on the overall organization.

Adding to its flexibility, the network flow model permits planners to include new positions and their costs in "what-if" analysis. Positions may be entered as elements even though the positions do not yet exist, appropriately linked to other positions, thereby providing planners with the impacts of the new positions on existing human resources, future availability, and costs.

The network flow model based on career planning data thus describes the reality of past and continuing force movement but is also an "optimization" model, which permits the testing of alternative policies—different career paths or changes in the elements and linkages of career paths—to reach desired goals. Although unwieldy for short-term forecasting, such models—adjusted for attrition—combine a commonsense approach to existing force movement with a capacity to intervene in the factors that will create human resources availability in the years ahead.

Other Human Resources Forecasting Techniques

In addition to the network flow model described above, there are many other techniques for human resources planning and forecasting, including Markov and renewal models. No one type of forecasting technique is necessarily superior to others, and often the model used is a combination of several types, designed to meet specific organizational needs or constraints.

Wheelwright and Makridakis list six major factors associated with forecasting techniques, each of which might be a "selection criterion" in choosing the most appropriate model:

- Time horizon
- Pattern of data
- Type of model
- Cost
- Accuracy
- Ease of application[3]

The time horizon should coincide as nearly as possible with the overall planning time frame, although shorter-range forecasts may be necessary in certain departments, to meet priority objectives, or simply because insufficient data exist to make long-term projections. In general, long-range forecasts incorporate more qualitative factors. In addition, the model used for long-range forecasting should be capable of producing a number of different forecasts—for each of several points in time or planning periods.

The pattern of data identified by the model should reflect actual business operations and not be an artificial construct that has been "force fitted" into the model. Some series of historical data, for example, depict a seasonal as well as an overall trend pattern; others present only average values with random fluctuations. Because different forecasting methods vary in their ability to identify different patterns, it is important to assure that this concept has not been overlooked.

Types of models vary according to their underlying assumptions. In some, for example, time is the critical variable; others rely mainly on regression analysis, or the identification of exact correlations among variables. Related to the choice of model type—which, of course, influences costs and effort expended—is the issue of "importance." How badly the organization needs accurate forecasts, or how much it will matter to overall objectives if forecasts are inaccurate, is a factor in choosing a model type.

The expense involved in selecting a model includes not only development costs but the costs of data storage and operation, as well as opportunity costs of alternative forecasting methods. Today's statistical models virtually require the use of computers, but the extent to which a forecasting system employs complex statistical models may vary.

Accuracy requirements often represent an area of trade-off with costs. Usually, accuracy requires a greater level of detail as well as a greater level of administrative effort to assure that data are current and valid, both of which cost money. In some organizations, an accuracy level of plus or minus 10 percent may be sufficient in order to meet needs, while in others—or for certain critical human resources—any inaccuracy that is greater than 5 percent could be disastrous.

Other important considerations that derive from organizational needs include the availability and timeliness of data. All of these matters must be examined in light of budgetary constraints and judged as to the importance to the organization of different levels or degrees of perfection.

Ease of application is another important criterion for choosing a statistical model, but it should be borne in mind that managers themselves need not understand the mathematics of the models in detail. Since managers will be held responsible for decisions based on forecasts, however, most will want to understand their basic assumptions, how variables are believed to be related, and what possibilities exist for manipulating the models in such activities as "what-if" planning.

The Role of Organizational Objectives

While the statistical factors that make one forecasting model different from another need not be completely clear to managers responsible for planning, no one else is—or should be—in a better position to analyze and express the organizational requirements that the model is expected to satisfy.

For example, our integrated planning system focuses primary attention on the internal availability of human resources. At this stage of its application, to identify the nature and extent of the gap between existing and needed human resources, the planner requires a forecasting model that shows what happens because of existing personnel development programs and practices, applied to known human resources or to those who might be introduced at entry levels in the near future. The network flow method described earlier in the chapter, which is based on career path data, responds to this need.

This is not the only objective of a forecasting approach, of course. In some organizations, demand factors—such as the personnel requirements of a totally new line of business—must be the focus of forecasts. Other organizations may have no career development program—just compensation, benefits, and a weekend softball team.

Thus, the critical question managers must answer before considering forecasting options is: What is being forecast? One aspect of this issue that relates to model types is whether or not the planner is trying to predict a continuance of a pattern already established or a turning point. In addition, some models more effectively allow for "optimization," the inclusion of goals and a working-backward process that points up least-cost alternatives for achieving those goals. (Optimization models are discussed later in this section.)

Most of the quantitative methods discussed below require vast amounts of historical and current data. In organizations with a comprehensive HRIS, this may not be an issue: A microprocessor downloaded with data from the personnel data base can supply the model with all that is needed. But some models may require more data elements than currently reside in the HRIS, and if all data must be collected and maintained "from scratch," the cost of the forecasting model may be prohibitive.

The following sections describe broad categories of human resources forecasting models, from simple forecasting techniques to more sophisticated statistical methods. As a rule, it may be wise for managers who are undertaking forecasting for the first time and to whom this is largely unfamiliar terrain to start by installing a relatively simple, generalized system and later upgrade to a more detailed, comprehensive, sophisticated system.

Simple Forecasting Methods: Qualitative and Quantitative

A forecasting technique does not need to be complex or statistically "elegant" in order to be effective and useful. In complex, rapidly changing, multivariate organizations where many factors can influence future human resources availability (and planners wish to test the impacts of changing variables), the method used is necessarily complex. But for organizations that are relatively stable or for short-term, subjective forecasting, simple forecasting tools that combine data and managerial judgment may be sufficient.

Examples of useful forecasting methods that have the virtue of simplicity include supervisor estimates, rules of thumb, replacement charts, and the Delphi technique. Any of these, or any combination of similarly simple methods, may be sufficient to the organization's human resources availability forecasting needs.

Supervisor estimates make use of the experience and intuition of persons closest to the actual jobs. Assuming supervisors have a clear understanding of operational needs, productivity, and "what it would take" to reach specified production goals, this knowledge can be the most reality-based data for short-term projections.

Rules of thumb are decision heuristics, intuitively known by supervisors and others or formally spelled out in job manuals, which posit certain basic relationships between human resources needs and levels of activity or production. For example, on a production line, when overtime costs rise above a certain level—say, $1,000 per week for four consecutive weeks—this may trigger the hiring of an additional worker.

At the management level, replacement charts are one form of simple, short-range forecasting. Replacement charts, showing who is ready to move into which positions as vacancies occur, can include data such as the incumbent's age, performance levels of all managers, promotability, and some indication of the degree of "readiness" of backup candidates. These data can be further supplemented by actuarial data, retirement trends, and other qualitative judgments about when and where vacancies may occur.

These simple approaches—supervisor estimates, rules, charts—can usefully incorporate both quantitative data and qualitative judgment, but each assumes that there is a status quo to human resources requirements and that this existing relationship will essentially prevail in the future. In some cases, these methods may be supplemented by a "forward-looking" Delphi technique, such as that described in Chapter 5. This method permits members of a Delphi panel to make estimates of future human resources needs, based on new products, technologies, shifting organizational objectives, and other elements of change. The experience and perceptions of individual supervisors and managers who make up the panel are incorporated with whatever firm data may be availabile—such as job requirement data furnished by professional associations or other industry standards—and the panel works its way to a consensus regarding human resources availability forecasts.

Statistical Models: General Classifications

The use of highly sophisticated statistical models of various kinds—often at the same time, in an integrated system—is not uncommon in major organizations seeking a clearer picture of force movement and its impacts on future human resources availability. The chief purpose of these models is to examine what has happened in the past in an effort to predict (and sometimes shape) the future. When used in "what-if" analysis, such models should be able to estimate the availability of future human resources on the bases of different variables—more compensation here, faster vesting there, a clearer path in one department, earlier retirement in another.

Availability forecasting models are frequently classified as being either "change models," which assess the impacts of past employment practices and attempt to project the availability of future human resources given certain assumptions about organizational change, or "optimization models," which introduce organizational goals—objectives of human resources costs, skills, tenure, or other desired attributes.

Change Models. Change models forecast future human resources flows and requirements by looking at what has happened in the organization up to the moment. The main statistical models used are probabilistic or stochastic: They assign probabilities—such as the likelihood that X number of engineers in a department will leave the company by a certain time—based on past conditions and events.

Markov models and renewal models are stochastic planning models based on what has happened to groups rather than individuals. They assume that the planner can forecast changes in staffing based on different classifications—or "states"—of groups of employees, such as all those in a given unit, at a certain salary, with so much tenure, in specific jobs, or in some other classification.

Markov models were originally developed for the U.S. Air Force in the early 1960s. The procedure is based on the calculation of "probabilities of transition" from one state to another, using historical records on employee attrition, promotion, and separation.[4]

As shown in Figure 9-2, there are at least five types of personnel movement in the organization: recruitment, promotion, transfer, demotion, and separation. In Markov modeling, data on the employees within each grouping selected for analysis permit this kind of calculation:

$$\text{Transition probability} = \frac{\text{Number who left position}}{\text{Total number in position}}$$

Figure 9-2. **Types of personnel moves.**

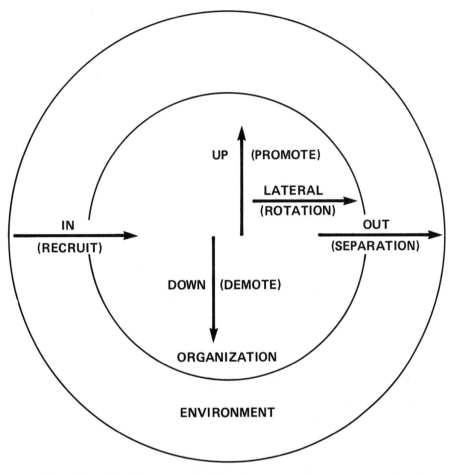

SOURCE: ANDREW O. MANZINI, "HUMAN RESOURCE PLANNING AND FORECASTING," IN *HUMAN RESOURCES MANAGEMENT AND DEVELOPMENT HANDBOOK*, ED. WILLIAM R. TRACEY, NEW YORK, AMACOM, (1985), p. 511.

Further analysis will reveal the probabilities for each type of personnel move. For example, suppose it was found that in the past, 60 percent of all employees in job 123 left that job for known reasons each year. Of that 60 percent, typically 55 percent were promoted, 15 percent were moved laterally, 15 percent initiated departure, 10 percent were terminated by the company, and 5 percent were demoted.

By multiplying the percentage of employees who leave job 123 by the probability of each type of personnel move, transition probabilities for each move can be calculated as follows:

Probability of promotion	=	.60 × .55 = 0.33
Probability of lateral move	=	.60 × .15 = 0.09
Probability of employee-initiated departure	=	.60 × .15 = 0.09
Probability of company-initiated departure	=	.60 × .10 = 0.06
Probability of demotion	=	.60 × .05 = 0.03
		Total = 0.60

Once transition probabilities have been determined, their effects on the distribution of employees in the organization can be projected into the future. These projections highlight areas of shortages or surpluses. By analyzing and manipulating appropriate policies on promotions, separations, recruitment, or other human resources activities, management can implement changes that will help achieve desired staffing levels.

For Markov models to be effective as forecasting tools, however, several conditions must apply:

- Types of employment moves must be known.
- Historical data on actual employees within positions must be known.
- The job groups or positions must be relatively homogeneous.
- Accurate data on force movement must be known.

Markov analysis assumes that personnel are "pushed" through the organization because of classifications (age, salary, job title, and so on) that have in the past led to certain kinds of movement. Renewal models, another probabilistic approach, assume that people are "pulled" through the organization because of vacancies. Replacement charts are a nonstatistical approach to the same concept: As people move up, certain patterns are formed by the vacancies created, and renewal models quantify the historic relationships between these patterns.

A commonly used statistical technique for forecasting human resources needs and availability—employed alone or in conjunction with change models—is regression analysis. Regression analysis measures the degree of correlation among variables—such as performance ratings and promotions—and assigns values to these correlations based on their occurrence in the past. Many planners have found, however, that staffing correlates often are "quantitative" in appearance only where job functions have not been precisely defined or where relationships are accidental or are consequences of unknown variables. Obviously, if the regression analysis process shows that the path to promotion invariably includes membership in a certain all-male, all-white private club, something is wrong with either the method or corporate promotion policies.

Of the two basic types of change models, Markov and renewal, renewal models are usually considered to be more susceptible to management intervention aimed at controlling force movement. Renewal models are, after all, based on progression patterns that have been established to fill vacancies. Through career planning interventions, management can assure that individuals in line for certain jobs have completed prescribed training and development programs, served in the right positions for the required lengths of time, or met other qualifications of succession planning.

Optimization Models: Goal-Oriented Analysis. Although often treated as another category of statistical models, optimization models that start with predetermined objectives (instead of starting with past experience) are a technically overlapping category of forecasting tools, often including Markov-type analysis and multiple regressions. Frequently, however, the additional technique of linear programming is applied in optimization models as well as a refinement of linear programming known as goal programming (discussed below).

Optimization models provide planners with an "ideal" or best solution to a given set of needs or constraints, such as the right combination of ingredients in a packaged cake mix—to achieve optimal color, taste, convenience in preparation, and cost. Applied to human resources, such models begin with ideal staffing patterns or goals for a future time—such as affirmative action plan goals and timetables for having specified proportions of protected-class employees in different jobs or at various levels in the organization. In other cases, the ideal might be the right mix of technical and marketing skills in a given department or a set of employment conditions or employees conducive to higher productivity or reduced turnover. Because they focus on a defined future, optimization models are clearly "planning" tools.

Linear programming is simply a mathematical technique for determining an "optimal" solution under a set of constraints or needs. It is a basic tool of operations research that assumes that all resources that are converted by operations have costs that are variable and constraints that can be stated as mathematical expressions. Where the relationships between variables are not linear, variations of the technique such as concave, convex, or quadratic programming are applied. In dynamic programming, another variation, optimization, is seen as a multistage goal: The optimal solution at each stage of a project or point in time is determined, based on overall constraints and goals.

As discussed in Chapter 6, on operational planning, linear programming and similar techniques treat human resources as essentially items of cost. The "optimization" sought is normally the lowest possible cost per unit, project, or level of services. To accomplish meaningful analysis, the variables expressed as inequalities must be related mathematically and may include a wide array of factors.

Goal Programming. Optimization models known as goal programming, a combination of linear and Markov techniques, were developed in the military to account for a range of possible constraints over many time periods. This approach can consider salary, budget data, and stipulated staffing floors and ceilings in each relevant period of the forecast horizon, for example, and can take into account such external constraints as labor pool availability—especially useful in EEO applications. The chief advantage of goal programming is its versatility: It can consider numerous different goals in a number of time frames, where goals cannot or should not be aggregated into a single objective.

Most of these models have been developed and applied in military or government settings. Reports of private-industry applications in human resources planning are relatively scanty in the literature, although Flast describes the use of goal programming for EEO,[5] and Patz demonstrates its use in a training situation.[6] For the most part, however, the state of knowledge about mathematical human resources modeling far outstrips its application.

Forecasting Attrition: Issues and Techniques

When human resources availability is viewed primarily as internal availability—the people now in the organization or entering training and development programs designed to create the human resources needed in the future—the issue of attrition, or turnover, assumes magnified importance. In order to forecast the availability of human resources at various levels, in different jobs, with different kinds of internally provided experience and development, the forecast must include some estimate of the kinds and numbers of people who will leave the organization in the planning time frame.

For forecasting purposes, in this phase of the application of the integrated system, the issues do not include "What can we do about turnover?" However, in order to analyze the most common form of attrition—voluntary separation— the forecasting process does require determinations about the causes of attrition, if only to develop different turnover-rate formulas for different "classes" of employees.

Employees leave the organization because of death or illness, retirement, dismissal, accidents, or mass layoffs, as well as voluntary separation. Over a long-term planning period, the majority of these nonquit departures can be accounted for and predicted with some accuracy—through actuarial tables, employment practices, retirement policies, and the known characteristics (such as average age) of employees. In most organizations, however, the leading cause of attrition is, as noted, voluntary separation, and the specific "determinants" of voluntary quitting are not always satisfactorily identifiable.

A partial listing of the factors, or determinants, of voluntary turnover would include, for example:

- *Compensation*, which generally means that turnover is highest in lowest-paying jobs but also means that employers paying less than comparable competitors will have higher quit rates
- *Age*, which numerous studies have found has a direct and linear relationship to quit rates
- *Tenure*, often closely related to age but enforcing its own influences on quit behavior, as employees in their early years make up the bulk of turnover and more experienced employees develop a "stake" in the organization, learn organization-specific skills, and establish personal roots
- *Educational attainment*, which, all else being equal, has been shown to have

a direct relationship to turnover, in part because graduates are under-employed but also because employment opportunities are greater for better-educated employees

- *Firm-specific training* or management development, which may mean that employees' skills are not "transferable" to other situations—at least not at the same compensation—hence reducing their rate of voluntary separation
- *Job opportunities*, a consideration that reflects the fact that a large share of voluntary separation is made up of people leaving for another job and that is evidenced both by relatively high turnover in periods of full employment and by high turnover for "in-demand" skills and qualifications
- *Pension policies*, which can have a positive or negative effect on turnover rates among vested employees
- *Size of the company*, shown to have an inverse relationship to turnover when otherwise comparable employers are matched
- *Employment conditions*, including union occupancy, real or perceived health and safety hazards, worktime arrangements, and other "hygiene" factors of jobs that can cause worker dissatisfaction

Some of these factors are clearly beyond the control of the organization—such as company size or union occupancy, of interest primarily to researchers seeking the causes of differences among organizations—and others are difficult to "model" usefully as a means of forecasting future attrition. Job opportunities, for example, depend not only on overall economic conditions and unemployment rates but on industry-specific demand, competitors' moves, local labor market conditions, and specialized demands for certain kinds of skills or educational qualifications.

Two types of attrition forecasting that take into account a number of the variables affecting voluntary turnover—and recognize the reality that different factors apply to different groups or types of employees—are log-probability curves and cohort analysis.

Log-Probability Curves

Employee turnover is strongly related to length of service. This one indicator, tenure, incorporates a number of the determinants known to have a relationship to turnover: age, obviously; wage rates, likely to be higher for longer-term employees; job-specific or firm-specific training and development; and beyond a certain time, pensions.

In general, a log-probability curve such as the one shown in Figure 9-3 can be constructed for human resources forecasting purposes.[7] Based on observed data, actual incidents of departure over time, the curve is both more simply developed and more readily understood than Markov modeling.

To ensure accuracy, however, a number of different curves for different

Figure 9-3. **Log-probability curve for attrition.**

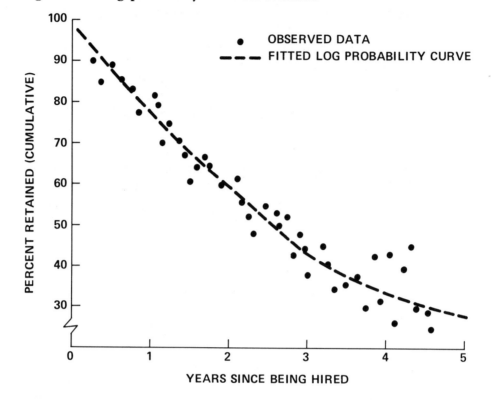

Source: United States Civil Service Commission (1977).

segments of the employee population should be constructed: one for each category of employee with discernibly different turnover rates. A curve that combines architects, for example (who seem to stay in place with great persistence), with computer systems analysts (who are the job gypsies of our time) provides meaningful forecasts about neither group.

Also, many organizations will have positions or departments with intrinsic turnover-causing characteristics—revolving-door jobs that could not be otherwise, such as seasonal work or manual labor. At the other extreme are managers and professionals in whom the firm has invested a great deal of time and money, whose turnover rates must be closely monitored and analyzed.

Finally, many organizations will find through turnover analysis that characteristics of individuals—such as age, sex, and education—play a role in turnover rates. Companies under court order to employ certain percentages of women in traditionally male jobs, for example, have experienced unprecedented turnover rates among women blue collar workers.

Although a number of different iterations may be required, log-probability curves based on tenure are essentially valid as predictors of future turnover.

Figure 9-4. Longevity data comparing employee- and company-initiated separations.

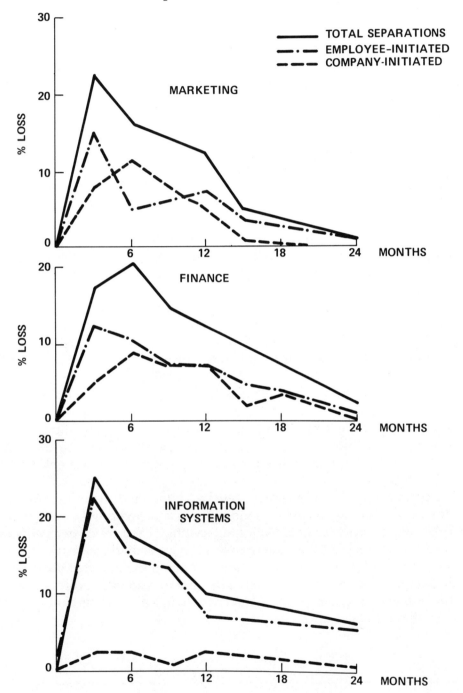

Numerous studies have found that a high percentage of quits occur in the first year or two of employment for all groups and that turnover declines rapidly when length of service exceeds five or ten years.

Cohort Analysis

Cohort analysis examines employees as groups, personnel "cohorts" hired at about the same time. In effect, the planner follows this group of employees throughout its employment, recording losses quarterly or monthly and plotting the data over time.

Commonly, the cohorts are broken up by departments or job functions, as shown in Figure 9-4. Here, a further distinction is made between employee-initiated quits and employer-initiated terminations, providing specific data on voluntary separations by departments over time.

The kind of detailed analysis shown in Figure 9-4 provides more than forecasting information, of course. For example, the first graph shows that after six months in the marketing training program, company-initiated separations increase markedly. A manager might ask: "Are the performance standards at six months too high? Or is this the critical weeding-out stage at which high standards are necessary?" Analysis of the job, compensation practices, and advancement and transfer opportunities—in conjunction with cohort analysis—may reveal critical causes of turnover and suggest remedial interventions. In addition, cohort analysis can examine similarly tenured employees by different individual characteristics, to help recruiters and career management professionals shape policies that will reduce unwanted turnover.

In selecting a technique for availability forecasting, human resources planners are today faced with an array of computer-bred statistical approaches that represent state-of-the-art modeling methodology but that have little relevance to existing human resources planning techniques, are difficult to understand, and provide limited opportunities for human resources department manipulation and control.

For organizations with a comprehensive, integrated planning system that includes a fully developed career planning program covering key employees, a network flow approach to availability forecasting based on career paths offers a commonsense, reality-based alternative to more esoteric statistical methods. Adjusted for attrition, such forecasts provide planning data that are more specifically accurate, can be readily grasped by human resources professionals, and lend themselves to planning exercises such as "what-if" analysis aimed at closing gaps at optimal costs.

PART IV

Integrating Strategic, Operational, and Human Resources Planning

When the overall human resources–based strategic planning system is fully operational, the integrated system makes possible the identification of "variance," or gaps between supply and demand of human resources of various types at different points in time, and provides management with the information needed to most effectively close those gaps using interventions consistent with organizational goals and constraints. Part IV begins with a chapter on the identification of variance and the types of interventions that may be necessary to close gaps. It concludes with a "system management" chapter on how to sell, develop, and implement the integrated system in your organization—followed by appendix material showing examples of project implementation instruments.

At the stage addressed in Chapter 10, the discussion assumes that most of the major parts of the overall planning system are in place, including strategic and operational planning processes that determine demand forecasts and the human resources planning and development programs that determine availability. Realistically, however, we realize that the implementation of a major, comprehensive planning system such as this cannot usually be accomplished overnight and that the "payoffs" to the organization cannot wait months or years until the complete system is in place as a fully integrated process.

Thus, in discussing each kind of human resources program in the previous chapters, we have attempted to present insights and effective techniques for the design and implementation of *any* appraisal, career management, succession planning, or forecasting approach—not just programs that "fit" the overall integrated system that is the subject of this book. Similarly, Chapter 10 is intended to provide useful guidelines that will improve forecasts, identification of surpluses and shortages, and methods of preventing the adverse effects of demand-supply gaps—whether the total planning system is in place or not.

Finally, Chapter 11 provides practical advice on how to gain and keep management support for the development of an integrated system and how to assure the involvement of operational managers and the commitment of your own human resources department in what may be a long, difficult period of development. This chapter closes with project development guidelines that have been helpful in our experience and is followed by an appendix of the types of forms and information-gathering instruments that may be useful in designing your own change effort.

Again, the ultimate goal of an integrated system is to link the demand requirements of strategic and operational planning with the availability of people produced by human resources programs. But while this systematic linkage in an integrated process is necessary to maximize the effectiveness of all facets of the planning effort, it is likely that more valid and effective "parts" can be created piecemeal when the overall goal of an integrated system guides development.

10

Identifying and Closing Supply-Demand Gaps

The variance identified by the strategic human resources planning system represents a shortage or surplus of people needed to do the work of the organization from now on, both in the short term and on the long-range planning horizon. Typically, the modern organization has not just one variance but a number of different supply-demand inequalities, by job skills, managerial needs, division or location, and at different points in time in the planning cycle. This chapter focuses on the identification of specific surpluses and shortages of skills, managers, and other identifiably discrete human resources (see Figure 10-1) and on practical methods of closing such gaps, through personnel policies and management interventions that are consistent with strategic business plans and human resources management goals.

Identifying and Reporting Supply-Demand Gaps

Variance estimates are necessary throughout the planning process. To test the viability of different strategies for future organizational direction, for example, preliminary estimates of the demand created by such strategies (and operational needs) must be compared with human resources availability, as created by human resources programs and planning. If the preliminary evaluation shows a variance that cannot feasibly be closed, the strategy creating this variance must be discarded.

The forecasting goals of an integrated strategic planning system are tripartite: to develop demand forecasts based on actual operational needs and strategic plans; to create availability forecasts based on existing human resources, development program outputs, and attrition estimates; and to develop human resources variance forecasts, a comparison of demand and availability forecasts.

The kind of comprehensive data collection and analysis needed for this forecasting effort in most large organizations will require the use of computerized information systems, as discussed in Chapter 3. The need to keep data current

Figure 10-1. **Identification of human resources variance.**

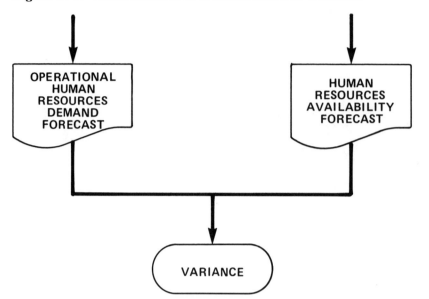

through regular updating, the ability to model "what-if" alternatives among related variables to see the effects of proposed change, and the need for what may be a broad range of different forecasts—breakouts by department, job skill, activity level, project mix, and other ways of isolating planning data—virtually necessitate the use of a mechanized system to maintain and report forecast data.

A hypothetical case study illustrating the application of the planning principles discussed earlier in this book—and using a microcomputer-based software system to process and integrate data in formats that produce forecasts of demand, availability, and variance—is provided in Appendix VII. There, the integrated system furnishes planning data needed for a growing organization with rising levels of human resources demand.

In all cases, however—regardless of whether human resources demand is growing, shrinking, or simply changing because of strategic and operational plans—the integration of the organization's three main planning systems is essential to the production of valid, comprehensive human resources forecasts. For example, the integrated system permits forecasts including:

- A clear picture of overall organizational demand and availability, with both summary and detailed reports based on existing needs, human resources, and planned expectations
- Forecasts by department, management level, job skill or function, location, or other category or qualification identified in the personnel data base
- Forecasts by level of activity—units of production, service levels, number of projects—and types of activity

- Time-dependent forecasts, relating planned changes in activity levels, force movement, and variable change in human resources availability and demand (among different departments, skills, or other categories) to different points in time in the future, according to strategic plans

Depending on the kinds of data collected and maintained in the system—which in turn depends on organizational needs and objectives—the mechanized forecast capabilities available to managers permit current analysis and decision-support information aimed at providing the answers to these kinds of questions:

- What job categories or management positions will become critical areas of surplus or shortage in the future? When and to what extent?
- What will be the characteristics of these variances, or gaps between demand and availability at different levels of activity—if more projects of certain types are undertaken, for example, or if production plans are revised?
- What training and development needs are identified as a result of the forecast?
- What turnover is expected in various departments, locations, or employee categories, and when is it likely to occur?
- To what extent can changes in programs affecting internal availability—career planning and development, revised succession planning, different criteria for appraisals, and so on—be expected to reconcile variances, and to what extent must gaps be closed by other alternatives, including hiring or reductions in force?

In many cases, of course, absolute precision in forecasting variance is not possible. While the goal of the system may be decision-support data that tell management, "We need to hire 47 new programmers to work in these six departments within 36 months," such precision is recognized as a target rather than an absolute condition of survival. Normally, the kind of human resources management interventions discussed later in this chapter—such as overtime scheduling or accelerated career succession—can make up for small differences in forecast supply and demand. (On the other hand, if your organization is an airline with 20 new planes scheduled for delivery, you know you will need at least 20 new crews to put the expanded fleet in the air.)

Typically, however, the analysis of variance points out to top management and human resources planners existing or potential surpluses and shortages far enough in advance to permit planning that will minimize the need for the most costly interventions. Where the variance is substantial, any or all driving factors in the demand-availability organizational picture may require revision: Strategic plans may have to be changed or modified; operational requirements may have to be changed (such as by the introduction of new technology); and human resources development programs affecting availability may need modification or complete overhaul. In the integrated system we proposed, these changes can be analyzed and tested for their impacts on one another and for their effects on the long-term forecast of human resources variance.

Variance Forecast Examples

Demand and availability forecasts are developed through separate procedures and projected independently in the integrated system. A summary program collects data from each and presents variance as the difference between demand and availability—by type of work, by department, at various times, and by other defined categories. Obviously, definitions of categories must be consistent throughout the system (to preclude the possibility of comparing apples and oranges), a function of data base administration in a mechanized human resource information system.

For example, the use of a position skill code is common. The code might combine salary bracket and job descriptions: 12CA, for example, might represent salary bracket 12 and the job title of claims adjuster. (The increased capacity of today's information system technology, including relatively inexpensive microcomputer-based systems, means that most computer codes can be represented in numbers and alphabetic characters that closely resemble existing scales and nomenclature.)[1]

The same position skill code—or code for department, location, job family, or other category used in planning—must of course be employed in both demand and availability forecasts, to assure the comparability of results. Other classifications of employees commonly used include:

- *Employee levels,* a one- or two-digit code that tells whether the employee is management or nonmanagement, level of management, or any one of a number of classifications such as executive, manager, supervisor, scientist, engineer, design, other professional, administrator, or clerical
- *Job family codes,* providing greater detail than employee levels but summarizing position skill codes in categories related by job descriptions or qualifications
- *Administrative codes,* which may be used to identify certain kinds of employees or types of skills for particular attention or specialized subsystems, such as affirmative action plans or technical training

Options available for presenting variance forecasts depend on organizational needs and the nature of work in the organization. One set of options is shown in Figure 10-2. Table 10-1 presents a section of one type of variance report, this one for the total organization by employee class. This summary is an aggregate of detailed demand and availability forecasts in all departments and includes new-hire estimates.

Variance Reports and Hire Forecasts

The processes of developing demand forecasts and availability forecasts in a growing organization, such as the hypothetical company used as a case history

Figure 10-2. **Variance forecast options: types of reports.**

Skills forecast by department

Job family forecast by department

Subtotal forecast by department

Project forecast by skill

Project forecast by department

Career path forecast

---

example in Appendix VII, results in a combined forecast that specifically indicates the number of people who will have to be hired by the firm to close variances and avoid human resources shortages. (Conversely, the variance may represent surpluses, and the forecast would be based on reductions in force or attrition rather than new hires.)

Forecasts of new hires that will close the gaps created by demand in excess of availability, such as the forecast in Table 10-2, show the exact number of new people who will have to be brought into the organization at different times in the future to meet planning needs. Other ways of presenting these data include forecasts by department, job family, skill level, management level, or specific project.

Forecasts such as these provide measures of the organization's ability to meet its future human resources needs. As indicated earlier, some forecasts may be firmly anchored in actual work underway or scheduled, and some may be projections based on one or more alternative strategies for the future.

In any case, the systematic consolidation of organization-specific data about human resources variance should provide virtually at-a-glance answers to such questions as:

- Do we have too many designers?
- Do we have too few quality control supervisors?
- Can we accomplish planned work with existing human resources?

In addition, the integrated system permits planners to assess the impacts of change as depicted by the human resources development systems. For example, the scheduled dates for succession planning present one picture of chang-

Table 10-1. Human resources forecast demand, availability, and variance by all companies, all departments, employee class code.

12/27/85   13:18:54
Report No. 1

	12/84 12/84	01/85 01/85	02/85 02/85	03/85 03/85	04/85 04/85	05/85 07/85	08/85 10/85	11/85 01/86	02/86 04/86	05/86 01/87	02/87 01/88	02/88 01/89	02/88 01/89	01/89 12/89	01/90 12/90
Co. all Dept. all Admin 99 000 Total												Dept. no. all companies all departments			
Demand	6,783.0	7,298.3	7,243.5	7,341.8	7,379.5	7,265.7	6,884.5	7,035.5	6,427.5	5,485.1	5,164.8	4,539.4	4,539.4	4,228.4	2,963.1
New hires	2.0	2.0	2.0	2.0	2.0	2.0	2.0	2.0	2.0	2.0	2.0	2.0	2.0	2.0	2.0
Planned avail.	7,814.3	7,770.5	7,705.7	7,603.4	7,539.0	7,465.8	7,262.3	7,077.7	6,914.6	6,737.4	6,290.3	5,774.1	5,774.1	5,402.1	5,022.4
Variance	1,031.3	472.2	402.2	261.8	159.5	200.1	377.8	42.2	487.1	1,252.3	1,125.5	1,234.7	1,234.7	1,173.7	2,059.3
Co. all Dept. all Admin 99 001 Executive												Dept. no. all companies all departments			
Demand	32.0	29.9	30.3	29.8	30.0	33.9	29.2	29.1	28.9	26.9	27.5	26.6	26.6	26.5	23.6
New hires															
Planned avail.	39.0	40.0	40.0	41.0	41.0	41.0	41.0	41.0	48.8	49.6	62.5	70.9	70.9	81.6	92.1
Variance	7.0	10.1	9.7	11.2	11.0	7.1	11.8	11.9	19.9	22.7	35.0	44.3	44.3	55.1	68.5
Co. all Dept. all Admin 99 002 Management												Dept. no. all companies all departments			
Demand	195.0	312.1	316.8	311.9	340.1	217.9	261.4	264.6	341.1	236.5	155.2	145.5	145.5	139.5	91.7
New hires															
Planned avail.	259.0	266.6	268.8	268.8	271.0	272.9	278.9	283.4	296.4	297.1	317.9	352.8	352.8	367.4	395.4
Variance	64.0	45.5-	48.0-	43.1-	69.1-	55.0	17.5	18.8	44.7-	60.6	162.7	207.3	207.3	227.9	303.7
Co. all Dept. all Admin 99 003 Scientific												Dept. no. all companies all departments			
Demand	54.0	170.6	175.0	172.3	200.2	122.2	134.3	127.7	234.6	135.9	56.6	52.5	52.5	50.8	31.2
New hires															
Planned avail.	86.0	82.8	63.0	61.4	57.8	57.3	51.5	46.2	43.9	43.1	38.8	31.6	31.6	27.8	21.5
Variance	12.0	107.8-	112.0-	110.9-	142.4-	64.9-	82.8-	81.5-	190.7-	92.8-	17.8-	20.9-	20.9-	23.0-	9.7-
Co. all Dept. all Admin 99 004 Engineering												Dept. no. all companies all departments			
Demand	1,953.0	2,206.0	2,221.3	2,239.4	2,278.7	2,066.9	2,149.1	2,214.1	1,838.9	1,548.5	1,414.6	1,148.0	1,148.0	1,097.2	583.1
New hires	2.0	2.0	2.0	2.0	2.0	2.0	2.0	2.0	2.0	2.0	2.0	2.0	2.0	2.0	2.0
Planned avail.	2,069.3	2,051.5	2,026.7	1,998.3	1,982.2	1,954.4	1,882.2	1,825.7	1,750.2	1,689.2	1,542.1	1,332.9	1,332.9	1,174.3	1,005.2
Variance	116.3	153.5-	194.6-	241.1-	296.5-	112.5-	266.3-	388.4-	88.7-	140.7	127.5	184.9	184.9	77.1	422.1

Table 10-2. Hire forecast based on current variance.

Report Date 09/28/86
Forecast For Department No.320/Mechanical Engineering

	09/86	10/86	11/86	12/86	1987	1988	1989	1990
Assistant chief engineer	1	0	0	0	0	0	0	0
Supervising engineer	5	5	7	6	5	6	6	7
Principal engineer	5	5	11	12	15	14	13	14
Senior engineer	8	10	15	15	14	18	17	18
Engineer	23	24	26	21	22	23	20	22
Associate engineer	3	4	5	4	4	3	5	5
Assistant engineer	13	12	14	18	22	21	15	14
Senior technician	1	1	1	2	2	2	2	2
Technician A	3	3	3	2	3	3	3	3
Engineering aide	0	0	1	1	2	1	2	1
Total personnel	62	64	83	81	89	91	83	86

Table 10-3. Career path forecast: example.

	9/86	10/86	11/86	12/86	1st Qtr. 1987	2d Qtr. 1987	3d Qtr. 1987	4th Qtr. 1987	1988	1989	1990	1991
Assistant engineer												
Demand	18	18	18	18	18	18	16	16	14	13	12	12
Availability	20	20	20	20	17	14	10	5	0	0	0	0
Variance	2	2	2	2	-1	-4	-6	-11	-14	-13	-12	-12
Associate engineer												
Demand	16	16	16	16	16	14	14	14	14	14	14	14
Availability	16	16	15	14	15	18	20	17	10	6	0	0
Variance	0	0	-1	-2	-1	4	6	3	-4	-8	-14	-14
Engineer												
Demand	10	10	10	10	14	14	14	14	18	18	18	16
Availability	8	8	9	9	9	10	12	16	22	18	16	13
Variance	-2	-2	-1	-1	-5	-4	-2	2	4	0	-2	-3
Senior engineer												
Demand	0	0	0	0	4	4	4	6	8	8	10	10
Availability	4	4	4	4	4	6	8	7	9	11	12	14
Variance	4	4	4	4	0	2	4	1	1	3	2	4
Principal engineer												
Demand	2	2	2	2	2	2	2	2	2	2	2	2
Availability	2	2	2	2	2	2	3	4	5	6	7	8
Variance	0	0	0	0	0	0	1	2	3	4	5	6
Chief engineer												
Demand	2	2	2	2	2	2	2	2	2	2	2	2
Availability	3	3	3	3	3	3	3	3	3	4	6	7
Variance	1	1	1	1	1	1	1	1	1	2	4	5

ing availability—and consequent variance changes—at management levels in the future.

Similarly, data from the career planning system can produce a "career path forecast," such as that shown in Table 10-3. Further analysis of these data will answer questions about future variance based on trends evident in career paths; for instance, are too many of our chemical engineers moving into management tracks, contributing to a future shortage of practicing chemical engineers? In an integrated system, of course, management intervention in the career planning process can correct any such imbalance—if intervention of this type is in fact more cost-effective and strategically "sound" (based on long-range organizational needs) than hiring from external labor markets.

Reports that combine specific availability factors—such as career path data, network flow forecasts, and attrition data—can be produced to provide further detail for management analysis.

The matching (or mismatching) in demand and availability of human resources leads to the development of strategies to address this variance, including the interventions described in the following sections.

Closing Supply-Demand Gaps

Personnel surpluses, unfortunately, have never been viewed as a human resources "problem" by most American organizations. The reasons have to do both with a labor relations history that has put wages and benefits ahead of job security and with the traditional "employment at will" doctrine applicable to exempt employees. The results of these past policies, which remain operative in today's employment relations, have generally been good, at least for the economy as a whole. Labor mobility, the response of labor markets to supply and demand, and the freedom of people to work where they choose—and the freedom of employers to dismiss noncontractual employees as they choose—are benefits we do not take lightly. For individual organizations, however, especially those with a major investment in human resources programs designed to develop and retain the key personnel required to meet increasingly challenging "people needs" in the years ahead, policies that use layoffs or mass dismissals to "solve" problems of surpluses may be both shortsighted and ultimately destructive of the human resources investment. Some interventions for avoiding precipitous or wholesale reductions in force are suggested in the following section, although the most effective means to this end is a strategically based human resources planning system that forecasts such surpluses well in advance of the need for layoffs or large-scale dismissals.

More commonly, the gap of greatest concern to human resources management is the variance between human resources availability in the organization, now and during the planning cycle, and organizational needs. Shortages of people—by skills, management level, location, or other attribute—call for management intervention that can take many forms, from increased hiring at entry levels to "pirating" competitors' managerial talent. Some of the more cost-effective long-range interventions are discussed in the final section of the chapter.

Ideally, most of these interventions to increase needed supply should be unnecessary: A "perfect" strategic human resources planning system would accurately predict the numbers and types of human resources dictated by strategic and operational plans and supply those human resources through integrated development, training, and other programs such as those discussed in Part III. But even if the system were "perfect," the world is not. Environmental factors beyond the control of organizations create change, and a flexible strategic planning system must accommodate changing management priorities, as well.

An effective planning system does, however, minimize fire fighting as a response to change. The management interventions recommended here as methods of closing the gap between supply and demand—especially the long-range interventions—merely underscore the importance of a business-based planning system that integrates human resources policies and programs with organizational needs. Over time, such a system is certain to assure that supply-demand gaps more closely resemble cracks than chasms and can be cost-effectively remedied by improved policies and sharply focused interventions.

Avoiding the Need for Layoffs

As a rule, layoffs and dismissals resulting from organizational change represent the ultimate failure of the human resources planning system. The goal of a system such as that proposed here is to forecast and create the human resources needed in the future to effectively meet organizational demands. If effective, such a system prevents both shortages and surpluses, for the most part, obviating the need to enter labor markets on an emergency basis or to inflict wholesale reductions in force—through layoffs or dismissals of surplus employees—on existing human resources.

For one thing, the human resources planning and management systems outlined in Part III represent a major investment of organizational resources and managerial commitment. If carefully laid career plans, effective appraisal systems, succession plans, and other human resources development and planning programs have any meaning at all, they assume the continuity of most managers' careers.

The underlying premise of effective human resources planning and development based on strategic plans is that the skills and talents of people *within* the organization will predominantly shape tomorrow's organization. Today's human resources—and those hired, trained, and developed by personnel programs now in place—represent the human assets needed to meet the strategic goals of the firm in the years ahead. How well that work is performed, and at what costs compared to value received, will depend on the organization's ability to attract, retain, and develop the best people to meet its objectives.

Thus, in an integrated human resources planning and development system, all human resources programs—from recruitment to pensions—are directed toward the accomplishment of organizational objectives in both the short term and the long range. Forecasts for future human resources are the result of "demand" requirements of strategic and operational planning and "availability" estimates created by internal human resources programs that will develop tomorrow's workforce.

Clearly, then, the need to undertake massive layoffs or dismissals—because supply or availability of personnel exceeds demand, a surfeit that must be addressed by reductions in force—is a failure of the HR planning process. But organizations that respond to this need by letting go a major part of the regular workforce are, in effect, throwing out the baby with the bathwater. Most of the investment in human resources development programs—and the skills, talents, and individual commitment they have been carefully designed to nurture—is lost forever to the organization or can be regained only through years of no-layoff policies and practices.

Even in the absence of a comprehensive, fully integrated human resources planning and development system, however, the costs of massive dismissals can include a broad range of immediate and longer-term expenses. These costs are more or less applicable to differently situated organizations. Some firms need not consider the costs of hiring employees and retraining people at a later date, for example, because the jobs in question have disappeared forever.

Also, there remain many areas of the economy where "warm bodies" are the primary human resources need. Where unskilled labor is available in an abundant market, the organization in this situation will probably have no human resources development programs to protect, no investment in training worth considering, and no particular problem recruiting employees at a moment's notice. Even companies in these industries, however—such as fast-food retailing—must remain competitive, and "swinging-door" employment policies are perceptibly disadvantageous to even the least-educated unskilled worker.

From an organizational human resources development perspective, layoffs or threats of layoffs have serious implications, although there remains much disagreement about how seriously layoffs affect companies. Where the massive introduction of new technology—such as factory robotization or complete office automation—makes a permanent layoff possible and desirable, there is no question of "whether or not" to lay people off—just how and when.

For the most part, however, technological change does not alter labor requirements "overnight" and can in any case be planned for in ways that reduce the need for dismissals and layoffs. Through planning and the implementation of some of the approaches discussed under "Interventions to Avoid Layoffs" (some of which are suggested by Richard Frantzreb) below, human resources policies that effectively promote a sense of job security—and reduce the real or perceived threat of layoffs that can be so harmful to the employee commitment necessary both for productivity improvement and for career development—can help the organization gain a reputation as "a good place to work," now and in the foreseeable future.

Costs of Layoffs and Dismissals

The reasons for avoiding large-scale dismissals and repeated layoffs are not strictly humanitarian but relate to actual bottom-line costs to the organization. Some are tangible, easily measured costs; others are intangible, but nonetheless real.

Some examples of the tangible costs include:

- Unemployment compensation taxes, which in some states equal the amount paid in benefits and which can be enormous after major layoffs
- Severance pay, for salaried employees
- Incentive payments or bonuses in exchange for resignation or early retirement, which can amount to a year or more in salary
- Administrative costs, such as benefits processing, exit interviews, and other paperwork
- Outplacement costs, where such services are offered by the organization
- Rehiring costs (if personnel dismissed are needed at some time in the future), which may include employment agency commissions, interviewing, and other expenses associated with the employment process

The intangible costs of precipitous reductions in force depend on the organization's need for skilled, talented, committed human resources—developed to reach their full potential over time—to meet organizational goals. Where the need is for "warm bodies" or unskilled labor in an abundant market, the organization will, as noted above, probably have no development programs to protect, no investment in training worth considering, and no particular problem recruiting employees at competitive compensation levels to meet future needs.

Interventions to Avoid Layoffs

Two kinds of interventions are available to companies seeking to avoid the need for layoffs: alternative staffing practices, which have the effect of minimizing high long-term employment levels that can create large surpluses; and alternatives to dismissal, a range of programs and policies that forestall the need for layoffs through redirection of human resources utilization in the organization.

Staffing Alternatives to Regular Employment. In personnel management, as in most other fields of endeavor, the best solutions to problems are often the preventive measures that preclude the emergence of such problems or reduce their severity when they do occur. As suggested earlier, the surest way to prevent both human resources shortages and surpluses is an effectively integrated HR planning and development system, but a number of short-term strategies—alternatives to regular hiring and employment practices—can help prevent the problem of personnel surpluses from one season or year to the next.

These strategies focus on policies and programs that minimize additions to the regular workforce, the people with career commitments to the organization who represent its long-term investment in professional, technical, and managerial skills and talents needed to reach strategic objectives and operational goals. This "regular" workforce may be differently defined in different industries or companies, but usually, it would include all who are participants in a fully developed career management program.

Alternative staffing practices work as short-term "surplus-prevention" techniques where the demand for additional human resources turns out to be transitory or seasonal or where it has been overestimated by managers faced with new production or service requirements. Instead of responding to such demands with traditional hiring and recruitment—which adds a range of new personnel costs that include not only payroll and benefits but reduced productivity for new employees in the early stages of "learning curves" on jobs—managers can opt for one or more of the following alternatives to meet short-term escalations in human resources demand.

- *Internal transfers.* A shortage of employees throughout a large, complex organization, while possible, is rare. More often, the shortage is in certain skills, departments, or locations. If skills or managerial competencies are available elsewhere in the organization, and are transferable with minimal retraining, lateral deployment can be effective. The high cost of relocation—and the problems posed by today's growth of two-career families—may be an issue, however. And such moves should be closely monitored for additional training costs and any consequent impacts on hiring patterns in the "sending" department or location.

- *Overtime scheduling.* Perhaps the most time-honored method of meeting temporary production peaks is the scheduling of overtime in affected departments or operations. Because existing employees—known commodities in terms of their skills and costs—are used, operational planning can accurately account for the cost of premium pay (which is usually far less than the costs of hiring and training new employees), and employees in most situations are favorably disposed toward the practice and its extra income. At some point, of course, if overtime scheduling continues over many months and is being applied to a significant share of the workforce (especially in work where employee fatigue is a factor), managers may have to decide that the demand increase is not short-term and that other alternatives or traditional hiring practices are necessary.

- *Recall of layoffs.* Temporary layoffs are a way of life in some industries, so much so that some companies—including major automakers in the United States—supplement regular unemployment compensation with company-paid benefits in order to assure that workers are on-hand in the labor force when needed again. In areas where a particular employer accounts for a large share of overall employment, or when an entire industry lays off employees at about the same time, most hourly workers can be expected to be available for recall. The recall of laid-off employees has obvious advantages for employers: Little or no training is required, the former employees know the organization and its conditions of employment, and recalled workers can be productive their first day back. Unless there exists a layoff-recall "pattern" in the area or industry or for the organization, however, there is little assurance that such workers will be available when needed. And white collar workers are usually not available.

- *Rehiring retirees.* As a short-term intervention to meet staff shortages at virtually any level in the company, management or nonmanagement, the rehiring of recently retired employees has many strong advantages. The skills, experience, company-specific knowledge, and abilities of retired workers represent an untapped reservoir of productive human resources for many firms. If adjustments can be made to pension systems, retired workers can be hired full-time or part-time at compensation levels that are highly attractive to retirees—especially in inflationary periods. For many companies, especially those located in the U.S. Sunbelt states, the older labor market has become an important source of skilled managerial and other talent.

- *Temporary and contract employees.* Temporary employees, often under contract individually or through contract agencies, provide short-term supplies of virtually every job description from clerical to professional. If the organization is engaged in a project with a known time frame, has unexpected production requirements, or needs some specialized skill for only a relatively short period of time, such employees are a viable option. Where a nonpermanent job specialty is required, however, the temporary employee is likely to be more expensive than regular employees. On the other hand, most temporary employees do not receive benefits, require training, or cost anything in employee development, as a rule.

- *Demand reductions.* Other short-term operational methods of reducing or closing the gap between human resources demand and supply involve actions to reduce the demand side of the equation, including:

> Inventory reduction
> Subcontracting of work
> Transfer of production within the organization
> Productivity improvement

In American industry as a whole, one of the first signs of recovery from a prolonged recession has usually been inventory reduction, which occurs before organizations begin staffing up to prerecessionary levels. The Japanese auto industry has made inventory reduction a deliberate policy, demonstrating how inventory levels of auto parts can be reduced to minimal levels by the kanban, or "just in time," system, which synchronizes parts production and delivery with their use in production lines. In any case, inventory reduction, under the right circumstances, can effectively lower the demand for certain human resources. This option is not available to most service companies, however.

Subcontracting of work normally done internally may be an intermittent "policy" in some organizations, a practice made necessary by great fluctuations in production requirements or predictable seasonal demands. In some cases, companies with contract deadlines or other time constraints may subcontract parts of jobs as a "last resort," a practice fraught with dangers to quality control, cost control, and the ability of the firm to grow in an orderly fashion.

Instead of transferring employees from other parts of the organization to increase supply in given areas, the work itself—or demand—may sometimes be transferred to less busy departments or locations. In some situations, plants with excess capacity can be fully utilized in this way, for example.

Productivity improvement is both a long-range and short-term concept in reducing demand-supply gaps in human resources. In the short term, it usually involves the introduction of a new process or readily used technology, production line acceleration, or the elimination of some parts of jobs to focus on output per hour. It can also include interventions that reduce the human resources requirements of work—such as superfluous inspections or formal meetings that have no direct bearing on work production. Longer-term reductions in operational demand for human resources may be obtainable through laborsaving technology such as office automation.

- *Accelerated development and leveraging.* Particularly among managers and professionals, these methods of extending the existing workforce are both techniques for addressing personnel shortage (see the next section of this chapter) and buffers against overstaffing.

Alternatives to Layoffs and Dismissals. Even in organizations where planning is conducted most carefully, unexpected developments can at least temporarily reduce human resources demands to a point where reductions in force appear to be essential to the continued health of the firm. In free-enterprise economies, after all, companies are not in business to provide employment, and long-range planning considerations become moot points if the firm does not survive the present. Where layoffs and massive dismissals are viewed as a "last resort," however, as they should be in the growing number of organizations where internally developed human resources are a vital business asset, a number of alternatives to layoffs can serve to reduce human resources supplies to economically feasible levels—while keeping the regular workforce needed to meet strategic goals intact.

Some of these alternatives to layoffs, such as the release of temporary employees, are more or less available according to previous staffing patterns; others, such as retraining, depend on the organization's resources and internal demand for retrained workers; and worktime alternatives may be suitable for some kinds of jobs and workers but not for others. For companies with a significant investment in human resources, however, and long-range needs to develop a committed, experienced workforce with organization-specific skills and capabilities, each of the following options should be considered as more cost-effective alternatives to massive layoffs or dismissals.

- *Nonregular workforce reductions.* To the extent that the organization has remained "lean" in its regular workforce by hiring temporary employees and contract workers to meet short-term demand increases, these employees can be released first when reductions in force are necessary, which may solve the surplus problem without further cuts.

- *Transfers and retraining.* Depending on the reasons for the surplus of human resources—which may affect only a few departments or locations, may be the result of new technology that has made certain skills obsolete, or may be occurring at a time when other operations in the organization require additional personnel—the options of transferring employees, and possibly retraining them for new jobs, may be viable alternatives. Where transfers require long-distance moves, however, the soaring costs of relocation and changing employee attitudes toward relocation—especially in two-career families—may mitigate against this alternative, as noted earlier.

- *Temporary leaves.* Short-term leaves or temporary layoffs have a long history among production workers in some industries—weeks or even months off with a return to work scheduled after plant retooling, process turnarounds, or maintenance. Other forms of temporary leave can be equally effective among managers and professionals. Schools have long given leaves of absence to tenured professors, for example. Extended vacations, partially reimbursed sabbaticals, or "loans" to nonprofit organizations are other alternatives.

- *Worktime reductions.* In periods of general economic decline, the share of the labor force working part-time invariably increases, as companies hire part-timers to replace more costly regular employees. In a few cases (for instance, New York Telephone in the recession of 1975), regular employees are asked to accept part-time schedules, temporarily, as an alternative to layoffs. In a somewhat different version, job sharing of a single position by two or more employees can effectively avoid layoffs while reducing personnel costs. Other industries can move workers to a four-day week.

- *Early retirement.* Increasingly popular in recent years, early retirement plans permit employees with a minimum time in the company to retire early with full benefits, a lump-sum bonus, or other incentives. Unfortunately, when such plans are offered across the board to managers—some of whom the company can afford to keep—it is "the best and brightest" who retire, those with opportunities to continue careers elsewhere.

Interventions to Cope with Shortages

The gaps or variances that become identifiable between strategic and operational demand and human resources availability or supply can represent either surpluses or shortages of people, but the chief concern of human resources managers and planners is usually shortages: What can we do to close the apparent gaps between today's skills and talents and those needed to meet strategic plans as well as the operational needs of the immediate future? The focus here is on management actions that address shortfalls that have emerged because of inadequate or inaccurate planning, the demands of unexpected (but welcome) business upturns, or environmental change—such as the emergence of a new competitor who is raiding your staff with irresistibly exorbitant pay offers.

Changing technology, as well as changing markets, can produce unplanned (and often unforseeable) demands for a different mix of skills than are being produced by the human resources development process. While some skills or professional competencies are becoming outworn or obsolete, other skills and qualifications may be needed in greater supply. The timing of technological change is not always easy to predict, another reason planning systems are imperfect.

Long-Term Methods of Addressing Shortages

An effectively integrated planning system will specifically identify future human resources gaps, but there remain many answers to the "what to do about it" question, especially when the gaps represent potentially debilitating shortages of the people needed to meet long-range strategic goals.

An attitude of "crossing that bridge when we come to it" can be disastrous for several reasons:

- Hiring and payroll cost escalation resulting from the need to acquire experienced or specially qualified people from the outside labor market is not only expensive but results in such dilemmas as wage and salary compression, disruption of compensation programs and their goals, and irreversible damage to the organization's credibility as a "partner" in career planning programs.
- Crash training and development programs are not only costly but may produce inferior skills and marginally competent managerial abilities—weaknesses that may come back to haunt the organization in the years ahead.
- The people needed may simply not be available, within or outside the company, and long-range strategies will have to be scrapped or changed because human resources planners failed to do their job.

For the most part, the particular management interventions that will be most effective for a given organization seeking to proactively plan for long-range shortages are highly "situational." Techniques or programs vary with specific needs, constraints, and opportunities. In general, however, the policies that most effectively address long-range people shortages in strategically integrated planning systems relate to turnover control, management development, training, and interventions in the external labor market. Some key perspectives in these areas are suggested below.

Turnover-Control Programs. To effectively address unwanted turnover, in the organization generally or in a specific job skill or department, the first question is "Why do they leave?" The answer to this question—and there may be more than one answer or different reasons for different types of employees—will point the way to the elements of a turnover-control program that will reduce quit rates.

Exit interviews are the basic tool for determining why people leave the organization, but employers often need supplemental data to "make sense" out of the reasons employees give interviewers for leaving the company.

The data required are the same kinds of information that may have been analyzed by planners in the identification of turnover as a problem—overall data from the personnel data base showing that an unacceptable percentage of people in a certain salary bracket, with so much tenure, are leaving voluntarily. The exit interviews alone may provide a gross, or unanalyzed, reason for departures—such as "poor opportunities for advancement." This "reason" may mean somewhat different things in different contexts, however, with different implications for the design of a turnover-control program.

For example, if the opportunities-for-advancement reason is reported as the cause of most voluntary separations among both recently hired data systems analysts with under two years of service and experienced managers at a given location who have been with the company for ten years or more, different kinds of intervention may be indicated. In the former case, the context suggests that the real reason for turnover may be opportunities elsewhere—at higher pay—combined with the typically high turnover rates of employees with little tenure. Increased salaries, earlier vesting in the pension program, or some other compensation tactic might be the appropriate intervention in this case.

For the experienced managers who are leaving in the latter case—and giving the same "reason" about advancement opportunities—compensation may have nothing to do with the problem or its solution. If these employees are mature professionals, for example, already in higher salary brackets, higher pay is probably less important to them than "the work itself." They may simply be bored by work they have been doing too long or may perceive that they are in dead-end jobs from which few are promoted to higher positions. In this case, the more effective interventions might include an improved career planning system or succession planning that is more clearly communicated and "sold" to managers.

Turnover control is at the heart of any human resources planning system that focuses on the internal availability of personnel and their development over the years to meet the long-range requirements of strategic plans. Some attrition of existing human resources is unavoidable, but voluntary separations can usually be reduced through policies and programs based on analysis of the reasons for unwanted turnover. And as indicated by the example, these reasons must be analyzed in the context in which turnover occurs.

Accelerated Management Development. The idea of the "field commission" in the heat of battle—the instant promotion of an enlisted man to officer because of the demands of combat leadership and an untimely shortage of regular officers—suggests one reason for accelerating managers' progress. At times, temporary or unexpected shortages of managers at a higher level may mean that the most efficient way to close the gap is by the premature promotion of leading candidates, along with intensified development.

Although the overall career development system and succession planning may assure orderly progression for most managers, there will always be a few at each level whose talents and abilities are underutilized. Another reason to accelerate the progress of these exceptional managers, of course, is to reduce the likelihood of their departure.

Because the maximization of human resources utilization is "the name of the game," exceptionally able managers should be challenged with positions of greater responsibility when *they* are ready, not only when a system says they are ready. Such accelerated development normally includes highly structured training or job experience along with increased responsibility, preferably under the tutelage of experienced managers. Done properly, with due respect for the overall succession system that will continue to apply to most managers, this kind of intervention can solve staff shortages economically, reduce turnover among "the cream of the crop" of young managers, and bring new enthusiasm and vigor to the upper levels of management. Moreover, if those selected for accelerated development are demonstrably exceptional, they can serve as an inspiration to other young managers.

"Leveraged" Technology. In many high-tech industries today, technology expertise at management levels is in increasingly short supply. In addition, plans may call for the rapid expansion of these human resources in the years ahead, or new levels of expertise may be required by rapidly changing technology.

One way of managing existing human resources—through intervention in the design of career management and succession planning systems—is to "leverage" technological skills. Instead of having all or most of the organization's most technologically advanced managers in a single department or in one hierarchy, these skills are leveraged, by spreading them across the organization in all relevant departments. If possible, the most technologically competent managers should supervise groups of average or less advanced people. In firms with a limited supply of outstanding scientists or other professionals, the utilization of these people as leaders can spread their skills and knowledge to a broader base.

Long-Range Retraining and Transfer. Increasingly, technological advances that displace workers, create job obsolescence, and will result in large surpluses of human resources are coming under the scrutiny of labor leaders and government officials who see "the menace of microelectronics" as being the cause of massive unemployment. The question of whether Information Age technology will turn out to be a boon to workers—creating more interesting, better-paying, easier work or shorter workweeks—or a disaster, as "jobless growth" creates armies of unemployed workers with obsolete skills, has not yet been conclusively answered.

European nations are concerned enough about the impacts of technology on jobs to insist on employer participation in government-sponsored retraining programs. In a few countries—Sweden, Norway, and West Germany—laws require employers to gain the approval of labor unions before introducing technology that could have an impact on jobs.

In the United States, where government intervention in long-range planning and training has had a sporadic and less pervasive history, a few labor unions and organizations have undertaken long-range retraining and redevelopment efforts aimed at employees displaced by technology. An early example occurred in the 1950s and 1960s at AT&T, where thousands of telephone operators were given the opportunity to learn other jobs as automatic dialing eliminated their function.

More recently, the 1984 United Auto Workers pacts with automobile companies provided for massive retraining funds—$1 billion over six years in the case of General Motors—to compensate for the expected introduction of labor-saving technology. President Owen Bieber of the UAW said of the GM pact, "We have never had a labor agreement in this country . . . that has provided this job security for its members."[2]

Few organizations have the size and resources of an AT&T or a GM, and virtually none in the United States has any contractual imperatives impelling retraining efforts for nonunion managers and professionals. Within the career development process, however, most employers have at hand the means of assuring that job skills are kept current through retraining, off-site education, and other development programs.

External Supply Interventions. To improve the long-term availability of human resources in the external environment, organizations have long participated in apprenticeship programs and conducted community relations programs in secondary schools, and some have a history of involvement in higher education. Although employer participation in skilled trades training is far more common in Europe than in the United States, some American organizations have become heavily committed to higher education; for example, the armed services through the service academies or General Motors through GM Tech. Many American universities, such as Carnegie and Sloan, specialize in curricula originally developed to provide supplies of managers and professionals to industries represented by major benefactors.

In small-town America, especially among firms dependent on local labor supplies, community relations programs—including "open-house" introduction to the organization, participation in vocational education, and other activities intended to improve attitudes toward the organization as a "good place to work"—have a long history.

Today's needs for better-educated managers and professionals with specialized degrees have focused increased attention on institutions of higher education, where organizations endow departments or chairs, provide scholarships, donate technological resources, and sponsor research. The purpose is not always to increase the available supply of human resources. At times, companies may merely be unloading obsolete technology on colleges (with tax benefits), and at other times, this form of altruism is tied to specific research results that will be used competitively by the benefactor.

More often, however, such efforts have tangible results in improving the overall external supply of human resources needed by an industry or a company. At the least, a reputation on campus as a concerned and generous employer should have positive effects on college recruitment efforts. And for organizations requiring highly specialized researchers and current access to state-of-the-art technology and science, a working relationship with one or more universities provides a valuable resource in terms of both information and people. If graduate students or faculty decide to enter industry, the organizations most familiar to them are likely to be among their first choices for employment interviews.

Outside of the military and a few organizations supporting technical schools or departments, American companies have traditionally left external human resources availability largely to the schools and the vagaries of labor market supply and demand, environmental factors affecting enrollments and fields of study, and the exigencies of competitive demand forces. However, this may no longer be enough for many organizations. If irrefutable evidence suggests a future shortage of skills or managerial competencies that are critical to the accomplishment of strategic plans, the organization will want to consider intervening in the external labor market in ways that improve human resources supply. For some, this may indicate a need for additional government funding—such as the *Sputnik*-inspired upsurge of federal aid to technical education in the 1960s. For others, the needs are seen as industrywide, calling for efforts by trade associations and business groups.

Even in the absence of funded educational efforts, costly endowments, or continuing working relationships with schools, employers can improve their ability to attract and retain graduates by being a good place to work. Such a reputation, of course, depends on the efficacy of the kinds of human resources programs discussed in Part III—programs that assure career opportunities, progression by merit, and a widely shared vision of strategic objectives.

Short-Term Methods of Closing Gaps

Short-term, or operational, methods of closing gaps that occur because of temporary or unexpected shortages of human resources are used by line supervisors in most organizations and are not usually the responsibility of human resources planning. If the planning system is effective, of course, such interventions should not represent a major share of employment practices. In seasonal industries or where workloads are volatile and subject to sudden surges in human resources requirements, the necessity for short-term increases in human resources supply may be a permanent, recurring operational need, however. In these cases, it becomes the responsibility of human resources planning to analyze the effects and costs of various methods of short-term intervention and be in a position to recommend the most effective methods of increasing human resources supply, which may differ for different jobs, locations, or time frames.

The major forms of short-term intervention to increase human resources supply were discussed earlier in this chapter (see "Staffing Alternatives to Regular Employment" under "Interventions to Avoid Layoffs" on page 245). Each of these types of intervention has advantages and disadvantages for specific organizations, work requirements, and personnel costs. And while human resources planners should have a hand in the development of policies that favor one or another method in different situations, the choice of method used should ultimately be an operational decision, because a short-term supply cap indicates that there is actual work that needs to be accomplished immediately—not a "capacity" for work that needs to be developed.

In addition to the aforementioned alternatives to hiring regular employees, there is, of course, the employment process. In fact, the time-honored approach to closing gaps between human resources demand and availability is simply to enter the labor market and hire more people, at levels above planned recruitment and hiring. As an expedient necessitated by unforecast demand, this is perhaps the most expensive and ultimately the least satisfactory method of closing gaps in the short term. In addition to payroll and benefits costs—which may be exorbitantly high for specialized skills or experienced managers—the organization normally incurs the costs of training, development, and reduced productivity during the "learning curve" inevitable in a new place of employment. Worse, as a means of countering short-term shortages, such employment is virtually certain to lead to reductions in force when the supply-demand picture returns to "normal" or productivity improvements permits the more complete utilization of skills. When the human resources "gap" shifts to the opposite side of the question—when there is a surplus of human resources that must be reduced to meet organizational objectives—a different set of issues must be addressed, as discussed above (see "Avoiding the Need for Layoffs").

Clearly, the chief benefit of an effective human resources planning system is to minimize shortages of the skills and talents needed by the organization—and the costly interventions required to correct such shortages. Inevitably, however, certain short-term gaps will emerge because of operational demand changes and unforeseen environmental change. If the shortage is clearly identifiable as short-term, however, planners and human resources managers should ensure that interventions taken to alleviate the shortage are also short-term. The lasting impacts of certain "remedies" may be more harmful to the company than the original complaint.

In summary, human resources planning and development create the organization of the future in many important respects. A phenomenon of the postindustrial era is that people in organizations are no longer interchangeable parts but require increasing levels of technical expertise, organizational commitment, ability to manage within organization-specific constraints, and leadership perspectives that comprehend and act to fulfill corporate goals. The characteristics that make organizations successful in their various fields—innovation, knowledge, service, reliability, and so forth—are characteristics of the people in the organization, and this is becoming more true every day as products proliferate, markets grow and diversify, and methods of providing goods and services are increasingly distinguishable by the costs and capabilities of human resources.

The most effective management response to these changing human resources needs is comprehensive, integrated human resources planning that takes into account the long-range strategic needs of the organization, short-term operational demand, and the availability of human resources as shaped by personnel programs such as training, career development, appraisals of performance and potential, and succession planning. Forecasts can then be made that identify gaps, or variances, between human resources supply and demand—shortages or surpluses by specific skills and management capabilities—and these variances can be addressed through changes in either demand requirements (such as the introduction of new laborsaving technology) or availability (such as accelerated career paths or new hiring and training efforts), or both.

Unforeseen events or new circumstances can create short-term "gaps" that even the most carefully constructed planning system will not anticipate, however. And when these gaps represent surpluses of people, a traditional response has been large-scale reductions in force, dismissals that putatively "cut costs" be removing people from payroll and benefits rosters.

Layoffs and widespread dismissals not only are more costly to the organization than is commonly supposed, but can be fatal to the human resources planning and development effort needed to achieve organizational goals. Worse, such reductions in force to meet temporary exigencies are largely avoidable, through the use of staffing strategies that maintain a "lean" regular workforce—the key human resources on which the planning and development system is based—and interventions that serve as alternatives to layoffs of regular employees.

11

How to Develop, Sell, and Implement a Strategic System Within the Organization

In the world of the modern organization, the effective introduction and implementation of new ideas with wide impacts often requires much more than the inherent virtue of the ideas themselves. Bureaucratic firms, almost by definition, resist change; the individual managers who run bureaucracies have vested interests in maintaining the status quo, resisting threats to their existing power or incursions into their managerial "turf," and—in profit-making organizations, at least—a vocational aversion to any new idea that will cost time and money without immediate "bottom-line" results.

A comprehensive, strategically driven human resources planning and development system such as the one outlined here meets all the qualifications for the kind of new idea that is most likely to be resisted in the organization. It will have wide impacts, require coordination and effort across the organization in all functions, and is definitionally "long-range," with results that may not become evident for five or ten years—and then only as costs that were *not* incurred or crises that were averted. Moreover, the person or function responsible for this new idea, the prime mover in the introduction and "selling" of the comprehensive system, is typically the representative of a relatively new activity in the organization: human resources planning. As discussed in Chapter 2, the human resources function has only recently been gaining legitimacy as a key participant in the strategic planning process.

In organizations where human resources departments are still confined to basic duties—hiring, firing, benefits administration, and payroll—the human resources planner is faced with a commensurately difficult campaign.

Despite these barriers, the human resources planner whose task it is to "sell" a comprehensive system such as this has one important advantage, if the planner chooses to use it: Organizational diagnosis, a process that in effect "presells" the system to managers who have had a hand in its creation, can be an effective approach both to developing the right kind of strategic human resources planning system for your organization and to gaining the management support needed initially as well as once the system is in operation. Throughout this book, and especially in Chapters 4 through 6, planners have been urged to focus on the specifics of their organization—its business needs, environment, operational requirements, and human resources needs for the future. The starting point for this approach is the organizational diagnosis. As Harry Levinson has observed:

> Before you do anything in your organization—whether introducing a compensation plan or a training program or a change in management procedures—you need to understand your organization. A company's history, character, value system, demographics, and characteristic ways of thinking and acting are the background against which any one element figures. If you understand the background, you can assess how a given program or procedure will fit into your organization. If you try to introduce changes before you understand the organization, you'll be making stabs in the dark. A program that works beautifully in one organization will fail in another where employees have different values, expectations, and needs.[1]

OD Techniques Are Critical. The diagnostic techniques recommended by organizational development advocates such as Levinson, supplemented by methods we developed in designing and implementing a comprehensive planning system at a major engineering and construction firm, can be critical in gaining top management approval and wide participation in the system. For example:

1. The choice of the diagnostic method—the first decision to be made once the need for change has been recognized—should be based on organization-specific needs and capabilities and should be made by a top management group or individual with ultimate responsibility for resource allocation in the firm.
2. Once the diagnostic method has been determined, an upper-management group composed of the top executives—such as an organizational development council—should be formally established. Its job will be to define the scope of the diagnostic effort and provide appropriate support and budgets.
3. Support of top managers alone is rarely sufficient to ensure the success of a comprehensive, systematic change effort. It is essential to harness the various power centers within the organization—people who can help or hinder change through overt or covert means. One effective approach is to identify the "critical mass" of leaders throughout the firm and enlist these managers and professionals in the diagnostic effort. (The way to identify such leaders is discussed in Chapter 4: Ask people who they think has power, then ask those named if they think they have power.)
4. The diagnostic team, made up of critical-mass leaders, can follow data collection procedures and other operational guidelines established by the planner or outside specialist, but its results should be presented to top

management by team members themselves. This reinforces ownership of the results, both for the diagnostic team and for top management.

5. *Comprehensive* is a key adjective in a diagnostic effort designed to point the way to the specific requirements of an integrated human resources planning and development system. As we have stressed repeatedly, effective human resources planning and development must be driven by strategic and operational demands.

6. Implementation of changes based on the diagnosis, especially in the early stages, should have the imprimatur of the diagnostic team of critical-mass managers. In this way, the system is perceived as being what it actually is: an integrated, strategic "business" system, not merely a human resources planning and development system.

Finally, it should be obvious that the degree of difficulty most planners will have in selling the system to top management will vary in inverse proportion to perceptions of "problems." The very use of the word *diagnosis* implies that there is an ailment to be treated—pain or the threat of pain that needs to be dealt with through change.

If no organizational problems are apparent or foreseeable, the planner's job may be more difficult. But increasingly, today's top managers know that organizations do not "just grow" like Topsy but require effective planning to meet the challenges of change.

Selling the System in Your Organization

In situations short of a crisis—where there are no "clear and present dangers" to the organization or general consensus on the need for redirection, reorganization, or planning for a different future—a strategic human resources planning system is considerably more difficult to "sell" within the firm. If the organization is running relatively smoothly, with little or no recognition of the importance of planning, the new system will be met with the same resistance that meets all change, in approximate proportion to the amount of money, time, and organizational change required to implement the system.

The costs of developing and implementing an integrated planning system are often only a superficial "reason" for opposition or a lack of enthusiasm among managers. In many modern organizations—especially those with existing management information systems, human resource information systems, and underutilized computer capacity—these costs need not be prohibitive.

The actual costs of developing a comprehensive, mechanized information system can vary from a few thousand to several hundred thousand dollars per year, depending on the size of the company, the amount of data already available, and the time required by the planning function to create the complete system. As discussed in earlier chapters, however, most of the data needed for an integrated planning system such as this are already available in the organization—or should be—and the job of the planning function is primarily one of identifying relevant information and establishing procedures for its incorporation in the integrated system.

Obviously, the only way a system such as this can cost hundreds of thousands of dollars to develop—without some highly "creative" accounting procedures—would be in the hypothetical situation of a major company where *no* strategic planning currently exists, where *no* operational data are being gathered on the costs of doing business, and where *nothing* is known about employees beyond what's on their paychecks. Realistically, this is never the case.

In any event, the planning system can be introduced incrementally, a piece at a time, utilizing inexpensive microcomputer technology or even manually gathered and processed data at first.

But managers who have other reasons for opposing the new system—and whose approval and active participation will be essential in the ongoing system—may often cite cost, including the cost of their time, as a reason for opposition. Generally, the real reasons for opposition point to the most effective approach for "selling" managers at different levels in the organization. Here are some examples.

■ Line managers will generally resist anything that seems likely to require additional data collection, analysis, and work, regardless of putative merits. If the status quo is sufficient to meet most operational needs, line managers will be skeptical of proposed change, unless the planner is able to sell "solutions" instead of merely a new system.

■ Human resources managers and professionals, those who logically should be most committed to a strategic human resources planning system and whose active involvement is the sine qua non of effective development, often are afflicted with a parochial view of their responsibilities or are unwilling to undertake the difficult tasks involved in exploring business and operational requirements in the organization. Some also resist computerization of data or any quantification of human resources skills, performance, potential, or careers.

■ Top management will generally resist any planning system that by definition involves long-term payoffs rather than instant gratification, or results that will be reflected in the next quarterly statement. In addition, any change is usually perceived as threatening to the existing power structure in the organization. This underscores the importance of identifying the "critical mass" of influential managers, whose support for a new system will be essential if resources are to be allocated and participation is to be widespread in key areas across the organization.

Each of these general categories of managers and professionals should be approached from a somewhat different perspective in "selling" the system in the organization. All are critical to the success of the ongoing system—although it may be possible to get started with only top management's approval—and wise planners will approach each category with situation-specific selling points. Also, of course, it should be borne in mind that systems that may require continuing effort, participation, and new budgets do not automatically "stay sold." Regular communication of benefits, cost savings, and a continuing set of mechanisms for participatory involvement in decision making may be required.

Selling and Involving Line Managers

In most organizations, no group is more important to the long-term success of the planning system than line managers, the operational heads who may have every reason to be suspicious of the latest "theoretical" approach being foisted upon them by "ivory tower" staff managers who have nothing better to do with their time than construct abstract rationales of organizational existence.

Too often, in the introduction of management systems generally and in strategic planning in particular, the needs and decision-making input of line managers have been treated as afterthoughts or given lip service only. Staff managers talking to one another, or writing a book or article on a new approach to strategic planning, invariably assert the "critical importance of bottom-up input of line managers, the people closest to actual production or service provision." But often, in these same organizations, line managers would be surprised to hear how important they are in the system. No one asked their advice before the system went into operation; they have never understood its jargon or overall objectives; and its only visible effect on their work is a time-consuming reporting system that periodically asks for data "that staff planners think are important" and recommendations that are rarely even acknowledged.

The problem is that line managers are likely to be "the toughest nut to crack" in gaining support for a new system, and there is an understandable tendency in the developmental stage to attempt to circumvent these managers, by focusing attention on top management. If the new system is approved, line managers have it presented to them as a *fait accompli*, something they will have to learn to live with—until the next new "theoretical" management or planning system catches the attention of headquarters staff.

The comprehensive strategic planning system proposed here not only accommodates line managers' participation, however; it *requires* it. At each stage of the planning process, the baseline estimates of operational planning—the demands for human resources that grow out of existing, scheduled, and anticipated operations—are the foundations of analysis. As discussed in Chapter 6, meaningful analysis and forecasts of human resources demand require an understanding of how human resources are used, what they contribute to the production of goods and services, and what they cost. Operational planning, because it is short-term and focuses primarily on the day-to-day costs of human (and other) resources, needs to be integrated with strategic and human resources planning in order for the organization to proactively plan for the future. But operational planning represents the "reality"—the production methods and procedures that define the organization's existence in the real world today.

As indicated in the examples in Chapter 6, the human resources planner is heavily dependent on line managers, supervisors, and operational analysts for data that must be incorporated in the planning system. If operational planning is fully developed in the organization, and information is available in standardized formats that can be integrated with other planning data—such as staffing tables that relate projects, time, and human resources needs—the planner's data collection efforts may merely involve a relatively simple systems interface. In other cases, planners may have to implement operations research techniques and mathematical modeling to create a framework for data collection.

At either extreme of the data collection effort—and across the intervening spectrum where most organizations will lie—the human resources planner must come to understand operational planning in greater detail than is typically the case. The guidelines, rules of thumb, statistical relationships, production constraints, time variables, and cost factors involved in the allocation of human resources to accomplish work must be systematically incorporated in planning if the system is to have relevance to actual organizational work.

Armed with this perspective—that line managers' commitment is essential to the overall planning process and that there is much to be learned from operational managers—the planner probably brings to meetings with line supervisors and operational analysts an attitude that is both refreshing and ultimately fruitful. But how does the planner "sell" a new planning system to line managers?

In the first place, planners in this position should not attempt to sell methods, techniques, or even a system, but rather *solutions*. The most effective points to be made to operational managers involve specific answers to their needs and opportunities: How much will productivity improve if turnover is reduced by *X* percent because of this planning system? What part of downtime is caused by inadequate levels of training? Why do skills requisitions take so long to get answered?

Once line managers are aware that the proposed system is not "ivory tower" but designed to apply to actual operational human resources demand and availability, the planner has acquired an "involved partner" in system development. Line managers assume a share of the ownership of the system, as they must if they will be responsible for the continuing flow of planning data, as soon as it becomes evident to them that they can reap operational benefits.

Human Resources Department Commitment

Although line managers are treated first in this chapter, because of their often-overlooked importance, the chronologically "first" people the planner must sell on the system are within the human resources department itself. Even if the planner is head of human resources, the commitment of colleagues and subordinates within personnel must be more than a superficial response, a going through the motions to satisfy the boss. The professional skills and functional capabilities of many different types of human resources activity may be involved—from training to retirement planning—and the establishment of a complete system is likely to create more administrative work, more analysis, new forms and procedures, and perhaps different priorities and budgets. In the last case—if the system is likely to shift budget allocations—the planner can expect resistance to a shift in the balance of power within the department.

If the planner is not the head of human resources, his or her boss—or boss's boss—is the primary target. In this case, the approach that will be most effective combines human resources–specific advantages with the kinds of arguments that will be effective in selling top management. In addition, it need hardly be added, the development of a comprehensive, integrated planning system based on strategic and operational objectives is virtually certain to enhance the prestige and influence of the human resources department (and of its chief officer) within the organization. The ultimate goal of such a system, to accomplish strategic business objectives through planning and development that create needed resources in the most cost-effective quantities and qualities, puts the human resources department at the heart of corporate decision making.

The surest path to acceptance of the system among human resources professionals, assuming the planned system "works" for the organization, is explication. By explaining the organization-specific objectives incorporated in the system, the role of human resources planning and development in achieving those objectives, and the clear need for a systematic approach, human resources managers and professionals may be forced to emerge from parochial concerns and narrow perspectives regarding their roles.

Succession planning, for example, becomes more than just a "numbers game" or a tool to placate ambitious managers. Driven by the systematically determined needs of strategic plans, succession planning becomes a way of shaping tomorrow's organization, of assuring that the right managers are available in the right place at the right time to achieve long-range goals.

Each human resources function, as discussed in greater detail in Part III, is an essentially creative process, designed and carried out to shape future human resources availability. Although there may be many different objectives at any one time—different numbers and types of people in different places at different times—all are systematically related in an integrated system, driven by overall strategic and operational demands.

Among variously specialized human resources managers, this approach implies a "team-building" talent on the part of the planner. Not all functional specialists will be expected to completely agree, however. Training people will still believe their function is more valuable to the organization than job rotation, for example. The important thing is for each function to recognize that its efficacy can be improved through integration and that no "value" accrues to any activity or policy that is not synchronous with overall organizational goals.

The continuing commitment of human resources people to the system can be expected to come from top management's approval of the system's results and continued allocation of resources to the personnel functions responsible for those results.

Gaining and Keeping Top Management Support

When the planning system has gained the official sanction of the human resources department, and its benefits have been explicated to the managers and professionals who will be involved, the planner can move into the organization to talk with others—at line and staff levels—concurrently. The key targets, as always, are those who make up "top management," the person or persons with budgetary control and ultimate decision-making responsibility for the development of a new planning system.

A logical starting point is the corporate or strategic planning department, where the planner can learn the present systems, procedures, and objectives of long-range business planning. At the same time, the planner should be able to present a case for the importance of human resources availability in achieving strategic plans and the potentially huge differences—in cost and quality—between external availability and human resources developed internally.

For top management generally, the following are among the arguments that may be most effective in "selling" the planning system:

1. The planning system can save the company significant amounts of money by anticipating staffing requirements and providing the lead time needed to cost-effectively acquire and develop the necessary people. Savings can come from the reduced use of employment agencies, less crash-basis training, the orderly assimilation of employees into operations, and reduced turnover costs.

2. Integrated human resources planning can improve the strategic planning process, especially if closely coordinated with both strategic and operational planning. Planning and development of the right people at the right time and place, at the lowest possible cost, is an essentially strategic objective.

3. Where the costs and time involved in developing the total system are prohibitive—and no business urgency makes these costs necessary in the minds of top managers—an incremental approach to system development may be necessary. For example, many organizations developed HRIS technology because of EEO requirements (see Chapter 3) and only later created other human resources programs using this technology. A planner might be able to "sell" top management on a succession planning system and later make a case for a formal career planning system, which would enhance the effectiveness of succession planning and add other capabilities. Often, overlapping development costs can be effectively "buried" in the approved budget, so that the additional program or subsystem can be presented as a partially completed effort.

4. Perhaps as a last resort, planners should have available the results of similar planning efforts in other organizations—preferably competitors. Often, fear of being at a competitive disadvantage motivates managers more than any other factor. In the final analysis, if the system is as ef-

fective as it should be, the relative weakness of this "reason" for installing the system won't matter.

If some of these arguments or methods seem deceptive, it is only that they recognize the fact that human resources planning as proposed here is in its infancy. Unfortunately, planners may need to be "creative" in order to do their jobs effectively.

Finally, it should be remembered that, as noted earlier, human resources planning does not "stay sold." Even with a mandate from top management, planners must overcome inertia to implement the system and must then continuously sell the program through communication, demonstration of its benefits, and activities that assure the continuing involvement of the key players and members of the critical mass.

The Development Process: Guidelines and Tools

Once the planner has a mandate to create an integrated human resources planning and development system, the question becomes: Where to start? The answer to this depends on whether the process of selling the system to management included the performance of an organizational diagnosis. If not, now is the time for this important process. (If the system is being developed incrementally and only the planner knows its overall "grand design," a scaled-down version of organizational diagnosis may be required. This would focus on the specifics of the "part" being introduced first, such as succession planning or the development of an HRIS.)

A tool such as the questionnaire shown in Appendix I is a useful instrument in the initial stages of development. Ideally, this questionnaire will have been prepared with the participation of key managers in the organization, the critical mass of influential executives and professionals. This questionnaire should be completed by all major departments and levels of management that may have responsibility for data collection, analysis, and evaluation of the final system. The involvement of these managers from the very beginning of the development process is important, as are the results of the questionnaire, which will further define system needs.

System Development Guidelines and Tools

Overall project management in the development and installation of an integrated planning system such as this is usually the responsibility of the planner, or should be. The pitfalls and potential for project-threatening delays, misdirection, and excessive costs are in direct proportion to the size of the project, and in organizations starting "from scratch," development may require a number of budget cycles.

The selection of a project management technique usually turns out to be a compromise between intrinsic project needs and what the planner knows about planning and scheduling projects. Bar charts, the project evaluation and review technique (PERT), critical path method (CPM) charts, and a broad range of manual or computerized techniques may be used successfully, however.

The overall development process typically includes these broad steps:

1. *Design the overall system.* The planner should develop a flowchart or other means of defining the various modules, input-output requirements for information flows, and interfaces.
2. *Decide sequences.* Decide which parts or part of the project need to be developed first, and sequence activities according to resource availability and other constraints.
3. *Define stages.* On the basis of the scope of the project, decide what activities can be grouped into various stages, with clearly defined completion points, as well as sequences and activities that can be performed simultaneously.
4. *Identify existing interfaces.* In most organizations, the planning system will not be developed "from the ground up" as a totally new entity. Existing management information systems, environmental scanning activities, operational research functions, and other systems will be integrated through interfaces.
5. *Prepare development budget.* Once all developmental activities have been identified, the time and costs of the activities can be estimated. These include costs outside of the planning organization as well as such costs as computer use, graphics, and documentation.
6. *Prepare development schedule.* A total project development schedule showing anticipated completion times of all major project elements, such as that presented in Appendix II, serves as a checklist for assuring compliance with time and cost estimates.
7. *Prepare implementation schedules.* For each major part of the project, an implementation schedule, such as the one shown in Appendix III, may be prepared.

The appendixes from I through VI show some of the kinds of forms and instruments useful in managing the implementation of a strategic human resources planning and development system. While not all-inclusive, these checklists provide an indication of the level of detail, main planning and scheduling requirements, and monitoring capabilities that should characterize developmental tools.

APPENDIX I

Human Resources Forecasting, Planning, and Development Questionnaire

The following questionnaire is intended to assist the HR planner in identifying the degree to which his or her organization needs to enhance its capability in human resources forecasting, planning, and development in order to maximize its effectiveness.

Questionnaire

Instructions: You are urged to answer all the questions to the fullest extent. At some point, you may wish to share this analysis with your colleagues, to ask for or give advice about its completion. This sharing, however, is entirely up to you. Your questionnaire will be treated in confidence, and no responses will be directly attributed to you without your written permission. The questionnaire should be completed and returned to the human resources department before _____. Depending on your position in the organization, it is possible that you might not have access to certain information requested by the questionnaire. Should this be the case, it may be helpful to ask your management to provide you with the data. Customary safeguards regarding confidentiality will apply.

Continued on next page

Appendix I (continued).

1. *What is the core mission of your organization?*

   Core mission is defined as your organization's *reason for being*. Making a profit is normally an objective, which by itself provides no clue as to the organization's purpose. Here is an example of a mission statement (previously mentioned in Chapter 4): The O. M. Scott Company spent one year deciding between two possible core missions: The first was "to make fertilizers"; the second was "to keep lawns green." Eventually, it decided to use the second statement as the core mission. This led the organization to invest in facilities to produce a variety of implements and chemicals, all designed to "keep lawns green"—a range of products far more sophisticated than the company's traditional product, chemical fertilizer.

   _____ I am not aware of my organization's core mission.

   I believe that my organization's core mission is as follows:

   _____
   _____
   _____
   _____
   _____
   _____

2. *What are your organization's main objectives, both short-range and long-range?*

   Examples: (1) to acquire a smaller organization to complement our present product line; (2) to open a new plant.

   _____ I am not aware of my organization's long-range objectives ($1\frac{1}{2}$ to 10 years).

   _____ I am not aware of my organization's short-range objectives (1 month to $1\frac{1}{2}$ years).

   I believe I know the following to be my organization's objectives:

   Short-range: _____
   _____
   _____
   _____
   _____

   Long-range: _____
   _____
   _____
   _____
   _____

3. *What are your organization's most significant policies in regard to its approach to business?*

   Examples: (1) Normally, it will not take government work. (2) Promotion of managers is always from internal resources.

   _____ I am not aware of my organization's significant policies.

   I believe I know the following to be my organization's significant policies:

   _____

   _____

   _____

   _____

   _____

   _____

4. *Does your organization have a long-range plan or a strategic plan?*

   _____ No.

   _____ Yes.

   If "Yes," briefly summarize its content:

   _____

   _____

   _____

   _____

   _____

5. *Does your organization assimilate market data, and is it aware of new and existing market trends?*

   _____ No.

   _____ I am not aware.

   _____ Yes.

   If "Yes," briefly summarize the most relevant information:

   _____

   _____

   _____

   _____

   _____

6. *Does your organization recognize that there may be more than one business environment to contend with? For example, does the organization seem to be considering more than one set of economic predictions, different impacts of technology, or other external changes affecting the business?*

   _____ No.

   _____ I am not aware.

   _____ Yes.

Continued on next page

Appendix I (continued)

7. *Does your organization develop various possible scenarios of economic and business environmental conditions that are likely to affect its existence?*

_____ No.

_____ I am not aware.

_____ Yes.

   If "Yes," briefly describe the major scenarios as you know them:

   _____

   _____

   _____

   _____

   _____

8. *If your organization has developed economic and environmental scenarios, has it developed response strategies designed specifically to respond to each scenario affecting your organization?*

_____ No.

_____ I am not aware.

_____ Yes.

   If "Yes," briefly describe your organization's response strategies:

   _____

   _____

   _____

   _____

   _____

9. *If your organization is a technical company or an organization that often performs major projects, has it developed a list of specific projects and groups of projects, each representative of the scope of work unique to its strategy?*

_____ No.

_____ I am not aware.

_____ Yes.

   If "Yes," briefly describe how this is done in your organization:

   _____

   _____

   _____

   _____

   _____

10. *For each of the major projects that your organization normally performs, do you have a standard model of human resources required to accomplish those projects?*

_____ No.

_____ I am not aware.

_____ Yes.

If "Yes," briefly describe the models:

_____

_____

_____

_____

_____

11. *Does your organization have the capability to produce computer-based demand forecasts in support of its strategic plans?*

_____ No.

_____ I am not aware.

_____ Yes.

    If "Yes," briefly describe how this is done:

_____

_____

_____

_____

_____

12. *Does your organization have on-line, interactive computer capability to rapidly examine scenarios, strategies, and relevant variables for alternative action plans?*

_____ No.

_____ I am not aware.

_____ Yes.

    If "Yes," briefly describe your organization's capabilities in this area:

_____

_____

_____

_____

_____

13. *If your organization has a business strategy, is it the only one, or are there alternative strategies to be employed if necessary?*

_____ No.

_____ I am not aware.

_____ Yes.

    If "Yes," briefly describe how your organization approaches this:

_____

_____

_____

_____

_____

Continued on next page

Appendix I (continued)

14. *Does your organization have a corporate data base to be used for operational and long-range planning as well as financial and human resources planning?*

_____ No.

_____ I am not aware.

_____ Yes.

   If "Yes," briefly describe your organization's system:

_____

_____

_____

_____

_____

15. *Does your organization utilize operational planning techniques (short-term planning, up to 1½ years)?*

_____ No.

_____ I am not aware.

_____ Yes.

   If "Yes," briefly describe your organization's system:

_____

_____

_____

_____

_____

16. *Is your organization capable of producing operational human resources demand forecasts so that human resources loading can be planned in a systematic fashion?*

_____ No.

_____ I am not aware.

_____ Yes.

   If "Yes," briefly describe your organization's system:

_____

_____

_____

_____

_____

17. *Does your organization have an employee performance evaluation program?*

_____ No.

_____ I am not aware.

_____ Yes.

18. *If your organization has an employee performance evaluation program, does it distinguish between managerial performance and performance of nonmanagerial employees?*

    _____ No.

    _____ I am not aware.

    _____ Yes.

19. *Does your organization have a career management program, so that career paths are developed for key employees?*

    _____ No.

    _____ I am not aware.

    _____ Yes.

    If "Yes," briefly describe your organization's system:

    _____

    _____

    _____

    _____

    _____

20. *Does your organization have the capability to train its own employees?*

    _____ No.

    _____ I am not aware.

    _____ Yes.

21. *If your organization has a training capability, does this address skills training as well as management development? Check one or both as applicable.*

    _____ Skills training.

    _____ Management development.

22. *Does your organization have a management succession plan?*

    _____ No.

    _____ I am not aware.

    _____ Yes.

    If "Yes," briefly describe how such planning is done in your organization, beginning with whether succession planning is developed manually or is computer-based:

    _____

    _____

    _____

    _____

    _____

23. *Does your organization have reliable statistics on past employee turnover?*

    _____ No.

    _____ I am not aware.

    _____ Yes.

Continued on next page

Appendix I (continued)

24. *To what extent is the management of your organization involved in human resources planning? Describe briefly:*

      ————————————————————————————————

      ————————————————————————————————

      ————————————————————————————————

      ————————————————————————————————

      ————————————————————————————————

      ————————————————————————————————

25. *Does your organization have a skills inventory?*

      —————— No.

      —————— I am not aware.

      —————— Yes.

26. *Does your organization have a list of people outside the company whom it might like to hire in the future?*

      —————— No.

      —————— I am not aware.

      —————— Yes.

27. *Does your organization have a computer-based employee records data base?*

      —————— No.

      —————— I am not aware.

      —————— Yes.

28. *Has your organization ever been exposed to formal organizational development activity (organizational diagnosis, team building, process consultation, and so on)?*

      —————— No.

      —————— I am not aware.

      —————— Yes.

      If "Yes," briefly describe the kinds of interventions that have taken place and approximately when:

      ————————————————————————————————

      ————————————————————————————————

      ————————————————————————————————

      ————————————————————————————————

      ————————————————————————————————

      ————————————————————————————————

29. *Does your organization have formal position descriptions for each significant job in the company?*

    _____ No.

    _____ I am not aware.

    _____ Yes.

30. *Does your organization have a formal program of compensation?*

    _____ No.

    _____ I am not aware.

    _____ Yes.

APPENDIX II

Human Resources Planning System Development Schedule

Function	Accomplished Date
1.0 *Staff the Human Resources Planning Function.*	
1.1 Identify the position requirements.	January
1.2 Prepare a position description.	January
1.3 Appoint an administrator, corporate manager of planning.	January
1.4 Select an administrative/clerical assistant.	January
1.5 Identify internal consultation resources.	January
1.6 Hold meeting between human resources planning staff and director to discuss relationship between human resources planning, personnel, and training development staffs.	January
2.0 *Coordinate all Human Resources Planning Information Resources.*	
2.1 Hold joint meeting of corporate human resources planning staff, systems, and personnel.	January
2.2 Hold meeting with personnel to discuss accessibility of needed historical human resources information.	January
2.3 Hold meeting with MIS staff to examine existing human resources forecasting model and feasibility of adding variables.	January
2.4 Hold meeting with human resources administrator to discuss accessibility of needed historical information.	January
2.5 Hold meetings with branch office personnel to discuss accessibility of needed historical human resources information.	January

Function	Accomplished Date
3.0 *Update Employee Skills Inventory.*	
3.1 Send skills inventory update form to all employees.	Out of scope
3.2 Authenticate revised skills inventory information on a random-sample basis.	Out of scope
3.3 Travel to locations where return of updated forms is slow.	February
3.4 Enter updated information into the computer.	March
4.0 *Expand Employee Skills Inventory.*	
4.1 Meet with personnel and MIS to discuss expansion of the training portion of the skills inventory.	January
4.2 Expand the skills inventory.	March
5.0 *Generate Department Managers' Interest in Human Resources Planning.*	
5.1 Director of human resources planning meets with all department managers to discuss their role in planning.	March
5.2 Director of human resources planning sends a memorandum to all remote managers indicating their role in human resources planning.	March
6.0 *Develop a Five-Year Human Resources Forecast.*	
6.1 Meet with individual department managers to determine their short-term and long-range needs.	2d year—February
6.2 Meet with corporate planning to explore corporate plans for expansion or contraction.	2d year—February
6.3 Examine historical personnel records to determine trends in employment and unemployment	2d year—February/March
6.4 Provide data to MIS personnel for input to their forecasting model.	2d year—April
6.5 Examine results of the model.	2d year—May
7.0 *Conduct Human Resources Inventory and Audit.*	
7.1 Examine position descriptions for currency.	Out of scope
7.2 Revise out-of-date position descriptions.	Out of scope
7.3 From the skills inventory, run a human resources inventory by position to determine matching of position against forecast need.	May
7.4 Determine human resources discrepancies.	May
7.5 Audit list of scheduled promotions and transfers.	March

Continued on next page

Appendix II (continued)

Function	Accomplished Date
8.0 *Develop Career Paths.*	
8.1 Meet with department managers to discuss historical career paths within their particular group.	May
8.1.1 Identify historical career paths of those scheduled for promotions or transfers.	March
8.2 Correlate managers' career path information against personnel records information.	June
8.2.1 Correlate historical career paths of those scheduled for promotions or transfers.	March
8.3 After correlating information, meet again with managers to discuss alternative paths that might have been uncovered.	July
8.4 Assure agreement with the department manager before finalizing career paths.	July
8.5 Send career path information to divisional vice-president for final approval.	September
8.5.1 Present career path information regarding scheduled promotions and transfers to divisional vice-president.	March
8.6 Meet with systems group to determine feasibility of computerizing career path information for professional employees.	March
8.7 Computerize career path information.	September
8.8 Verify career path information.	2d year— March
9.0 *Develop Management Succession Charts.*	
9.0.1 Develop model of management succession integration.	March
9.1 Integrate already developed management succession information with current needs.	July
9.2 Develop an up-to-date position description with each person on the chart.	July
9.3 Develop a set of human resources specifications by discussing with the individuals the pertinent qualifications needed to fill that position should it become vacant.	August
9.4 Have each individual nominate at least one and preferably two replacements: an emergency replacement and a planned replacement to be available within two years.	July
9.5 Have each manager, in consultation with a human resources planning consultant, develop a training and development program for each of the key replacements to fill the gaps in background.	2d year— March

Function			Accomplished Date
	9.6	If there is no potential replacement on board who can be ready in two years, request that the manager hire an outside backup within one year.	September
	9.7	The results of the above will be plotted on a confidential planning board displaying management readiness and succession.	September
10.0		***Provide Career Planning.***	
	10.1	Design career planning workshop for professional employees.	August
	10.2	Design career planning workshop for nonprofessional employees.	September
	10.3	Train the training staff to conduct each workshop.	October
	10.4	Trial-run each workshop.	October
	10.5	Offer career planning workshops on a voluntary basis.	November
	10.6	Match corporate requirements against career path alternatives and desires.	December
		10.6.1 Select career path alternatives of those scheduled for promotions or transfers that will meet short- and long-term career objectives.	April
	10.7	Formulate individuals' career objectives.	November
		10.7.1 Interview those scheduled for promotions or transfers.	March
	10.8	Offer ongoing career counseling services.	December
11.0		***Develop Management Development Plan.***	
	11.1	Identify requirements on management succession/ replacement charts for training and development.	August
	11.2	Identify professionals on career paths and their educational requirements.	September
		11.2.1 Identify career path skill requirements of those scheduled for promotions or transfers through interviewing of incumbents.	April
	11.3	Identify annual requirements for training and development.	November
		11.3.1 Formalize a training schedule for those scheduled for promotions or transfers.	April
	11.4	Meet with systems group to determine feasibility of computerizing training needs.	March
12.0		***Integrate Performance Plans and Appraisal Information with Human Resources Planning.***	
	12.1	Meet with systems group to determine feasibility of computerizing performance appraisal and planning data.	February

Continued on next page

Appendix II (continued)

Function	Accomplished Date
12.2 Design a mechanism whereby training and development information can be communicated to department managers at appropriate performance planning periods.	February
12.3 Develop a procedure for gaining access to performance appraisals for purposes of updating computer on fulfillment of training and development requirements.	2d year— February
12.4 Redevelop performance appraisal form to include potential and performance coding symbols.	February
12.5 Begin communication of training and development needs to individual professional employees.	November
13.0 *Administrative Functions.*	
13.1 Develop human resources planning forms.	February
13.2 Develop human resources planning procedures.	February
13.3 Develop and approve human resources planning policies.	July
13.4 Develop human resources planning objectives.	May
13.5 Evaluate computer-generated human resources planning reports.	June

APPENDIX III

Plans for Development and Implementation of Management Succession: Ongoing Computer Implementation

Individual Responsible		Estimated Completion Date	Revised Completion Date	Completion
WL	1. Identify additional requirements of management succession system.			
WL	2. Define components in detail. Determine feasibility from programmers. Detail input, output, run procedure, and system considerations.			
WL AG	3. Review Nos. 1 and 2 above with AG. Modify as required.			
WL AG	4. If required, define and review additional managment sucession details with CS and OM.			
WL	5. Submit specifications to computer staff.			
WL	6. Monitor progress computer staff is making in implementing specifications. Report as necessary.			
WL AG	7. Debug system, review specifications, and adjust target dates as needed. Report as necessary.			

Continued on next page

281

Appendix III (continued)

Individual Responsible		Estimated Completion Date	Revised Completion Date	Completion
WL AG	8. Assign staff to review and proof system outputs. Correct as required.			
	9. Incorporate new management succession programming into existing system. Check for accuracy, then release outputs to management for its use.			

APPENDIX IV

Plans for Development and Implementation of High-Potential (HP) Identification List

Individual Reponsible		Estimated Completion Date	Revised Completion Date	Completion
WL	1. Identify need for and potential uses of HP list.			
WL	2. Define components of computerized system—that is, mechanisms for entering, generating, displaying, and updating the data.			
WL AG	3. Review Nos. 1 and 2 with AG.			
WL AG	4. Present findings and recommendations to OM and CS for their review.			
WL	5. On the basis of No. 4, submit specifications within target dates for completion.			
WL	6. Monitor progress computer staff is making in implementing specifications within target dates. Notify OM and CS.			
WL	7. On the basis of No. 6, debug system, review specifications, and adjust target dates as needed. Notify OM and CS.			

Continued on next page

Appendix IV (continued)

Individual Reponsible		Estimated Completion Date	Revised Completion Date	Completion
WL AG	8. Assign staff to review and proof computerized HP list once it is available to obtain a "clean run."			
WL	9. Submit computerized HP list to executive staff with guidelines for its use and updating.			

APPENDIX V

Plans for Development and Implementation of Demand and Availability Forecasts

Individual Responsible		Estimated Completion Date	Revised Completion Date	Completion
WL	1. Continue to monitor and review computer staff implementation.			
WL	2. Clarify and revise system specifications as systems, outputs, and operating procedures are defined. Advise AG.			
WL	3. If necessary, report changes in specifications and report completion progress to OM and CS.			
WL	4. Review outputs and assign staff to check accuracy.			
WL AG	5. Using staff, develop initial career path data, based on current positions and/or management succession data.			
WL	6. Review initial results prior to release of first forecasts to management.			

APPENDIX VI

Plans for Development and Implementation of Performance Appraisal System

A. Timing of Performance Appraisals

Individual Responsible		Estimated Completion Date	Revised Completion Date	Completion
AG	1. Summarize survey results (see OM memo to all officers and department heads No. 12345).			
AG	2. On the basis of survey comments, come up with recommendations on when performance appraisals should occur as well as strategies for implementing the system (timing). Review with WL.			
AG	3. Schedule meeting with OM and CS to present survey results, recommendations, and strategies for implementation.			
AG	4. Once consensus is obtained on timing of performance appraisals, brief administrators and communicate decision to organization (that is, memo to "All Officers and Department Heads") and/or schedule briefing session with executive staff.			

Individual Responsible		Estimated Completion Date	Revised Completion Date	Completion
AG	5. Install procedures for human resources development's timely processing of performance appraisal forms out to the organization as well as procedures for monitoring the timely return of forms to human resources development.			

B. Project and Department Head Evaluation Forms and Procedures

Individual Responsible		Estimated Completion Date	Revised Completion Date	Completion
AG	1. Summarize comments of individuals who reviewed the forms and procedures (see OM memo No. 12346).			
AG	2. On the basis of reviewers' comments, own observations, and input from administrators, redesign forms and develop alternative procedures. Review with WL.			
AG	3. Schedule meeting with WL and CS to present recommendations for changes in forms and procedures.			
AG	4. Once consensus is obtained on changes, send forms and procedures to section chiefs, for distribution to and use by project managers and for human resources development's monitoring of the evaluation system.			

Continued on next page

Appendix VI (continued)

C. Design and Development of New System and Forms for Performance Appraisal

Individual Responsible		Estimated Completion Date	Revised Completion Date	Completion
AG	1. Schedule meetings with administrators, OM, and CS to review history and current status of performance appraisal system.			
AG	2. Review existing forms for all levels.			
AG	3. On the basis of own observations/experience and specific company requirements, begin redesign of forms for all levels. Review with WL.			
AG	4. Identify problem areas that require clarification by department heads or officers. Advise OM. Schedule individual and/or group meetings and incorporate comments into redesign of forms.			
AG	5. Schedule meeting with OM and CS to present initial recommendations on redesign of forms.			
AG	6. Complete redesign of forms and submit to OM for review and approval.			
AG	7. Once consensus is obtained on redesign of forms, send draft copies to officers and department heads for their comments.			
AG	8. Inspect comments and changes received and incorporate them into forms, where possible. Come up with final draft of forms.			

Individual Responsible		Estimated Completion Date	Revised Completion Date	Completion
AG	9. Work with administrators and trainers on development of training programs aimed at instructing individuals in how to: (1) complete (fill out) new forms; (2) conduct performance appraisal feedback sessions with subordinates; and (3) develop performance plans with subordinates.			
AG	10. Pilot-test training programs.			
AG	11. Implement training programs on companywide basis.			
AG	12. Implement procedures for assuring timeliness of performance appraisal information provided by department heads.			
AG	13. Develop and implement procedure for integrating performance appraisal review system into human resources planning model data base.			

APPENDIX VII

Case Study: How ACS, Inc. Applies the Strategic Human Resources Forecasting System Using a Microcomputer

(This case study of a hypothetical company, Aggressive Computer Systems, Inc., illustrates the actual application of the recommended approach to human resources forecasting, in this instance using a microcomputer-based software system to process and integrate data from the three main planning systems of the organization: strategic planning, operational planning, and human resources planning. The principles and definitions involved at each stage of the model flowchart for integrated planning and forecasting (see Chapter 1, Figure 1-1) are applied to the hypothetical company's situation, to help illustrate the processes, relationships, constraints, and results of the system.

In this instance, the hypothetical organization is a "growth" company, whose business strategies require a planning approach that more effectively forecasts the human resources needed to accomplish various levels and types of increased production and sales. The same principles and relationships exemplified here, however, apply to forecasting based on other strategies, if human resources forecasting is to be systematically and effectively integrated with long-term strategic goals and the realities of operational human resources requirements.)

Aggressive Computer Systems, Inc. (ACS) began in 1980 as a backyard operation run by its two founding partners, Paul Saunders and Jack Lawrence. Like many of their contemporaries in the computer business, both founders had been "renegades" who left larger companies to start off on their own, primarily because they felt they had a better idea that could not be properly exploited in a large, bureaucratic organization. In this case, their "better idea" was a specialized software package that anticipated the advent of computer-assisted design (CAD), a method of integrating engineering data so that the object or structure could be displayed on the computer screen as a three-dimensional figure that took into account all relevant parameters.

From the initial software package, which our heroes sold to a dozen small engineering firms, sufficient profits were realized to purchase a powerful minicomputer. This they modified to accept an even more sophisticated version of their CAD software, and the complete package was sold as a product in its own right. The partners were successful in establishing their small organization as a pioneer in the field, and by the end of 1983, the company's staff had grown to 1,800 people.

Not content with their accomplishments thus far, Paul and Jack decided to pursue a strategy of aggressive growth and started to design their own personal computer, capable of running both IBM MS-DOS and Apple CP/M operating systems. To a certain extent, it could be said that the ACS people emulated past Japanese business tactics. Even though ACS was technologically up-to-date, its strength was in taking an existing concept or design and refining and improving it so that the resulting application worked better than the original. Whether this philosophy was to continue depended on the strategic plan that the company was about to develop.

By the end of 1985, ACS had grown to over 4,000 employees and, much to the chagrin of its "renegade" founders, had become large enough to require a formal administrative system with staff groups, operating units, titles, and organization charts. The company was now made up of three main operating divisions: engineering, manufacturing, and research. A small corporate group provided all the support services: finance, administration, marketing, and legal.

It was at this time that management recognized it needed help in charting the future course of the firm. Even though management had a good understanding of the market, it had difficulty staffing its projects and was constantly reminded of the fact that skilled people in its business were not always available to be bought on demand. As is typical in the computer industry, the company experienced a high degree of attrition, which was expensive both in recruiting costs and in lost productivity.

To obtain help, the firm hired two consultants with experience in human resources planning and proceeded to design and to implement its own strategic human resources planning and development system.

The Planning Process

ACS decided to use a microcomputer system based on the Lotus 1-2-3 spreadsheet package to follow the planning model (see Chapter 1, Figure 1-1) closely and proceeded step-by-step according to the flowchart. Since a data base had to be established from scratch, the company started with the human resources planning cycle, then proceeded to operational planning, and finally to strategic planning. Each of the following subheadings refers to the corresponding step in the Figure 1-1 model flowchart.

Human Resources Planning

Human Resources Pool

As of January 1, 1986, the company had 3,725 employees in its operating divisions (986 in engineering, 142 in research, and 2,597 in manufacturing). In addition, it counted 410 staff people in finance, administration, marketing, and the legal department. (See Figure A-1.)

Employee Population Characteristics

Except for the staff people, the majority of the employees are generally of a technical background. They are highly educated, and often their skills are in demand in the marketplace. This necessitates competitive compensation and benefits.

Figure A-1. **Human resources pool: Aggressive Computer Systems, Inc.**

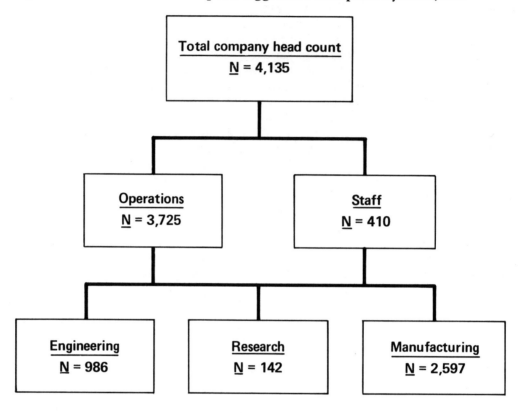

Availability Forecast

Of the options available for structuring the task of availability forecasting, the company chose to use the network flow model. This necessitated the design of standard career paths for the three operating departments. (Since the employees in the technical departments were considered the most critical resources, these are the ones that the firm decided to plan for in detail. The staff groups would be considered in the form of appropriate ratios.)

A hypothetical career path for the engineering department at ACS is shown in Figure A-2. Data include the position name, identification codes, and an estimate of the time an individual spends in each position. In our example, we have estimated that it takes an entry-level junior engineer 16 years to become a chief engineer.

An application of these computerized career path data is shown in the illustrations in the balance of this appendix, which were developed using the popular commercial spreadsheet software called Lotus 1-2-3, running on an IBM PC. Even though large forecasting applications generally require a mainframe package, a micro-based program often is quite adequate.

Despite the fact that the formulas used to develop the spreadsheets are not shown here, anyone with some microcomputer experience can readily develop similar approaches.

Table A-1 illustrates how a standard career path framework was created. Starting

Figure A-2. **Standard career path: ACS engineering department.**

Position	Skill code	Time in position
Junior engineer	9AHV	2 years
Associate engineer	10AHT	2 years
Engineer	11RT	3 years
Senior engineer	13RT	2 years
Principal engineer	14RT	2 years
Supervising engineer	16RT	3 years
Assistant chief engineer	17FR	2 years
Chief engineer	18DA	I
		16 years

with the entry-level position of junior engineer 9AHV (*9* for salary bracket and *AHV* as the code identifying this particular position), a matrix representing nine time periods horizontally (P1 through P9) and seven positions vertically (9AHV through 17FR) was constructed. For purposes of this illustration, let's assume that the time periods are years.

The actual head count for junior engineers (in this case, 390) was entered for year

Table A-1. Actual employee count—engineering.

Engineers		P1	P2	P3	P4	P5	P6	P7	P8
Jr. engineer									
	9AHV	390	390	0	0	0	0	0	0
	10AHT			390	390	0	0	0	0
	11RT					390	390	390	0
	13RT								390
	14RT								
	16RT								
Engineer									
	9AHV				no entry at this level				
	10AHT	268	268	0	0	0	0	0	0
	11RT			268	268	268	0	0	0
	13RT						268	268	0
	14RT								268
	16RT								
	17FR								

Table A-2. Total employee availability by department.

		P1	P2	P3	P4	P5	P6	P7	P8
182	*Dept. No. 730*								
183	*Central Engineering*								
184									
185	9AHV	390	390	0	0	0	0	0	0
186	10AHT	268	268	390	390	0	0	0	0
187	11RT	187	187	455	268	658	390	390	0
188	13RT	98	98	0	187	187	268	268	390
189	14RT	42	42	98	98	0	187	187	268
190	16RT	1	1	43	42	140	98	98	187
191	17FR	0	0	0	1	2	43	42	98
192	18DA	0	0	0	0	0	1	1	43
193									
194	Availability total	986	986	986	986	987	987	986	986
195									
196	Forecast (initial)	986	986	986	986	987	987	986	986
197	Forecast (adjusted)			907	835	768	706	650	598
198	Turnover 8%	0	79	73	67	61	57	52	48
199									
200	Adjusted availability	986	907	835	768	706	650	598	550

1. This number is then spread throughout the various positions, consistent with past patterns, which indicated that a junior engineer could expect to stay in this position for two years. He or she would then be promoted to other positions (10AHT, 11RT, and 13RT) and stay in each of them for a specified period of time, as shown in Figure A-2.

The next step would be promotion to 14RT, where the junior engineer would spend two years, until year 9. Since our planning does not go beyond this, the time that a person would spend in this job is not clearly indicated.

The same process is repeated for the next position in the hierarchy, engineer (10AHT). Table A-1 (line 194) indicates that in this matrix, no entry is made at the 9AHV level, since it has already been done in the matrix for the junior engineer position. This step indicates that, at present, 268 employees with this classification are available. The rest of the matrix extends this availability through time until year 9.

Similar data entries are made for the rest of the identified positions, creating a summary of all career path matrixes in the central engineering department, which enables a computation of total availability, shown in Table A-2.

Table A-2 clearly illustrates how the availability numbers are arranged so that movement of the employee population can be traced through time, based on past experience. It also surfaces some anomalies, such as the unusual peaks in availability for the 11RT positions in cells P3 186 and P5 186 and the total absence of people in cell P3 187. This is a factor of the time in position for those particular skills, which will need to be modified in the future in order to allow a smoother availability curve.

The initial forecast in cell P1 196 indicates that the present head count for all job classifications in engineering is 986 employees. The rest of the numbers on this line are not valid, because they do not account for turnover. This is dealt with in line 198, which applies a correction factor of 8 percent turnover per year after the first year. The attrition factor is based on historical experience. The adjusted availability, then, is shown on line 200.

Table A-3. Consolidated employee availability—all departments (turnover: 8 percent).

Department	P1	P2	P3	P4	P5	P6	P7	P8
Staff	410	377	347	319	294	270	248	229
Engineering	986	907	835	768	706	650	598	550
Research	142	131	120	111	102	94	86	79
Manufacturing	2,597	2,389	2,198	2,022	1,860	1,712	1,575	1,449
TOTAL	4,135	3,804	3,500	3,220	2,963	2,725	2,507	2,307

Exactly the same process is repeated for the two remaining departments, applied research and manufacturing, resulting in a consolidated employee availability as illustrated in Table A-3.

In essence, Table A-3 indicates that according to the present organizational structure, taking into account historical attrition experience and given no interventions (such as recruiting or layoffs) to change availability, the company can expect to have the specified number of employees available at each of the points in time shown.

The impact of attrition on availability can be significant. For example, if turnover assumptions for two departments were changed to 12 percent for engineering and 15 percent for manufacturing, the net availability would be as shown in Table A-4. If planning is being done for a company that has experienced different turnover rates among different departments, such variables should be reflected in the forecast to ensure the greatest possible accuracy.

The next step in the creation of the data base is the development of standard staffing packages. To illustrate this, we will move to the operational planning section of the Figure 1-1 flowchart.

Table A-4. Consolidated employee availability—all departments (turnover: 8 percent—staff and research; 12 percent—engineering; 15 percent—manufacturing).

Department	P1	P2	P3	P4	P5	P6	P7
Staff @ 8% attrition	410	377	347	319	294	270	248
Engineering @ 12%	986	868	764	672	591	520	458
Research @ 8%	142	131	120	111	102	94	86
Manufacturing @ 15%	2,597	2,207	1,876	1,595	1,356	1,152	979
TOTAL	4,135	3,583	3,107	2,697	2,343	2,036	1,771
Original forecast at 8%	4,098	3,770	3,468	3,191	2,935	2,701	2,485
Difference	38	-187	-361	-494	-593	-665	-713

Operational Planning

Sales

To date, the company has booked sales levels of 3,000 ACS-1 microcomputers, 400 ACS-2 minicomputers, and 10 ACS-5 mainframe machines for the next eight time periods.

Production Planning

Production planning is a department within the manufacturing group. Its charge is to compute the resources required to manufacture products and to schedule production in the most effective manner. The main device for computing human resources requirements is the staffing package technique.

Standard staffing models have been developed for all of the company's products. Employing historical experience regarding how many and what kinds of people were utilized over the course of an identified project or production run, the company had a good baseline to use in its estimate of resource requirements.

Table A-5 illustrates a staffing package that engineering uses as a guide for determining human resources requirements for supporting the development and production of ACS-1 microcomputers at 1,000-units-per-year levels, projected to eight years. The gradually decreasing staffing requirements, from 86 to 64, reflect an expectation that over time, with experience, the manufacturing process will become more efficient, thus enabling a gradual reduction of employee demand to meet the stated level of production.

This particular staffing model uses eight time periods, and for the sake of simplicity, we will regard them as years. In an actual situation, however, it is more likely that a mix of time periods would be used. The following is one example of this multiple-time-period approach:

1. The first six months and two last quarters for the current year, such as:

1986
Jan Feb Mar Apr May June 3d Qtr 4th Qtr

Table A-5. Standard staffing model for engineering—based on 1,000 microcomputer units/year.

Type 1: ACS Microcomputer									
Skill	Code	P1	P2	P3	P4	P5	P6	P7	P8
Chief engr.	16RT	1	1	1	1	1	1	1	1
Pr. engr.	14RT	2	2	2	2	1	1	1	1
Sr. engr.	13RT	3	3	3	2	2	2	2	2
Engineer	11RT	15	12	12	11	11	10	9	9
Assoc. engr.	10AHT	30	23	22	22	22	21	20	20
Jr. engr.	9AHV	35	34	33	32	31	30	28	30
TOTAL		86	75	73	70	68	65	61	64

Table A-6. Standard staffing model for all departments—based on 1,000 microcomputer units/year.

Type 1: ACS-1 Microcomputer *Skill*	*P1*	*P2*	*P3*	*P4*	*P5*	*P6*	*P7*	*P8*
Staff	35	36	38	42	43	42	41	36
Engineering	86	75	73	70	68	65	61	64
Research	86	66	66	63	65	65	64	64
Manufacturing	264	200	196	191	188	184	177	172
Total 1000/year	471	377	373	366	364	356	343	336
Ratio for multiples of each additional 1000 units/year	298	229	224	219	216	211	203	198
(100% manufacturing + 15% research + 20% engineering + 10% staff)								

2. Plus four quarters for the next year, such as:

1987

1st Qtr 2d Qtr 3d Qtr 4th Qtr

3. Plus single years for subsequent periods:

1988 1989 1990 1991 1992 1993

Again, for simplicity, in our case each time period will be regarded as a year.

In standard staffing models (Table A-5), the various skills required—such as chief engineer—are listed vertically, along with the numbers of each that the planners anticipate will be required. Similar staffing packages have been prepared for the other departments involved in production: applied research and manufacturing. In addition, staffing packages for all three departments have been prepared for the other current products. The total resource requirements for each product are then summarized.

Table A-6 illustrates the consolidated standard staffing model for producing 1,000 units of the microcomputer. The consolidated standard staffing model for producing 100 units of the minicomputer is illustrated in Table A-7. A third consolidated standard staffing model for the mainframe computer is similarly constructed. However, since the product is larger and more complex, it uses standard production criteria of ten units per year.

Production unit specifications are convenient, because they set standard criteria for computation. For purposes of this example, we will use multiples rounded off to the nearest hundred rather than exact quantities, such as 1,276, as would be the case in an actual situation.

Immediate Production Requirements

Immediate production requirements indicate the production that is presently in the system, usually called *active* or *ongoing*. The graph in Figure A-3 illustrates the firm's personnel requirements to maintain current production levels. The supporting data in Table A-8, the operational human resources demand forecast, indicate that the company

Table A-7. Standard staffing model for all departments—based on 100 microcomputer units/year.

Type 2: ACS-2 Minicomputer Skill	P1	P2	P3	P4	P5	P6	P7	P8
Staff	47	50	52	55	54	49	47	46
Engineering	129	108	101	94	88	81	75	95
Research	96	78	80	85	82	79	82	78
Manufacturing	380	271	269	263	258	254	248	245
Total 100/year	652	507	502	497	482	463	452	464
Ratio for multiples of each additional 100 units/year	425	309	306	300	293	287	280	280
(100% manufacturing + 15% research + 20% engineering + 10% staff)								

is now currently involved in the production of 3,000 microcomputers, 400 minis, and 10 mainframe units per year (lines 108–110). The total personnel requirement to meet the needs of active work is 4,096 employees at the present time (cell P1 106).

Upcoming Production Requirements (Scheduled Production)

Upcoming production requirements are generated from sales that have been booked. Table A-8 includes not only what is being manufactured now but also the *scheduled* production or *backlog*, which extends into the future. The human resources requirements to produce this volume are again computed, using the applicable staffing packages. Line 112, Table A-8, summarizes the demand for meeting scheduled production for the planning periods from P2 to P8.

These numbers are developed by multiplying the applicable staffing packages by the number of standard units to be produced, corrected to account for economies of scale. For example, the values in Table A-8, cell P1 109 (active production for the minicomputer) and cells P2 115 through P8 115 (scheduled production for the minicomputer), are developed by multiplying the consolidated standard staffing model for the minicomputer by the number of units that have to be produced.

But it will not be a straight multiplication of the entire staffing package by 4 since when production rises beyond 100 minis (100 being the basic unit of production on which the model is based), it takes fewer added people to support that production level.

Referring again to the standard staffing model for the minicomputer, the minimum number of workers necessary to produce 100 units for the first year is 652 (Table A-7, cell P1 94).

For each multiple of 100 that we add to production, however, we will have to add only an extra 425 workers, the assumption being that even though the increment must include 100 percent of the manufacturing people, we need add only 15 percent for research, 20 percent for engineering, and 10 percent for staff. This adjustment is extended to subsequent time periods, as well.

For a level of 400 units, then, we would start with 652 employees, then add only 425 for the next three multiples. The result:

$$652 + (425 \times 3) = 1,927$$

Figure A-3. **Personnel required for active and scheduled work.**

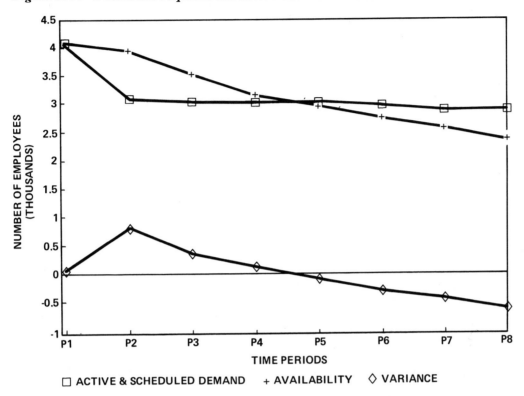

Table A-8. Operational human resources demand forecast for active and scheduled production.

		P1	*P2*	*P3*	*P4*	*P5*	*P6*	*P7*	*P8*
105 *Time Periods*									
106									
107 Active prod.	units	4,096	0	0	0	0	0	0	0
108 ACS-1 micro	3,000	1,066	0	0	0	0	0	0	0
109 ACS-2 mini	400	1,927	0	0	0	0	0	0	0
110 ACS-5 main	10	1,103	0	0	0	0	0	0	0
111									
112 Scheduled prod.		0	3,192	3,160	3,104	3,046	2,967	2,894	2,901
113 (backlog units)									
114 ACS-1 micro	3,000	0	834	822	803	795	778	749	732
115 ACS-2 mini	400	0	1,435	1,421	1,397	1,362	1,324	1,292	1,305
116 ACS-5 main	10	0	923	917	904	889	865	853	864
117									
118 Total act. + sched.		4,096	3,192	3,160	3,104	3,046	2,967	2,894	2,901
119 Availability		4,135	3,804	3,500	3,220	2,963	2,725	2,507	2,307
120 Variance		39	612	340	115	-84	-242	-387	-594

This is the number of employees necessary to produce 400 units. Had we not corrected demand by this simple device, we could have reached the erroneous conclusion that we needed 652 × 4 = 2,608 employees, an error of 681.

Strategic Planning

The previous work in setting up staffing models in the data base enables us to proceed with determining demand for personnel arising from strategic plans.

Develop Economic and Environmental Scenarios

On the basis of an evaluation of the business environment, three scenarios have been developed (optimistic, pessimistic, and most likely), discussed below.

Develop Preliminary Strategies

Preliminary strategic plans will attempt to position the company so that it can achieve the most rapid growth possible and avoid the need to issue stock or equity outside of the existing circle of owners.

Optimistic Strategy. The first strategy to be considered assumes very positive business conditions, resulting in a high demand for the firm's products (illustrated by the graph in Figure A-4). In order to evaluate the resource requirements of this strategy, a spreadsheet listing those products and the anticipated demand for them is prepared (Table A-9, lines 128 through 135).

In this case, the human resources demand for executing this strategy is a total of 4,096 for period 1 (P1 137). Not surprisingly, this is the same as the demand for active work, because indeed that's what it is (P1 128). In addition, we must add the resources already identified for the accomplishment of scheduled production (P2 129 through P8 129). Line 130, P2 through P8, summarizes the potential demand to meet the assumed

Table A-9. Strategic project mix: optimistic scenario.

126						Strategy: A34			
127	*Staff Model*		*P1*	*P2*	*P3*	*P4*	*P5*	*P6*	*P7*	*P8*
128	Active prod.		4,096	0	0	0	0	0	0	0
129	Sched. prod.		0	3,192	3,160	3,104	3,046	2,967	2,894	2,901
130	Potl. prod.		0	4,764	3,714	3,675	3,613	3,551	3,462	3,385
131										
132	Models	units								
133	Type 1 micro	3,000	0	1,066	834	822	803	795	778	749
134	Type 2 mini	400	0	1,927	1,435	1,421	1,397	1,362	1,324	1,292
135	Type 3 main	20	0	1,771	1,445	1,432	1,412	1,393	1,360	1,345
136										
137	Total demand		4,096	7,956	6,874	6,780	6,659	6,517	6,356	6,286
138	Availability		4,135	3,804	3,500	3,220	2,963	2,725	2,507	2,307
139	Variance		39	-4,152	-3,374	-3,560	-3,697	-3,792	-3,849	-3,979

140 **Note:** Potential production = type 1 + type 2 + type 5

Figure A-4. **Personnel required in optimistic scenario.**

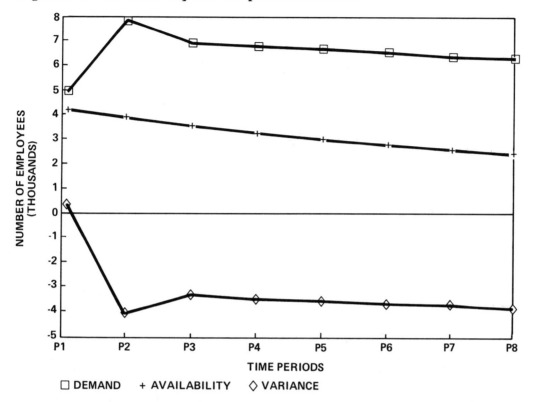

production requirements of this scenario, displayed under "units." At this time, we will postpone comparing this demand with availability, because we do not want to prejudice decision making by a premature examination of resource demand.

Pessimistic Scenario. The next case examines the resource requirements of a pessimistic scenario, illustrated by the graph in Figure A-5 and the accompanying spreadsheet in Table A-10.

In Table A-10, we see that the human resources demand for active production remains the same, 4,096. However, the projected demand generated by this particular strategy is considerably and understandably less than the demand generated by the optimistic strategy, as reflected by the demand shown in the potential summary (line 153). Moreover, it is assumed that something could happen to the scheduled backlog, reducing the number of units to be produced and the corresponding demand for people (line 148). Whereas the optimistic scenario (Table A-9) demanded 7,956 people for P2, the pessimistic strategy requires only 3,499, a significant difference.

Most Likely Scenario. The third scenario and strategy obviously involves a set of conditions that fall in between optimistic and pessimistic. For lack of a better word, let's call this the most likely scenario. The graph in Figure A-6 and the accompanying spreadsheet in Table A-11 summarize the total human resources requirements of the strategy designed to deal with these conditions.

It should be noticed again that demand due to active (4,096) and scheduled (3,192) production is the same as the previously discussed operational demand forecast (Table

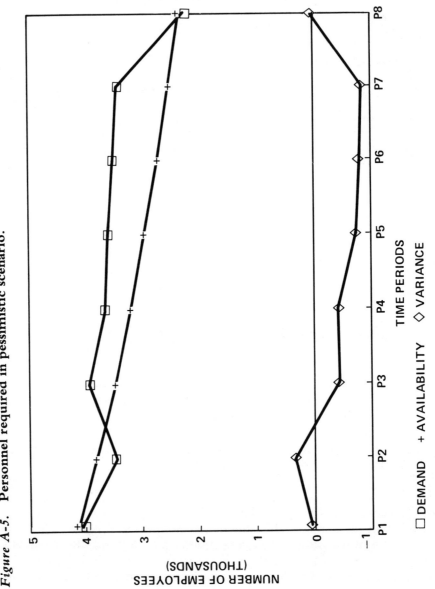

Figure A-5. Personnel required in pessimistic scenario.

Table A-10. Strategic project mix: pessimistic scenario.

		Strategy: B22							
146	*Staff Model*	*P1*	*P2*	*P3*	*P4*	*P5*	*P6*	*P7*	*P8*
147	Active prod.	4,096	0	0	0	0	0	0	0
148	Sched. prod. units	0	1,574	1,300	1,290	1,270	1,253	1,221	1,196
149	Type 1 micro 1,000	0	471	377	373	366	364	356	343
150	Type 2 mini 0	0	0	0	0	0	0	0	0
151	Type 5 main 10	0	1,103	923	917	904	889	865	853
152									
153	Potl. prod. units	0	1,925	2,643	2,364	2,335	2,292	2,224	1,093
154	Type 1 micro 1,000		471	377	373	366	364	356	343
155	Type 2 mini 200			1,077	816	808	797	775	750
156	Type 5 main 0				0	0	0	0	0
157									
158	Total demand	4,096	3,499	3,943	3,654	3,605	3,545	3,445	2,289
159	Availability	4,135	3,804	3,500	3,220	2,963	2,725	2,507	2,307
160	Variance	39	305	-443	-434	-643	-820	-939	18

A-8). The demand generated by the potential production forecast, however, reflects the demands imposed by the particular mix of production that this most likely case is expected to generate.

Test Strategies

The main test of a strategy is whether the organization can generate the resources necessary to execute it successfully. The fact that a particular case demands resources that are presently not available does not necessarily mean that it is not possible to find ways to acquire them. The contrary may also be true: Such demands may be entirely out of the realm of possibility. The only way to find out for sure is to test several scenarios and variables.

Standard and/or Estimated Staffing Criteria

As was previously indicated, initial demand calculations require the assimilation of data indicating what resources, how many, and over what period of time will be required to accomplish a certain volume of work. If the products or projects in question have been dealt with before, then standard staffing criteria should be available. The staffing packages are an example of this. However, it is possible that strategic planning could require staffing projections for products and processes that may be new for the organization. In this case, the staffing package techniques can still be utilized to project human resources requirements. The only difference is that instead of historical staffing patterns, we will have human resources demand that reflects the "best estimate" of the appropriate line managers, given reasonable specifications of what will need to be done. To keep our case study simple, we will assume that our staffing criteria will be standard throughout.

Figure A-6. **Personnel required in most likely scenario.**

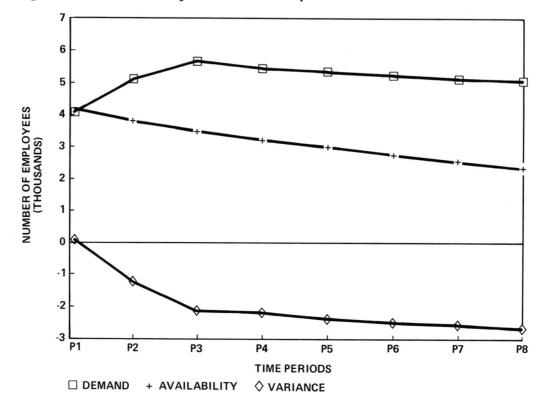

Demand Forecasting Options

Standard Staffing Packages

Our standard staffing packages will remain the same: There will be three departments (engineering, research, and manufacturing), each with a staffing package appli-

Table A-11. Strategic project mix: most likely scenario.

					Strategy: C34			
Staff Model		*P1*	*P2*	*P3*	*P4*	*P5*	*P6*	*P7*	*P8*
Active prod.		4,096	0	0	0	0	0	0	0
Sched. prod.		0	3,192	3,160	3,104	3,046	2,967	2,894	2,901
Potl. prod.	units	0	1,846	2,525	2,329	2,299	2,259	2,206	2,143
Type 1 micro	2,000		769	606	597	585	580	567	546
Type 2 mini	2,000		1,077	816	808	797	775	750	732
Type 5 main	1			1,103	923	917	904	889	865
Total demand		4,096	5,037	5,685	5,433	5,345	5,226	5,100	5,044
Availability		4,135	3,804	3,500	3,220	2,963	2,725	2,507	2,307
Variance		39	-1,233	-2,185	-2,214	-2,382	-2,501	-2,593	-2,737

Figure A-7. **Personnel requirements compared by strategy.**

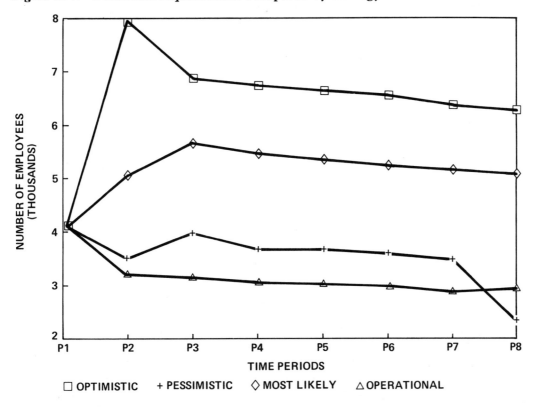

cable to an established product—in this case, the microcomputer (PC), minicomputer, and mainframe machine. Thus, we are working with a total of nine packages.

Estimated Staffing Packages

As previously indicated, to keep things simple, we will assume that estimated staffing packages will not be necessary because the product line is established and will continue indefinitely, albeit with gradual technical improvements to keep it current.

Statistical Demand Techniques

Management decided that statistical demand techniques would not be appropriate in this situation.

Preliminary Demand for Each Strategy

The graph in Figure A-7 and the accompanying spreadsheet in Table A-12 summarize the preliminary demand for each strategy. In Table A-12, we find that the people demand for all strategies remains the same (4,096) for P1 (period 1, or the immediate production run). This is understandable because this is production in progress, not likely to change. A close review of the operational human resources demand (line 170) also indicates a

Table A-12. Comparison of preliminary demand by strategy.

168		*Human Resources Demand*						
169	*Strategy*	*P1*	*P2*	*P3*	*P4*	*P5*	*P6*	*P7*	*P8*
170	Operational	4,096	3,192	3,160	3,104	3,046	2,967	2,894	2,901
171	Optimistic	4,096	7,956	6,874	6,780	6,659	6,517	6,356	6,286
172	Pessimistic	4,096	3,499	3,943	3,654	3,605	3,545	3,445	2,289
173	Most likely	4,096	5,037	5,685	5,433	5,345	5,226	5,100	5,044

gradual reduction in demand in every period after P1 because the remaining work in progress (scheduled production or backlog) gradually gets accomplished, and fewer workers are needed.

Test for Resource Adequacy

Are Resources Adequate?

Table A-13 provides a consolidated forecast for all strategies. In all cases, the initial employee head count of 4,135 will drop in subsequent periods since there will be only 8 percent attrition. This has to be reviewed in context with the demand generated by each strategy. In the optimistic case, demand will grow from 4,096 in P1 to 7,956 in P2, resulting in an initial shortage of 4,152 people and a shortage of about 3,500 thereafter. Considering the present base of 4,135 employees, it is highly unlikely that the company will be able to hire, train, and assimilate that many people over that period of time. This means that, however much we like it, this strategy may have to be discarded as nonimplementable.

A similar review of the pessimistic case indicates an employee surplus of 305 in P2, but still a moderate shortage beyond that. There doesn't seem to be any doubt that from a staffing perspective, the scenario is feasible. However, management can be expected

Table A-13. Consolidated forecast for all strategies.

	Human Resources Forecast	*P1*	*P2*	*P3*	*P4*	*P5*	*P6*	*P7*	*P8*
126		*Optimistic*							
127	Demand	4,096	7,956	6,874	6,780	6,659	6,517	6,356	6,286
128	Availability	4,135	3,804	3,500	2,963	2,963	2,725	2,507	2,307
129	Variance	39	-4,152	-3,374	-3,697	-3,697	-3,792	-3,849	-3,979
130									
131		*Pessimistic*							
132	Demand	4,096	3,499	3,943	3,654	3,605	3,545	3,445	2,289
133	Availability	4,135	3,804	3,500	3,220	2,963	2,725	2,507	2,307
134	Variance	39	305	-443	-434	-643	-820	-939	18
135									
136		*Most likely*							
137	Demand	4,096	5,037	5,685	5,433	5,345	5,226	5,100	5,044
138	Availability	4,135	3,804	3,500	3,220	2,963	2,725	2,507	2,307
139	Variance	39	-1,233	-2,185	-2,214	-2,382	-2,501	-2,593	-2,737

to make every effort to seek a profitable environment and to look further toward scenarios that are ambitious without making excessive demands on the firm's ability to provide resources.

The end result will be the refinement of the third strategy, based on the most likely scenario, which has the best chance of reconciling strategic objectives with the realities of the business environment and resource limitations. Lines 137–139 summarize the impact of such a strategy.

Here, indications are that there will be a shortage of 1,233 employees starting with P2. Even though this shortfall is substantial, it appears that, given its resource base, the organization will be able to hire, train, and assimilate that many new employees every year.

Discard Nonfeasible Strategies

A close review obviously leads to the conclusion that the optimistic strategy requires far too many resources to be considered feasible. It will have to be dropped, even though this action may mean giving up some opportunities. The only way to achieve the required staffing level would be merging with another organization, something that the company owners are not willing to do.

The pessimistic strategy is definitely implementable, but it will also be set aside in favor of the most likely scenario and strategy.

Upgrade Strategies

The pessimistic strategy will be retained as a contingency plan should adverse business conditions affect the firm. Refinements will also be made to the most likely strategy.

Optimize

The remaining most likely strategy will be further refined and optimized to ensure its implementability. At this time, factors such as human resources availability in the environment, possible changes in the expected attrition factors, and the cost of recruiting will be taken into consideration.

Select Alternative Scenarios and Strategies

In this case, the pessimistic scenario will be used as an alternative strategy. This means that the organization should be able to implement the plan should conditions dictate its use.

Select Most Likely Scenario and Strategy

Obviously, the most likely scenario and strategy that has been optimized will be used for developing a primary plan.

Corporate Data Base for Operational and Long-Range Planning

The corporate data base for operational and long-range planning will be made up of the most likely scenario and strategy, along with the applicable business plan, goals and objectives for the key managers, and applicable budgets. Minimum resources to meet the requirements of the pessimistic strategy will also be planned for on a contingency basis.

Operational Human Resources Demand Forecasts

The operational human resources demand forecasts summarize the concrete categories of demand: (1) active work and (2) scheduled work.

Human Resources Loading Schedule

Once the forecast has been developed, the production planners will prepare a list of people for assignment to active and scheduled work.

Consolidated Forecast

The consolidated forecast includes demand, availability, and variance for all departments at various levels of detail.

Variance

The comparison of demand and availability will give us the variance. This is the number that will need to be addressed, because we have reached a point at which action will need to be taken.

Feedback to Department Heads

The various forecasts are distributed to the department heads for review and to provide action plans for dealing with identified variances.

Plan to Address Variance

Now that the most likely, or high-probability, scenario has been identified and a strategy reflecting the human resources requirements has been developed, it will be necessary to examine just how the variance—the difference between what is needed and what is available—can be closed. A review of the three-line forecast for the most likely case provides a summary of demand, availability, and variance for periods 1 through 8 (Table A-14).

The immediate task at this point is to compute exactly how many people should be brought into the organization in order to close the variance. Line 350, the variance, provides a base for creating a specific plan for recruitment.

In order to achieve the best possible balance between demand and availability of employees during every time period, only those employees necessary to meet the demand will be hired during each period. Thus, lines 352 through 358 are added to the spreadsheet. This will be an aid to indicating how many new hires are necessary and when. For purposes of this illustration, it is initially assumed that there will be seven groups of new hires, staggered as indicated.

Period 1. Since this period indicates a surplus of 39, no additional recruiting is

Table A-14. Detailed forecast—period 1.

Strategy: B22 High Probability Scenario
Availability Method: Career Path + New Hires

		P1	*P2*	*P3*	*P4*	*P5*	*P6*	*P7*	*P8*
348	Demand	4,096	5,037	5,685	5,433	5,345	5,226	5,100	5,044
349	Availability 8%	4,135	3,804	3,500	3,220	2,963	2,725	2,507	2,307
350	Variance	39	-1,233	-2,185	-2,214	-2,382	-2,501	-2,593	-2,737
351									
352	+ New hires (1st group)		0	0	0	0	0	0	0
353	+ New hires (2d group)			0	0	0	0	0	0
354	+ New hires (3d group)				0	0	0	0	0
355	+ New hires (4th group)					0	0	0	0
356	+ New hires (5th group)						0	0	0
357	+ New hires (6th group)							0	0
358	+ New hires (7th group)								0
359									
360	Total new hires	0	0	0	0	0	0	0	0
361	Adjusted availability	4,135	3,804	3,500	3,220	2,963	2,725	2,507	2,307
362	Adjusted variance	39	-1,233	-2,185	-2,214	-2,382	-2,501	-2,593	-2,737

necessary. Due to the fact that shortages are expected in subsequent periods, the employees are retained and assigned to meaningful work on the overhead budget.

Period 2. Here, the variance forecast clearly indicates a shortage of 1,233 employees, and the hiring of that amount is reflected in Table A-15, cell P2 352.

At this point, an important principle about the impact of turnover rates needs to be discussed. If the 1,233 employees were to be retained without any losses due to attrition, we could indicate the availability of these additional 1,233 employees in every period from P2 to P8. But in fact, a group of new employees will experience significant

Table A-15. Detailed forecast—period 2.

Strategy: B22 High Probability Scenario
Availability Method: Career Path + New Hires

		P1	*P2*	*P3*	*P4*	*P5*	*P6*	*P7*	*P8*
348	Demand	4,096	5,037	5,685	5,433	5,345	5,226	5,100	5,044
349	Availability 8%	4,135	3,804	3,500	3,220	2,963	2,725	2,507	2,307
350	Variance	39	-1,233	-2,185	-2,214	-2,382	-2,501	-2,593	-2,737
351									
352	+ New hires (1st group)		1,233	0	0	0	0	0	0
353	+ New hires (2d group)			0	0	0	0	0	0
354	+ New hires (3d group)				0	0	0	0	0
355	+ New hires (4th group)					0	0	0	0
356	+ New hires (5th group)						0	0	0
357	+ New hires (6th group)							0	0
358	+ New hires (7th group)								0
359									
360	Total new hires	0	1,233	0	0	0	0	0	0
361	Adjusted availability	4,135	3,804	3,500	3,220	2,963	2,725	2,507	2,307
362	Adjusted variance	39	0	-2,185	-2,214	-2,382	-2,501	-2,593	-2,737

Table A-16.   Detailed forecast—period 2 (adjusted for turnover).

Strategy: B22 High Probability Scenario
   Availability Method: Career Path + New Hires

		P1	P2	P3	P4	P5	P6	P7	P8
348	Demand	4,096	5,037	5,685	5,433	5,345	5,226	5,100	5,044
349	Availability 8%	4,135	3,804	3,500	3,220	2,963	2,725	2,507	2,307
350	Variance	39	-1,233	-2,185	-2,214	-2,382	-2,501	-2,593	-2,737
351									
352	+ New hires (1st group)		1,233	925	851	783	720	662	609
353	+ New hires (2d group)			0	0	0	0	0	0
354	+ New hires (3d group)				0	0	0	0	0
355	+ New hires (4th group)					0	0	0	0
356	+ New hires (5th group)						0	0	0
357	+ New hires (6th group)							0	0
358	+ New hires (7th group)								0
359									
360	Total new hires	0	1,233	925	851	783	720	662	609
361	Adjusted availability	4,135	5,037	4,425	4,070	3,745	3,445	3,169	2,916
362	Adjusted variance	39	0	-1,260	-1,363	-1,600	-1,781	-1,931	-2,127

turnover during the early part of employment, and such a loss must be reflected in the plan. In this case, we will assume a loss of 25 percent for all newly hired employees during the first period after joining the company. For the subsequent periods, new hires will acquire the characteristics of the existing employee population and will experience its attrition rate of 8 percent. The result is reflected in Table A-16, line 352.

Given our assumptions, all 1,233 new hires will be available in P2. During the subsequent period, this group will experience 25 percent turnover ($1,233 \times .25 = 308$), which is subtracted from the total, leaving us 925 employees in P3. After this point, these employees become part of the existing employee group and experience the same turnover rate of 8 percent. Therefore:

$$925 \times .08 = 74$$

$$925 - 74 = 851$$

The loss of 74 employees leaves an availability of 851 in P4.

This calculation on the new base of 851 is repeated, leaving 783 employees in P5, 720 in P6, 662 in P7, and 609 in P8.

The hiring of the first group enabled the reduction of the variance in P2 to zero (cell P2 364). The adjusted variance for the next period (cell P3 362) now indicates that 1,260 new hires are necessary to zero out the adjusted variance. Thus, 1,260 are hired in P3, and the usual attrition calculations compute the impact of adding that second group to the employee pool. This process is repeated for all remaining periods, resulting in the hiring plan shown in Table A-17.

A summary forecast for the high-probability scenario is then developed (Table A-18). This figure clearly demonstrates how the initial variance (line 334) can be zeroed out by hiring a precise number of employees at specific points in time (line 335).

Other sections of the plan will provide additional details necessary for precise staff-

Table A-17. Detailed forecast—hiring plan.

Strategy: B22 High Probability Scenario
Availability Method: Career Path + New Hires

	P1	*P2*	*P3*	*P4*	*P5*	*P6*	*P7*	*P8*
Demand	4,096	5,037	5,685	5,433	5,345	5,226	5,100	5,044
Availability 8%	4,135	3,804	3,500	3,220	2,963	2,725	2,507	2,307
Variance	39	-1,233	-2,185	-2,214	-2,382	-2,501	-2,593	-2,737
+ New hires (1st group)		1,233	925	851	783	720	662	609
+ New hires (2d group)			1,260	945	869	800	736	677
+ New hires (3d group)				418	314	288	265	244
+ New hires (4th group)					417	313	288	265
+ New hires (5th group)						380	285	262
+ New hires (6th group)							357	268
+ New hires (7th group)								412
Total new hires	0	1,233	2,185	2,214	2,383	2,501	2,593	2,737
Adjusted availability	4,135	5,037	5,685	5,433	5,345	5,226	5,100	5,044
Adjusted variance	39	0	0	0	0	0	0	0

ing analysis at department, subunit, and skill levels. In fact, the most useful forecasts will be those that provide the most detail. For example, Table A-19 is representative of a departmental forecast.

The completed plans—which may involve hiring, transfers, training, and selected terminations—are forwarded to top management for review.

Review by Top Management

Top management reviews the staffing plans for consistency and feasibility.

Directed Staffing Level

The final plan, approved by top management, directs an official staffing level consistent with the adjusted availability of the plan, which averages about 5,000 employees per

Table A-18. Summary forecast.

Strategy: B22 High Probability Scenario (Most Likely)
Availability Method: Network Flow + New Hires

	P1	*P2*	*P3*	*P4*	*P5*	*P6*	*P7*	*P8*
Demand	4,096	5,037	5,685	5,433	5,345	5,226	5,100	5,044
Availability @ 8% annual attrition rate	4,135	3,804	3,500	3,220	2,963	2,725	2,507	2,307
Variance	39	-1,233	-2,185	-2,214	-2,382	-2,501	-2,593	-2,737
+ New hires @ 25%/8%	0	1,233	1,260	418	417	380	357	412
Adjusted availability	4,135	5,037	5,685	5,433	5,345	5,226	5,100	5,044
Adjusted variance	39	0	0	0	0	0	0	0

Table A-19. Departmental forecast: department No. 730—central engineering.

Availability Method: Network Flow + New Hires

	P1	P2	P3	P4	P5	P6	P7	P8
Demand	1,065	1,310	1,478	1,413	1,390	1,359	1,326	1,311
Availability @ 8% annual attrition rate	986	907	835	768	706	650	598	550
Variance	-79	-403	-643	-645	-683	-709	-728	-761
+ New hires	79	343	332	-60	-311	-515	-690	-895
Adjusted availability	1,065	1,309	1,478	1,413	1,390	1,359	1,326	1,311
Adjusted variance	0	0	0	0	0	0	0	0

year. In addition, management authorizes actions necessary for implementation, including recruitment, adjustment of standard career path patterns to smooth out availability curves, accelerated development of high-potential personnel, and the establishment of a formal management succession program. Recognizing the dynamic nature of such a system, management directs that the planning process be made permanent, thus enabling "on-line" updates as necessary to reflect the impact of actions that modify demand and availability.

Conclusion

This relatively simple example demonstrates how much can be done with a commonly accepted—and relatively inexpensive—microcomputer and a popular spreadsheet package. All the key concepts were used, starting with a simple application of the network flow model for availability forecasting, standard staffing models for demand forecasting, operational demand forecasts, the three basic strategies, and the human resources demand associated with them. We also demonstrated how adding current demand to scheduled and potential demand resulted in a complete forecast of employee requirements for each strategy. The impact of attrition on availability was examined, and a distinction was drawn between turnover characteristics of existing employees and new hires.

While a permanent application should utilize a thoroughly tested micro-based program or a customized program running on a company's mainframe, significant preliminary work can be done with a spreadsheet package to ensure proper file structures and a better definition of appropriate variables, thus facilitating the development of a permanent program that will ultimately be more timely and cost-effective.

NOTES

Chapter 2

1. "The Professionalization of the U.S. Labor Force," *Scientific American* (March 1979).
2. Thomas H. Patten, Jr., *Manpower Planning and the Development of Human Resources* (New York: John Wiley & Sons, 1971).
3. A. D. Szilagyi and M. J. Wallace, *Organizational Behavior and Performance* (Santa Monica, California: Goodyear Publishing Company, 1980).
4. Frederick Herzberg, "One More Time: How Do You Motivate Employees?" *Harvard Business Review* (January–February 1968).
5. Szilagyi and Wallace, *Organizational Behavior*.
6. E. E. Ghiselli, *The Validity of Occupational Aptitude Tests* (New York: John Wiley & Sons, 1966).
7. Anne Anastasi, *Psychological Testing* (New York: Macmillan, 1954); R. D. Arvey, *Fairness in Selecting Employees* (Reading, Massachusetts: Addison-Wesley, 1979); R. M. Guion, *Personnel Testing* (New York: McGraw-Hill, 1965).
8. Patten, *Manpower Planning*.
9. J. A. Craft, "A Critical Perspective on Human Resource Planning," *Human Resource Planning*, Vol. 3, No. 2 (1980), pp. 39–52.

Chapter 3

1. Alfred J. Walker, *HRIS Development: A Project Team Guide to Building an Effective Personnel Information System* (New York: Van Nostrand Reinhold, 1982).
2. Walker, *HRIS Development*.
3. Walker, *HRIS Development*, p. 25.

Part II—Introduction

1. Peter Lorange and Richard F. Vancil, *Strategic Planning Systems* (Englewood Cliffs, New Jersey: Prentice-Hall, 1977).

Chapter 4

1. *Business Week* (May 24, 1982).
2. Harry Levinson, *Organizational Diagnosis* (Cambridge, Massachusetts: Harvard University Press, 1972).
3. "When Bosses Look Back to See Ahead," *Business Week* (January 16, 1979), pp. 60–

61; "Engineering Organizational Change," *The Levinson Letter* (published by Harry Levinson).

4. Richard Beckhard and Reuben T. Harris, *Organizational Transitions: Managing Complex Change* (Reading, Massachusetts: Addison-Wesley, 1977).

5. "The O. M. Scott and Sons Company," Harvard Business School case, HBS Case Services No. 209–102 (Boston: 1964).

6. William F. Glueck, *Business Policy: Strategy Information and Management Action* (New York: McGraw-Hill, 1976).

Chapter 5

1. Among its earliest uses is this citation in *Dictionary of Music* (1883): "an Italian term, meaning a sketch of the scenes and main points of an opera libretto, drawn up and settled preliminary to filling in the detail." *Oxford English Dictionary* (1971).

2. *Webster's New Collegiate Dictionary* (1976).

3. Rochelle O'Connor, *Planning Under Uncertainty: Multiple Scenarios and Contingency Planning*, Report No. 741 (New York: The Conference Board, 1978).

4. E. Kirby Warren, *Long Range-Planning: The Executive Viewpoint* (Englewood Cliffs, New Jersey: Prentice-Hall, 1966).

5. John Chandler and Paul Cockle, *Techniques of Scenario Planning* (London: McGraw-Hill, 1982).

6. Harold W. Henry, *Long Range Planning Practices in 45 Industrial Companies* (Englewood Cliffs, New Jersey: Prentice-Hall, 1967); "Formal Planning in Major U.S. Corporations," *Long Range Planning* (October 1977).

7. Robert E. Linneman and Harold E. Klein, "The Use of Multiple Scenarios by U.S. Industrial Companies: A Comparison Study, 1977–1981," *Long Range Planning* (December 1983).

8. Even the U.S. government's long-range economic forecasts "are notable for only one thing—their inaccuracy." In 1977, for example, the Ford administration projected an average annual real growth rate of 4.8 percent during the 1977–82 period, while the Congressional Budget Office projected a 5.2 percent growth rate for that same period. The actual 1977–82 growth rate turned out to be 2.3 percent annually. Clyde Farnsworth, *The New York Times* (August 13, 1984).

9. W. H. Newman, "Selecting a Company Strategy," *Journal of Business Policy*, Vol. 2, No. 1 (1971).

10. William F. Glueck, *Business Policy: Strategy Information and Management Action* (New York: McGraw-Hill, 1976).

11. Charles J. McMillan, "From Quality Control to Quality Management: Lessons from Japan," *Business Quarterly* (Spring 1982). W. Edwards Deming, who helped teach Japanese industry military procurement standards beginning in 1958, and J. Duran, who lectured extensively in Japan after 1954, are considered pioneers in the quality of work life movement.

12. *The Wall Street Journal* (August 5, 1982).

13. *The Wall Street Journal* (June 10, 1982).

Chapter 6

1. James L. Riggs and Michael S. Inoue, *Introduction to Operations Research and Management Science: A General Systems Approach* (New York: McGraw-Hill, 1975).

2. Edward J. Ignall, "A Review of Assembly Line Balancing," Chapter 15 in *Operations Management: Selected Readings*, ed. Gene K. Groff and John F. Muth (Homewood, Illinois: Richard D. Irwin, 1969); M. E. Salveson, "The Assembly Line Balancing Problem," *Journal of Industrial Engineering*, Vol. 6, No. 3 (May–June 1955).

3. James W. Walker, *Human Resource Planning* (New York: McGraw-Hill, 1980).

4. Don R. Bryant, Michael J. Maggard, and Robert P. Taylor, "Manpower Planning Models and Technology; A Descriptive Survey," *Business Horizons* (April 1973), reprinted in G. E. Biles and S. R. Holmberg, *Strategic Human Resource Planning* (Glen Ridge, New Jersey: Thomas Horton and Daughters, 1980), p. 121.

5. W. J. McLarney and W. M. Berliner, *Management Training: Cases and Principles* (Homewood, Illinois: Richard D. Erwin, 1970).

6. B. M. Radcliffe, D. E. Kawal, and R. J. Stephenson, *Critical Path Method* (Boston: Cahners Publishing Company, 1967).

7. "Planning and Scheduling with PERT and CPM" (Newburyport, Massachusetts: Entelek Incorporated, 1973).

8. R. C. Shroeder, *Operations Management* (New York: McGraw-Hill, 1981), pp. 342–348, 484–485.

Chapter 8

1. K. P. Schneider and D. I. Hawk, "The Performance Appraisal Process: A Selected Bibliography," Special Report (Greensboro, North Carolina: Center for Creative Leadership, March 1980).

2. A. K. Korman, "The Prediction of Managerial Performance: A Review," *Personnel Psychology*, Vol. 21, No. 3 (1968), p. 319.

3. Robert J. Sternberg, *Intelligence, Information Processing, and Analogical Reasoning: The Componential Analysis of Human Abilities* (Hillside, New Jersey: Lawrence Erlbaum Associates, 1977).

4. Elliott Jaques, *The Changing Culture of a Factory* (London: Tavistock Publications, Ltd., 1951), *Measurement of Responsibility* (London: Tavistock Publications, Ltd., 1956), and *A General Theory of Bureaucracy* (London: Heinemann, 1976). Figures 8-5 and 8-6 are copyright © Heinemann Ltd. and are used by permission.

5. Manuel London and Stephen A. Stumpf, *Managing Careers* (Reading, Massachusetts: Addison-Wesley, 1982).

6. Edgar H. Schein, *Career Dynamics: Matching Individuals and Organizational Needs* (Reading, Massachusetts: Addison-Wesley, 1978).

Chapter 9

1. Michael J. Feuer, Richard J. Niehaus, and James A. Sheridan, "Human Resource Forecasting: A Survey of Practice and Potential," *Human Resource Planning*, Vol. 27, No. 2 (1984).

2. James W. Walker, *Human Resource Planning* (New York: McGraw-Hill, 1980).

3. Steven C. Wheelwright and Spyros Makridakis, *Forecasting Methods for Management*, 2d ed. (New York: John Wiley & Sons, 1977).

4. John A. Hooper and Ralph F. Catalenello, "Markov Analysis Applied to Forecasting Technical Personnel," *Human Resource Planning*, Vol. 4, No. 2 (1981), pp. 41–47.

5. Robert H. Flast, "Taking the Guesswork Out of Affirmative Action Planning," *Personnel Journal* (February 1977).

6. A. L. Patz, "Linear Programming Applied to Manpower Management," *Industrial Management Review*, Vol. 11, No. 2 (Winter 1970).

7. A detailed explanation of the methods for deriving the log-normal curve is addressed in the handbook *Planning Your Staffing Needs: A Handbook for Personnel Workers* by Harry L. Clark and Donna R. Thurston (Washington, D.C.: U.S. Civil Service Commission, Bureau of Policies and Standards, 1977).

Chapter 10

1. Ren Nardoni, "The Building Blocks of a Successful Microcomputer System," *Personnel Journal* (January 1985).

2. *The New York Times* (September 30, 1984).

Chapter 11

1. Harry Levinson, *Organizational Diagnosis* (Cambridge, Massachusetts: Harvard University Press, 1972), pp. 22ff.

BIBLIOGRAPHY

Alfred, Theodore M., "Checkers or Choice in Manpower Management," *Harvard Business Review* (January–February 1967).

Alpander, Guvenc G., *Human Resources Management Planning*. New York: AMACOM, 1982.

Anastasi, Anne, *Psychological Testing*. New York: Macmillan, 1954.

Angle, H. L., "Integrating Human Resource Management and Corporate Strategy: A Preview of the 3M Story," *Human Resource Management* (Spring 1985).

Ansoff, H. Igor, *From Strategic Planning to Strategic Management*. New York: John Wiley & Sons, 1976.

Arvey, R. D., *Fairness in Selecting Employees*. Reading, Massachusetts: Addison-Wesley, 1979.

Beckhard, Richard, *Organization Development: Strategies and Models*. Reading, Massachusetts: Addison-Wesley, 1969.

Beckhard, Richard, and R. T. Harris, *Organizational Transitions: Managing Complex Change*. Reading, Massachusetts: Addison-Wesley, 1978.

Biles, George E., and Stevan R. Holmberg, *Strategic Human Resource Planning*. Glen Ridge, New Jersey: Thomas Horton and Daughters, 1980.

Blum, John M., *et al.*, *The National Experience*. New York: Harcourt Brace and World, 1963.

Bourgeois, L. J., "Strategic Goals, Perceived Uncertainty, and Economic Performance in Volatile Environments," *Academy of Management Journal* (September 1985).

Bray, Douglas W., "The Assessment Center Method," Chapter 16 in *Training and Development Handbook*, ed. Robert L. Craig, New York: McGraw-Hill, 1976.

Bray, Douglas W., and Donald L. Grant, "The Assessment Center in the Measurement of Potential for Business Management," *Psychological Monographs*, Vol. 80, No. 17 (1966).

Bryant, Don R., Michael J. Maggard, and Robert P. Taylor, "Manpower Planning Models and Technology: A Descriptive Survey," *Business Horizons* (April 1973). Reprinted in G. E. Biles and S. R. Holmberg, eds., *Strategic Human Resource Planning*. Glen Ridge, New Jersey: Thomas Horton and Daughters, 1980, p. 121.

Burack, Elmer H., and Nicholas J. Mathys, *Career Management in Organizations: A Practical Human Resource Planning Approach*. Lake Forest, Illinois: Brace-Park Press, 1979.

——, *Human Resource Planning: A Pragmatic Approach to Manpower, Staffing and Development*. Lake Forest, Illinois: Brace-Park Press, 1981.

Camillus, J. C., and A. L. Lederer, "Corporate Strategy and the Design of Computerized Information Systems," *Sloan Management Review* (Spring 1985).

Campbell, John P., *et. al.*, *Managerial Behavior, Performance, and Effectiveness*. New York: McGraw-Hill, 1970.

Carnazza, Joseph P., *Succession/Replacement Programs and Practices: A Report.* New York: Center for Research in Career Development, Columbia Business School, 1981.

Chambers, J. C., "Coupling Corporate Strategy and R & D Planning," *Management Planning* (May-June 1985).

Chandler, John, and Paul Cockle, *Techniques of Scenario Planning.* London: McGraw-Hill Book Company, Ltd., 1982.

Clark, Harry L., and Donna R. Thurston, *Planning Your Staffing Needs: A Handbook for Personnel Workers.* Washington, D. C.: U.S. Civil Service Commission, Bureau of Policies and Standards, 1977.

Cleland, David I., ed., *Matrix Management Systems Handbook,* New York: Van Nostrand Reinhold, 1984.

The Conference Board, *Appraising Managerial Performance,* No. 723. New York: The Conference Board, 1977, pp. 95, 99–100, 113–15, 120.

———, *Manpower Planning: Evolving Systems,* No. 521. New York: The Conference Board, 1971, pp. 19, 21, 34, 44–45.

Craft, J. A., "A Critical Perspective on Human Resource Planning," *Human Resource Planning,* Vol. 3, No. 2 (1980), pp. 39–52.

The Dartnell Corporation, *How to Review and Evaluate Employee Performance.* Chicago: Dartnell Press, 1976, p. 53.

DeRijcke, J., "Strategy Formulation and Implementation During Purchasing of Production Materials," *Journal of Business Research* (February 1985).

Dimma, W. A., "Ten Ways to Cope with Change," *Canadian Business Review* (Spring 1985).

Dreher, George F., and Paul R. Sackett, "Some Problems with Applying Content Validity Evidence to Assessment Center Procedures," *Academy of Management Review* (October 1981).

Drucker, Peter F., "Long Range Planning," *Management Science* (April 1951).

———, *Management: Tasks, Practices, Responsibilities.* New York: Harper & Row, 1974.

Emerson, Ralph Waldo, "Self Reliance," in Bliss Perry, ed., *Selections from the Prose Works of Ralph Waldo Emerson,* Boston: Houghton Mifflin, 1926.

Feuer, Michael J., Richard J. Niehaus, and James A. Sheridan, "Human Resource Forecasting: A Survey of Practice and Potential," *Human Resource Planning,* Vol. 7, No. 2 (1984).

Flast, Robert H., "Taking the Guesswork Out of Affirmative Action Planning," *Personnel Journal* (February 1977).

Frantzreb, Richard B., "Human Resource Planning: Forecasting Manpower Needs," *Personnel Journal,* Vol. 60, No. 1 (1981), pp. 852–55.

———, *Manpower Planning Newsletter,* Vol. 1, Nos. 9 and 10 (1977); Vol. 2, No. 10 (1978); Vol. 4, Nos. 5 and 6 (1982). Sunnyvale, California: Advanced Personnel Systems.

Friedman, Barry A., and Robert W. Mann, "Employee Assessment Methods Assessed," *Personnel* (November/December 1981).

Gaballa, A., and W. Pearce, "Telephone Sales Manpower Planning at Qantas," *Interfaces,* Vol. 9, No. 3 (May 1979).

Ghiselli, E. E., *The Validity of Occupational Aptitude Tests.* New York: John Wiley & Sons, 1966.

Ginzberg, Eli, "The Professionalization of the U.S. Labor Force," *Scientific American* (March 1979).

Ginzberg, Eli and George Vojta, *Beyond Human Scale, The Large Corporation at Risk,* New York: Basic Books, 1985.

Glueck, William F., *Business Policy: Strategy Information and Management Action.* New York: McGraw-Hill, 1976.

Gould, R., "Conjoint Executive Assessment for Strategic Planning," *Personnel Administrator* (April 1985).

Gray, B., and S. S. Ariss, "Politics and Strategic Change Across Organizational Life Cycles," *Academy of Management Review* (October 1985).

Gridley, John D., "Mergers and Acquisitions, I: Premerger Human Resources Planning," *Personnel,* September 1986.

Gridley, John D., "Who Will Be Where When? Forecast the Easy Way," *Personnel,* May 1986.

Guion, R. M., *Personnel Testing.* New York: McGraw-Hill, 1965.

Haire, M., "Managing Management Manpower," *Business Horizons* (Winter 1977), pp. 23–28.

Hall, Douglas T., *Careers in Organizations.* Pacific Palisades, California: Goodyear Publishing Company, 1976.

Hansen, G. B., "Preventing Layoffs: Developing an Effective Job Security and Economic Adjustment Program," *Employee Relations Law Journal* (August 1985).

Henry, Harold W., "Formal Planning in Major U.S. Corporations," *Long Range Planning* (October 1977).

———, *Long Range Planning Practices in 45 Industrial Companies.* Englewood Cliffs, New Jersey: Prentice-Hall, 1967.

Herzberg, Frederick, "One More Time: How Do You Motivate Employees?" *Harvard Business Review* (January–February 1968).

Hoffman, N. H., and L. L. Wyatt, "Human Resources Planning," *Personnel Administrator,* Vol. 22, No. 1 (1977), pp. 19–23.

Hooper, John A., and Ralph F. Catalenello, "Markov Analysis Applied to Forecasting Technical Personnel," *Human Resource Planning,* Vol. 4, No. 2 (1981), pp. 41–47.

Hrebiniak, L. G. and W. F. Joyce, "Organizational Adaptation: Strategic Choice and Environmental Determinism," *Administrative Science Quarterly* (September 1985).

Ignall, Edward J., "A Review of Assembly Line Balancing," Chapter 15 in *Operations Management: Selected Readings,* ed. Gene K. Groff and John F. Muth. Homewood, Illinois: Richard D. Irwin, 1969.

Jaques, Elliott, *The Changing Culture of a Factory.* London: Tavistock Publications, Ltd., 1951.

———, *A General Theory of Bureaucracy.* London: Heinemann, 1976.

———, *Levels of Abstraction in Logic and Human Action.* London: Heinemann, 1978.

———, *Measurement of Responsibility.* London: Tavistock Publications, Ltd., 1956.

Jenkins, M. L. and G. Lloyd, "How Corporate Philosophy and Strategy Shape the Use of HR Information Systems," *Personnel* (May 1985).

Kaumeyer, Richard A., Jr., *Planning and Using a Total Personnel System.* New York: Van Nostrand Reinhold, 1982.

Kelleher, E. J., and K. L. Cotter, "An Integrative Method for Human Resource Planning," *Human Resource Planning,* Vol. 5, No. 1 (1982), pp. 15–27.

Kimberly, John R. and Robert E. Quinn, *New Futures: The Challenge of Managing Corporate Transitions,* Homewood, Illinois: Dow Jones-Irwin, 1984.

Korman, A. K., "The Prediction of Managerial Performance: A Review," *Personnel Psychology,* Vol. 21, No. 3 (1968), p. 319.

Lawrie, John, "Appraisal, Assessment, and HRD," *Personnel Journal* (January 1984).

Levinson, Harry, *Organizational Diagnosis*. Cambridge, Massachusetts: Harvard University Press, 1972.

Levinson, Harry, and Stuart Rosenthal, *CEO: Corporate Leadership in Action*, New York: Basic Books, 1984.

Linkow, P., "HRD at the Roots of Corporate Strategy," *Training & Development Journal* (May 1985).

Linneman, Robert E., and Harold E. Klein, "The Use of Multiple Scenarios by U.S. Industrial Companies: A Comparison Study, 1977–1981," *Long Range Planning* (December 1983).

Lippitt, Gordon L., Petter Langseth, and Jack Mossop, *Implementing Organizational Change*, San Francisco: Jossey-Bass, 1985.

London, Manuel, and Stephen A. Stumpf, *Managing Careers*. Reading, Massachusetts: Addison-Wesley, 1982.

Lopez, F. E., B. W. Rockmore, and G. A. Kesselman, "The Development of an Integrated Career Planning Program at Gulf Power Company," *Personnel Administrator*, Vol. 25, No. 10 (1980), pp. 21–29, 75–76.

Lopez, F. M., *Evaluating Executive Decision Making: The In-Basket Technique*," AMA Research Study 75 (1966).

Lorange, Peter, and Richard F. Vancil, *Strategic Planning Systems*. Englewood Cliffs, New Jersey: Prentice-Hall, 1977.

Lowman, J., and T. Snediker, "Pinpointing Avoidable Turnover with 'Cohort Analysis,'" *Personnel Journal*, Vol. 59, No. 4 (1980), pp. 310–15.

Lubben, G. I., D. E. Thompson, and C. R. Klasson, "Performance Appraisal: The Legal Implications of Title VII," *Personnel* (May–June 1980).

Lucas, H. C., *Information Systems Concepts for Management*. New York: McGraw-Hill, 1982.

Lundberg, C. C., "Toward a Contextual Model of Human Resource Strategy: Lessons from the Reynolds Corporation," *Human Resource Management* (Spring 1985).

McLarney, W. J., and W. M. Berliner, *Management Training: Cases and Principles*. Homewood, Illinois: Richard D. Erwin, 1970.

McMillan, Charles J., "From Quality Control to Quality Management: Lessons from Japan," *Business Quarterly* (Spring 1982).

Makridakis, Spyros, and Steven C. Wheelright, *Interactive Forecasting*. Palo Alto, California: Scientific Press, 1974.

Manzini, Andrew O., "Enhancing the Effectiveness of Matrix Management with Organization Development Interventions," in *Matrix Management Systems Handbook*, New York: Van Nostrand Reinhold, 1984.

Manzini, Andrew O., and John D. Gridley, "The False Economies of Unplanned Layoffs," *Personnel* (March 1986).

Murphy, Gardner, *Historical Introduction to Modern Psychology*. New York: Harcourt, Brace and Company, 1949.

Nardoni, Ren, "The Building Blocks of a Successful Microcomputer System," *Personnel Journal* (January 1985).

———, "Screening Optical Scanners for Personnel," *Personnel Journal* (October 1983).

Newman, W. H., "Selecting a Company Strategy," *Journal of Business Policy*, Vol. 2, No. 1 (1971).

Nunnaly, Jum C., *Tests and Measurements*. New York: McGraw-Hill, 1970.

Oberg, Winston, "Make Performance Appraisal Relevant," *Harvard Business Review*, No. 72110 (January–February 1972).

O'Connor, Rochelle, *Planning Under Uncertainty: Multiple Scenarios and Contingency Planning*, Report No. 741. New York: The Conference Board, 1978.

Patten, Thomas H., Jr., *Manpower Planning and the Development of Human Resources*. New York: John Wiley & Sons, 1971.

Patz, A. L., "Linear Programming Applied to Manpower Management," *Industrial Management Review*, Vol. 11, No. 2 (Winter 1970).

Porter, Lyman W., and R. M. Steers, "Organization, Work and Personal Factors in Employee Turnover," *Psychology Bulletin*, Vol. 80, No. 2 (1973), pp. 151–76.

Portwood, J. D., "Organizational Career Management: The Need for a Systems Approach," *Human Resource Planning*, Vol. 4, No. 1 (1981), pp. 47–59.

Psychological Associates, *Effective Appraisals Through Psychology*. St. Louis, Missouri: Psychological Associates, 1975.

Radcliffe, B. M., D. E. Kawal, and R. J. Stephenson, *Critical Path Method*. Boston: Cahners Publishing Company, 1967.

Riggs, James L., and Michael S. Inoue, *Introduction to Operations Research and Management Science: A General Systems Approach*. New York: McGraw-Hill, 1975.

Salveson, M. E., "The Assembly Line Balancing Problem," *Journal of Industrial Engineering*, Vol. 6, No. 3 (May–June 1955).

Schein, Edgar H., *Career Dynamics: Matching Individuals and Organizational Needs*. Reading, Massachusetts: Addison-Wesley, 1978.

Schneider, K. P., and D. I. Hawk, "The Performance Appraisal Process: A Selected Bibliography," Special Report. Greensboro, North Carolina: Center for Creative Leadership, March 1980.

Schroeder, R. C., *Operations Management*. New York: McGraw-Hill, 1981, pp. 342–48, 484–85.

Skipton, M. D., "Helping Managers to Develop Strategies," *Long Range Planning* (April 1985).

Smith, H. P., and P. J. Brouwer, *Performance Appraisal and Human Development: A Practical Guide to Effective Managing*. Reading, Massachusetts: Addison-Wesley, 1977.

Steiner, George A., *Strategic Planning—What Every Manager Must Know*. New York: Free Press (Macmillan Publishing Company), 1979.

Steiner, George A., and John B. Miner, *Management Policy and Strategy*, New York: Free Press (MacMillan Publishing Company), 1977.

Sternberg, Robert J., *Intelligence, Information Processing, and Analogical Reasoning: The Componential Analysis of Human Abilities*. Hillside, New Jersey: Lawrence Erlbaum Associates, 1977.

Subramaniam, S., "Engineering Manpower Planning in an Airline," *Long Range Planning*, Vol. 10 (August 1977).

Szilagyi, A. D., and M. J. Wallace, *Organizational Behavior and Performance*. Santa Monica, California: Goodyear Publishing Company, 1980.

Taylor, B., and J. R. Sparkes, *Corporate Strategy and Planning*. New York: John Wiley & Sons, 1977.

Taylor, Frederick Winslow, *Principles of Scientific Management*, New York: Harper & Brothers, 1911.

Walker, Alfred J., *HRIS Development: A Project Team Guide to Building an Effective Personnel Information System*. New York: Van Nostrand Reinhold, 1982.

Walker, James W., *Human Resource Planning*. New York: McGraw-Hill, 1980.

———, "Let's Get Realistic About Career Paths," *Human Resources Management*, Vol. 55 (Fall 1976).

————, "Personal and Career Development," in D. Yoder and H. G. Heneman, eds., *Training and Development*, ASPA Handbook of Personnel and Industrial Relations (Vol. 5), Washington, D.C.: Bureau of National Affairs, 1977.

Walker, James W., and Thomas G. Gutteridge, *Career Planning Practices: An AMA Survey Report*. New York: AMACOM, 1979.

Warren, E. Kirby, *Long-Range Planning: The Executive Viewpoint*. Englewood Cliffs, New Jersey: Prentice-Hall, 1966.

Weisbord, M. R., *Organizational Diagnosis: A Workbook of Theory and Practice*. Reading, Massachusetts: Addison-Wesley, 1978.

Wheelwright, Steven C., and Spyros Makridakis, *Forecasting Methods for Management*, 2d ed. New York: John Wiley & Sons, 1977.

Zaleznik, Abraham, "Managers and Leaders: Are They Different?" *Harvard Business Review*, Vol. 55, No. 3 (May–June 1977), pp. 67–78.

Zaltman, Gerald, *Strategies for Planned Change*. New York: John Wiley & Sons, 1977.

INDEX

line managers, and planning system
  involvement with, 261–262
  opposition to, 260
linear programming techniques, 120, 132, 227
liquidity goals, 70
load schedule, human resources, 125, 308
log-probability curves, for attrition
    forecasting, 229–232
long-range planning, 96
  data base for, 307–308
Lorange, Peter, on planning teams, 66

Makridakis, Spyros, on forecasting
    techniques, 221
management
  continuity of, 11
  participative, 23
  see also top management
management-by-objectives approach, 184
  rating scales from, 180–182
management development
  accelerated, 252
  as factor in voluntary turnover, 229
  strategic implications of, 177–212
  see also training
management information systems, 35
management potential, appraisal of, 187–189
management succession, development and
    computer implementation of, 281–282
managers
  analogical reasoning in, 191–192
  availability forecast of, 209
  core mission and, 77
  "critical mass" of, 6, 258, 260
  evaluation potential for, 11
  knowledge of promotion possibilities, 198
  opposition of, to planning system, 260
  in organizational diagnosis process, 76
  perceptions of unwelcome change by, 92
  performance appraisal systems for, 180–182
  profiles of, 198
  time-span capacity in, 192–194
Manpower Development and Training Act
    (MDTA) of 1964, 26
manpower planning, 19
  see also human resources planning
manufacturing, operational planning in, 126–
    130
market conditions, and technology decisions,
    73
marketing data, collection of, 90–91
Markov models, 215, 224–226
Marshall, George, 26

Marshall Plan, 26
Maslow, Abraham, needs hierarchy of, 23
material flow control sequence, 127–129
materials in manufacturing, operational
    planning for, 126–127
material usage variance, 127
mathematical models, 214
  for project-based operational planning, 135
matrix approach to performance appraisal,
    184
matrix organizations, performance appraisal
    in, 185
Mayo, Elton, 22
McMillan, Charles J., on Japanese labor
    relations, 103
MDTA (Manpower Development and
    Training Act of 1964), 26
measurement, with information system, 32
microcomputers, 40
  for data retrieval, 38
  for human resources planning, 312
microprocessors, 17
military establishment, 89
  personnel testing by, 24
models, 221–222
  costs of, 221
  definition of, 214
  descriptive, 218
  Markov, 215, 224–226
  mathematical, 135, 214
  for planning human resources, 15–16
  queuing theory, 132–133
  renewal, 215, 224, 226
  statistical, 224–228
  stochastic planning, 224
  see also forecasting models
module of information system, definition of,
    42–43
motivation, 187
  pay as, 21
Munsterberg, Hugo, personnel test
    development by, 24

National Cash Register Corp., 72
needs analysis, 40
  for human resources data base, 37
  for information system, and accuracy
    standards, 38
needs hierarchy (Maslow), 23
network flow method of forecasting, 215–220
  in case study, 292
networks, partial, 139
non-verbal tests, 24